18/4/05

CW00730661

PATERNOSTER THEOLOGICAL M

A Theology of Work

Work and the New Creation

*To Ruth
all Blessings
David*

PATERNOSTER THEOLOGICAL MONOGRAPHS

A full listing of titles in this series
appears at the end of this book

A Theology of Work

Work and the New Creation

Darrell Cosden

Foreword by Jürgen Moltmann

PATERNOSTER PRESS

First published 2004 by Paternoster Press

Paternoster Press is an imprint of Authentic Media
P.O. Box 300, Carlisle, Cumbria, CA3 0QS, UK
and
P.O. Box 1047, Waynesboro, GA 30830–2047, USA

10 09 08 07 06 05 04   7 6 5 4 3 2 1

British Library Cataloguing in Publication Data
A catalogue record for this book is available from the British Library

ISBN 1–84227–332–9

Typeset by J.E. Jeacocke
Printed and bound in Great Britain
for Paternoster Publishing
by Nottingham Alpha Graphics

Series Preface

In the West the churches may be declining, but theology—serious, academic (mostly doctoral level) and mainstream orthodox in evaluative commitment—shows no sign of withering on the vine. This series of Paternoster Theological Monographs extends the expertise of the Press especially to first-time authors whose work stands broadly within the parameters created by fidelity to Scripture and has satisfied the critical scrutiny of respected assessors in the academy. Such theology may come in several distinct intellectual disciplines—historical, dogmatic, pastoral, apologetic, missional, aesthetic and no doubt others also. The series will be particularly hospitable to promising constructive theology within an evangelical frame, for it is of this that the church's need seems to be greatest. Quality writing will be published across the confessions—Anabaptist, Episcopalian, Reformed, Arminian and Orthodox—across the ages—patristic, medieval, reformation, modern and counter-modern—and across the continents. The aim of the series is theology written in the twofold conviction that the church needs theology and theology needs the church—which in reality means theology done for the glory of God.

To Brenton and Kayleigh

Contents

FOREWORD

I am delighted that Darrell Cosden has undertaken to develop a new theology of work and it is a great honour that he has done so in critical dialogue with me and the few things that I have had to say on the subject. Ever since Miroslav Volf wrote his excellent dissertation *Work in the Spirit: Toward a Theology of Work* (Oxford University Press), when studying under me in Tübingen in 1988, I have waited for a young theologian to take this topic further. Here he is, and so it is with much pleasure that I am writing this Foreword.

It is good that Dr Cosden begins, as I do, with the view that human work can no longer be located only in the protology of the creation and preservation of the world, and grounds a specifically Christian theology of work in the concept of the new creation and collaboration with the kingdom of God. In this way he introduces a teleological dynamic into the concept of work. In Part I he develops the idea of a threefold nature of work: instrumental, relational and ontological. He thus puts the instrumental view of work as a means to an end, which predominates in the modern world, in a wider framework than we are accustomed to, and limits it to a degree that is tolerable for human beings. He gives human work in the other dimensions a more positive sense than the negative evaluations that abound today in which work is something that has to be reduced or replaced by machines.

So as to show just a few theological dimensions of the existing process of work, in Part II, in contrast to the Catholic tradition, which he calls the 'ontology of work', he sets human work in the wider contexts of anthropology, the doctrine of creation and eschatology. That not only sheds a theological light on work but also illuminates theology as a whole from the perspective of work. The summaries that he gives at the end show the fertility of his approach and his method. This study on the theology of work has something to say.

Because Dr Cosden has written this book in critical dialogue with me and my theology, inevitably I enter in to this dialogue, but in my remarks here I do not want to abandon the character of a Foreword, which is meant to invite readers to study the book. I have never claimed to have written a comprehensive and consistent theology of work, nor have I wanted to. My remarks on work and play, on the right to work and on meaningful work, which he reports and vigorously criticizes, are occasional remarks. In other words they are remarks which belong in a particular context, a given *kairos* and an identifiable society. They are not elements of a theory at the meta-level of a universal ethics. I wrote my study 'The First Freed Persons of Creation' in 1971 at the height of the student unrest and of Western European neo-Marxism. In its American edition this short work was put in a different context of 'play theology' and published along with contributions by Sam Keen, David Miller and Bob Neale. The English edition discreetly backed away from this and was called *Theology and Joy*, which sounds more serious.

The second text, 'The Right of Meaningful Work', was written in 1979 for a conference of the Society of Protestant Theology in Wuppertal. It was a contribution to the German discussion of the time about the insertion of the 'right to work' into the Basic Law of the Federal Republic of Germany, on the model of the 1948 Universal Declaration of Human Rights, Article 23.

If such remarks made on particular occasions are taken out of their context and regarded as elements of a universal theory, of course they seem inadequate. That is quite natural. So I can agree with the criticism which Dr Cosden makes. It was not my intention in those texts to provide what he was looking for in them. His distinction between 'work' and 'labour' cannot be expressed well in German, because we only have one word, '*Arbeit*'. 'Work', translated as '*Werk*', means more the result of work, whereas 'labour' used to be associated more with 'toil and labour'. In the German tradition from Moses Hess to Erich Fromm his distinction between 'being' and 'having' is seen not as an ontological hierarchy but as an anthropological dialectic. I later wrote at length on the relationship between justification and sanctification and spiritual growth in *The Spirit of Life* (1992); I think that Dr Cosden would agree with what I said. In describing the debate on justification and sanctification between Count Zinzendorf and John Wesley I took Wesley's side.

By contrast, I feel that I am understood and described very well in Part II. The author has understood and developed admirably the relational and ecological anthropology of the image of God in human beings in the context of the earthly community of creation. I would like to draw attention in particular to his teleological orientation of human work on the eschatological expectation of the kingdom of God. All too often the eschatological concept of the future is set against the teleological concept and in this way the present experience of life and work is robbed of any hopeful meaning. After this book that is no longer possible. The eschatological future of God motivates the ways in which we shape the present and at the same time criticizes them in order to improve them. That gives rise to a concept of human work which goes beyond paid work and also speaks to all those who are excluded from earning a living by unemployment. Our whole life consists in shaping the present in the light of our expectations of the future, and these expectations of the future in Christianity are eternal life, the kingdom of God and the creation of all things new.

Tübingen, 6 August 2004   Jürgen Moltmann

PREFACE

I was desperate for a theology of work when in January 1991 I moved to the Soviet Union to serve God and his people there. Unfortunately though, I did not know that I was. In fact I did not even know there was, could be, or should be such a thing. What I did come quickly to know, however, was that the vast majority of people I encountered, Christian and non-Christian alike, were struggling to make sense of their daily lives and especially their daily working activities in and for a society and economy that was crumbling around them.

With my Christian friends the problem became especially acute. Their daily work was to them meaningless and definitely not a place to find God or anything else remotely meaningful. Church on Sunday or church meetings during the week were the only places they expected to meet with God and become themselves the new creatures that they now were. Daily work only got in the way. In fact, public testimonies of many new believers usually proclaimed that they looked forward to the day when they would grow spiritually to the place where they, like the missionaries, could cast off the burden of their daily work and go out and serve God.

Such experiences gave me a deep sense that something was wrong, not just with their theology but also with the one I brought with me from America. Essentially, they were just making explicit what lay at the heart of the theology in my own tradition from America. 'Professional Christian work' was somehow more spiritual, a higher calling, the place where you could really serve God and others, and thus become more Christlike. Ordinary, daily, mundane work was at best a mission field, and at worst a distraction in the spiritual life.

A few years later as my angst within this situation increased I saw advertised at the Schloss Mittersill Study Center in Austria a two-week course entitled 'A Theology of Work'. I still did not know what a theology of work was, but I immediately knew that this was what I was searching for.

As I began to reflect upon and develop the ideas introduced to me at the Schloss by Dr Carl Armerding, especially while I was teaching theological ethics at the Donetsk Christian University in Ukraine, I realised the vital importance of this much neglected subject. So in 1995, driven by the pressing need I saw and felt, we moved to the University of St Andrews in Scotland where I undertook my PhD research on a theology of work under the supervision of Rev. J. Michael Keeling. To Michael's tutelage I owe more than I can ever express and probably more than I will ever know.

This book is a subtle reworking of that PhD thesis and the fruit of several years of my work. It is my attempt to make a contribution to this worthy area of study. The book is written in such a way that it should be read through in order. Omitting a chapter (or Part 1) will make the argument hard to follow. It is hoped that the book can also be used as an example of *doing* theology: it is not just a set of conclusions with the working hidden.

It is my sincere hope that the academic pursuit of a theology of work will be served in some way by this book. I also hope that through some of these ideas Christian people in various parts of the world will be encouraged to see that their daily work is a place to meet, worship and co-create with God and a place to realise more of who they were made to become. Indeed, this surely will require folk to be agents of change in their workplaces so that they and others can genuinely have such experiences. Yet, that is the whole point of this book anyway.

Of course, this book would not have been possible without the help of many people. To all of you I want to say in writing, thank you. First, to the authors from whom I learnt and with whom I interacted and here I would like to thank especially Professor Jürgen Moltmann for graciously continuing this interaction with his contribution of a Foreword to this volume. I am also indebted to the various groups of students who have allowed me to experiment on them with this material: my students at Donetsk Christian University in Ukraine, The International Christian College in Glasgow and Gordon Conwell Theological Seminary in the USA. Without your thoughtful and honest comments I may not have had the courage to take this material through to publication.

To all those who have helped me prepare this manuscript for publication I owe a great deal of thanks. Thanks to Janice Brown for reading the manuscript and patiently labouring to get me to sort out much of my awkward writing and many of my hopelessly complex sentences. Likewise thanks to Jeremy at Paternoster. Your patience with me is much appreciated.

I also owe a special thanks to Dr. John Jeacocke whose friendship and countless hours spent in reading, commenting on, editing, and formatting this book for publication has meant that these ideas might now be meaningfully read by others. Of course any mistakes and errors that remain in this book are wholly my own.

Finally I want to thank my family, Kristy, Brenton and Kayleigh, for simply being my family and keeping me rooted in reality (to the degree that I am) even at those times when my ideas would seem to take me elsewhere.

PART 1

Work in Christian Theology:
The Threefold Nature of Work

CHAPTER 1

Introduction

According to Pope John Paul II the 'key, probably the essential key, to the whole social question' is to be found in the phenomenon that we call human work.[1] He means that while the solution to humanity's social ethical problems will be sought through our gradually 'making life more human', this humanization process itself will be accomplished primarily through our human work. Thus, not surprisingly human work 'acquires fundamental and decisive importance.'[2]

For Pope John Paul II this high estimation of the significance of work stems not only from its practical consequences, but also derives from work's nature as 'a perennial and fundamental' aspect of human existence on earth. Accordingly, since it is so grounded in human existence, the activity which we call work becomes central to the life and mission of the Church. Work, through its connection to man, becomes a part of 'the primary and fundamental way for the Church'. Work is 'always relevant and constantly demands renewed attention and decisive witness.'[3]

The conviction that the phenomenon of human work must occupy at least part of the center stage in current social ethics is likewise propounded by the American sociologist Robert Bellah. In his ground-breaking book *Habits of Heart*, (1985) after extensively evaluating the social ills in American life which stem from modernist individualistic attitudes, Bellah in his conclusion suggests that 'work that is intrinsically interesting and valuable is one of the central requirements for a revitalized social ecology.' (p.288.) He argues further that for American society to be positively transformed (and, I would suggest for any society shaped by the values of modernity) there must be a deeply rooted change in the way that the society understands the meaning of work. Fine-tuning our essentially modern economic institutions alone will not be enough. (p.289.) What is needed is a fundamental reevaluation of what we understand human work to be.

Of course, one might want to challenge any or all of these claims. However, they do suggest the appropriateness and importance of efforts focused on prob-

---

[1] *Laborem Exercens*, (1981), 3.
[2] Ibid., 3.
[3] Ibid., 1.

ing the deeper nature and meaning of work. Clearly for Christian theology these observations mean that continued and deeper theological reflection on the nature of work and on an ethics of work is always in order. Since human work (with human life in general) is constantly changing, we will need to constantly exert ourselves to develop a more nuanced and insightful theological understanding of work's nature and ultimate meaning.

Toward a Christian Theology of Work

A Deepening Theological Understanding of Work

In this book I am taking up the challenge that both the broader Christian Church and the societies which today are part of what we call the 'global village' need to change the way in which we understand the nature and meaning of work. I suggest and will be demonstrating in what follows, that the resources needed for this change can be found in Christian theology. This does not mean that the task is simply to draw together and restate what has already been said theologically about work, helpful as that in itself might be. Rather, what is needed is a further probing, and where necessary, addition to the available resources. This book then, is intended to be an exploration of and contribution to a deeper theological understanding of work.

Specifically, rather than offering a narrower work ethics or random theological insights for work, I am working toward a more comprehensive theological construct called a 'theology of work.' What then, is a theology of work and how does it differ from other theological reflection on work or a work ethics?

The Concept of a Theology of Work: A Genitive Theology

Although theological reflection on work is as old as Christian theology itself, the concept of a 'theology of work' is a quite recent development. Lothar Roos comments in his article *On a Theology and Ethics of Work,* that 'French [Catholic] theologians after World War II were the first to ask whether there was a "theology of secular realities" and thus also a "theology of work."'[4] Catholic theologian M.-D. Chenu, in one of the first attempts at a theology of

---

[4] Roos, (1984), p.102. Here Roos is referring to G. Thils, M.-D. Chenu, and H. Rondet. Of course following WWII Roman Catholic theologians were not alone in their concern about Christianity's engagement with 'secular realities'. Following Bonhoeffer's broader reflections and cryptic comment in *Letters and Papers from Prison* about 'religionless Christianity' an entire industry emerged with this concern. Nevertheless the 'genitive' methodology being discussed here emerged from post war Catholic thinking.

work, pointed out that the phrase itself had only been 'recently-coined'.[5] In 1955 he claimed that it had only been around for five or six years.[6]

The creation of this new phrase, a theology of work, by Catholic theologians as a new way toward a theological understanding of the nature and meaning of work, introduced, according to Miroslav Volf, 'an important shift in the theological approach to the problem of work.'[7] This shift is what points to the difference between a theology of work and other theological reflection on work, or an ethics of work. Unlike other approaches, a theology of work attempts to be a comprehensive theological study, dogmatically reflecting on the nature and place of the phenomenon of work in God's universe; that is, in both human life and in the non-human creation. It is a theological exploration of work itself undertaken by exploring work with reference to a multitude of doctrines within a systematic theology. A theology of work thus defined is a genitive theology which methodologically means that it is a theology 'of *something*', or, a comprehensive theological explanation of something.[8]

A theology of work then, is not merely a discussion of how one should carry out work, or a discussion of how to resolve specific difficulties and problems faced in the working world. This would essentially be an ethics of work. Nor is a theology of work satisfied with only making theological comments about work as they arise within a discussion of some other broader point of doctrine. This would constitute a theological reflection on work. A theology of work is a much broader concept. It is a recent theological methodology developed for comprehensively exploring the phenomenon of work itself as a part of created reality.

Focusing Explorations for this Theology of Work

Interestingly, since the advent of the theology of work model / genre in the

---

[5] Chenu, (1963), p.2.

[6] Ibid., p.3.

[7] Volf, (1991), p.71.

[8] For additional discussion of the concept and possibility of a 'genitive theology' compare Juros, (1984), pp.138-139 with the discussion by Volf, (1991), pp. 75-76.
I have adopted Volf's perspective that a 'genitive theology' (particularly of work) is different from, for instance, a theology of liberation. The difference lies in its nature and methodology. In the latter, the object 'liberation' becomes elevated to the level of *the* methodological principle for the whole of theological reflection. (Volf p.75.) In this case Volf states (p.75.), building on his analysis in "Doing and Interpreting", (1983) that a 'Theology of liberation is not a theological reflection on a particular aspect of human life (a genitive theology), but a new way of doing theology as a whole.' A theology of work is best understood as a genitive theology rather than a 'contextual' theology in that 'it does not seek to make work the governing theological theme, but to treat it from a dogmatic perspective.' (Volf, 1991, p.75.)

1950's there have been relatively few explicit attempts to produce one. Articles calling for a new theology of work abound. These however, most often just suggest particulars that the author wants included in one when it is developed. Few substantial or developed examples in the genre exist.

Miroslav Volf's *Work in the Spirit* is an exception. Here is the most comprehensive, systematic, and the most theologically developed 'theology of work' thus far. Its scope and depth, surpass anything yet attempted within the genre. Volf demonstrated that, rather than simply promising (Chenu), the very methodology of a theology of work is appropriate and productive. Indeed Volf has now set the standard within this genre. While not needing to agree with Volf, any further explorations toward a 'theology of work' will need to take into account the contributions and advances he has made.

Given this, and since Volf's theological orientation is quite similar to my own, I have chosen to use *Work in the Spirit* both as an orientation point and a point of departure for my project. Although I will only occasionally make direct reference to Volf's theology of work as my views are developed, his work has had formative and far reaching influences on the whole of my project. Primarily, four themes outlined in *Work in the Spirit* have provided the focus and direction for my research into a theology of work.

WORK AND THE NEW CREATION.

Volf's theology of work is twofold in its intention. First, he wants to move away from the traditionally Protestant 'vocational understanding of work developed within the framework of the doctrine of creation to a pneumatological one developed within the framework of the doctrine of the last things.' (p. ix.) Volf wants to reconceive work by swapping the older static concept of calling (vocation) for the more dynamic concept of *charisma* (gifts). He secondly wants to shift the focus of the discussion of work from the doctrine of creation (protology) (where it has been discussed almost exclusively) toward the doctrine of the last things (eschatology).

In this book I have specifically taken up the second rather than first of these called-for shifts. Of course, whether the category of gift better serves the world of work than vocation is an interesting question. Volf is convinced that it does, but his argument and preliminary reflections on the subject throughout the book suggest that further theological work in this area is needed. Whether or not the vocational understanding of work is really a 'dead hand', (p.vii.) a more fundamental question is whether the gifts and talents used by everyone in ordinary work are really the same in kind as the specifically 'spiritual' gifts in the New Testament.[9] Although Volf may have pointed us in a potentially fruitful direction, more theological evaluation will be needed for working out the particulars.

However, my concern lies not with this question, but rather with his call for

---

[9] For some initial thoughts in this area see: Hardy, (1993), pp.191-196.

a theology of work based on the concept of new creation. (p.79.) In his preface Volf admits that his reflection on eschatology in the book is 'rather terse.' (p.ix.) He does later reveal that the 'eschatological realism' that he is operating with basically follows Moltmann's eschatology, (pp. ix, 79.) but he does not provide a detailed justification for his adopting this eschatology. Nor does he intend to provide a detailed unfolding (beyond pp. 89-102.) of this eschatology's implications for understanding human work. (p.79.) Since he also states that developing a full-scale eschatology may help others to understand him better, and, since he has likewise suggested that his book is a rough draft and that others are free to build their own structures upon its foundation, I have chosen in this book specifically to provide a more detailed unfolding of the implications of this eschatological realism for a theology of work. (pp. ix, viii, x.) The second half of this project works toward this goal.

WORK AND THEOLOGICAL ANTHROPOLOGY

A second important section in the book for my purposes is Volf's discussion of work in relation to human beings (within nature). (Ch. 5.) Earlier in the book when discussing the inadequacy of only considering work ethically in terms of spiritual sanctification, Volf states

> Ethical reflection on work traditionally done in the framework of the doctrine of sanctification also needs to be supplemented with reflection from the perspective of anthropology. (p.74.)

In chapter 5 Volf takes up this challenge but admits that a more comprehensive theology of work 'would need to discuss these issues much more exhaustively than I am able to do here.' (p.123.) Herein lies another point of departure for this book. While essentially agreeing with Volf's conclusions in this chapter, I want to explore and develop the theology upon which these types of conclusions are built. The second half of this book, while exploring and further developing an understanding of work with respect to the new creation, is devoted to probing and developing work more deeply within a theological anthropology.

THE CRITERIA FOR OUR CHRISTIAN THEOLOGY OF WORK

In chapter 3, when discussing the 'crafting' of a theology of work, Volf outlines what he calls the 'formal features' of his own theology of work based on the concept of new creation. (p.79.) Here I present a summary of these 'formal features', as I have adopted them as the generic criteria for guiding and evaluating my own project of a Christian theology of work. I am using these features firstly, as a way to define and focus more precisely what I mean methodologically by the phrase 'a theology of work', and secondly, I will constantly be working in this book toward the definitive standards established by each of these criteria.

The first feature which Volf outlines is that the theology of work which both he and I am espousing is *Christian*. This means 'that it is developed on the basis of a specifically Christian soteriology and eschatology, essential to which is the anticipatory experience of God's new creation and a hope of its future consummation.' (p.79.) What I want to do in broad terms, is to build a theology of work from within a Christian metaphysics. Specifically, I (like Volf) want to take the theology of the new creation as the goal toward which my theology of work is oriented.

The second feature suggested is that a 'theology of work based on the concept of new creation purports to be a *normative* understanding of work.' (p.81.) Here Volf argues that we are concerned with what all 'human beings *should* desire their work to be.' (p.81.)

> New creation is the end of all God's purposes with the universe, and as such, either explicitly or implicitly is the necessary criterion of all human action that can be considered good. For this reason, normative principles are implied in the concept of new creation, which should guide Christians in structuring the reality of human work. (p.81.)

Thus, 'normative' means that the prescriptions involved in this theology of work are to be universal in scope, growing out of God's ultimate purposes with the universe.

The next feature Volf suggests is that a theology of work should be transformative. It should be able to lead and move the experience of work towards its normative ethical implications. Here, 'its task is not merely to interpret the world of work in a particular way, but to lead the present world of work "towards the promised and hoped-for transformation" in the new creation.' (p.83.) As such, the practical consequences (either positive or negative) of our theologizing on work must be constantly and carefully considered.

Volf's fourth feature is that a 'theology of work based on the concept of new creation needs to be *comprehensive*.' (p.84.) It needs to be able to answer 'how human work is related to all of reality: to God, human beings, and their nonhuman environment.' (p.84-85.) It needs to be 'a *global* theology... reflecting on work in a global context which is "cross-cultural," "cross-historical" and "pan-human".' (p.85, 86.)

Finally, Volf argues that a theology of work must be able to take seriously any society's historical changes and development. That is to say it must allow for the particulars present within '*individual cultural units.*' (p.86.) Hence, as Volf puts it, the 'variety of cultural forms and their partial preservation in the new creation implies that a diversity of valid theologies of work conditioned partly by the character and the understanding of work in a given culture could exist.' (p.86.) This leads him to the position that his theology of work should be contextualized (while nevertheless having a 'universalizing tendency') for industrializing and industrialized societies. (p.87.) Of course, this must be the case for any theology of work in a similar context.

WHAT IS WORK

A final point of departure with reference to Volf's theology of work is related to the meaning of work. Work is a notoriously difficult concept to define. Most of us tacitly sense the meaning of work but when we are asked to define it we begin to stumble. Volf's definition suggests that,

> work is honest, purposeful, and methodologically specified social activity whose primary goal is the creation of products or states of affairs that can satisfy the needs of working individuals or their co-creatures, or (if primarily an end in itself) activity that is necessary in order for acting individuals to satisfy their needs apart from the need for the activity itself. (pp.10-11.)

While sympathetic to and finding merit with this definition, I have concluded that it is less than adequate. The main criticism is that here work is finally only an instrumental activity (even though it is also called an end in itself). Why I find this to be unsatisfactory will be more clearly seen shortly when I lay out the threefold hypothesis for this book. Here however, the point is that work is defined as always undertaken to satisfy some need. While not denying that work necessarily does always satisfy some need, I suggest that there is more to the very nature (and thus definition) of work than its instrumentality however depicted.

When Volf discusses work as 'an end in itself' he has captured an important and necessary insight. His attempt however to make this concept meaningful is slightly less satisfying. Volf states that,

> an activity cannot lose its instrumental character and still be considered work. But one can still choose things for their own sake under the condition of their instrumentality. (p.196.)

Generally this idea is both helpful and true. However, when he further tries to clarify what this means a problem arises. Volf argues of work that 'while it cannot objectively be done as an end in itself, subjectively it can be experienced as such.' (p.196.) I will in my hypothesis however suggest that work 'is' both an instrumental activity and an end in itself. It is not simply that work 'is' an instrumental activity which we can somehow experience 'as if it were' really an end in itself. Again, Volf's basis for regarding this experience of work as an end in itself, that 'work is a fundamental dimension of human existence' (p.197.) is conceded and I will demonstrate in due course that this is true. However, precisely because this is so it does not seem necessary for Volf to relegate work 'as an end in itself' solely to the category of subjective experience. Of course we can have this experience, but ultimately such an experience is possible because work really 'is' also an end in itself.

I will defend this idea later in my argument. Here my concern is with how this conception skews Volf's definition of work. I believe that a definition of work is needed which can meaningfully preserve both work's instrumentality and its non-instrumentality in a creative way without subordinating either aspect to the other. To find this definition without falling into self-contradiction is another important task of this project.

The Quest for a Theological Definition of Work

In this introduction I will not offer a definition of work. That would be begging the question. Instead I will offer a hypothesis concerning what might for Christian theology be a way to describe work's essential nature and meaning. The body of this book will attempt to demonstrate the truth and usefulness of this hypothesis.

The Threefold Nature of Work: Instrumental, Relational, and Ontological

The hypothesis that this research will explore and test is that the normative theological understanding of work is best construed threefold as a dynamic inter-relationship of instrumental, relational, and ontological aspects. In fact, herein lies a double hypothesis. The first part says that truly human work, i.e. work as it ought to be, is constituted when each of these three aspects (instrumental, relational, and ontological) exist together in a mutual and interdependent relationship. To test this idea I will look at and evaluate how contemporary theology has attempted to understand work.[10] I will examine, from the Church's vast theological resources and especially from its theological reflections on work, whether something like each of these aspects appears and how they are related, or, whether the insights which do arise call for a summarization according to these three dynamically related categories. This task forms the first half of the book.

The second part of the hypothesis, the part that will require particular attention theologically is that work is, and must be construed as, ontological. Of course, if this part of the hypothesis fails so too will the first part.

Why in opposition to definitions by Volf and others is it essential that work in its very essence be construed as something more than only an instrumental activity? There are two responses to this question. First, I grant that work always serves some end; it is always an instrumental activity in that it will always

---

[10] For a biblical analysis, or, a 'biblical theology' of work see: G. Agrell *Work, Toil and Sustenance* (1976), Walter Bienert *Die Arbeit nach der Lehre der Bibel* (1954), F. Hauck *Die Stellung des Urchristentumas zur Arbeit und Geld* (1921), H. Preisker *Das Ethos der Arbeit im Neuen Testament* (1936), H. Preisker *Das Ethos des Urchristentums* (1949), A.T. Geoghegan *The Attitude towards Labor in Early Christianity and Ancient Culture* (1945), A. Richardson *The Biblical Doctrine of Work.* (1952). G. Wittenberg, 'Old Testament Perspectives on Labour' in Cochrane, (1991), pp.91-108.

by necessity have some effect outside of itself (be that on the worker, on others or nature, be that spiritual or mundane, personal or social in nature). If however, work by definition is only a means through which we achieve some subsequent end or effect beyond the activity of work itself, then much, if not most, of our human life takes on only a secondary value. That is to say if work is understood and experienced only as a means to some other end, (economic, spiritual, social, or existential) then much of life loses its immediate and intrinsic value and thus its broader 'existence' meaning. Human life with its activity ceases to be 'gift' (a gift from God). Life itself becomes an object to be achieved and in the process of working to achieve it persons become cut off from themselves and their lives. One primary result of life and work experienced as only a means to an end is the frantic, panicked form of existence that so characterizes our contemporary world.[11]

This dehumanization will happen even if to some degree we are able to subjectively experience our productive activity or work 'as if it were' an end in itself. If work is not also by definition something more than an instrumental activity, (an end in itself), any basis for experiencing it as such is sacrificed. The concept 'as if it were' cannot help us, since to be ultimately authentic (real) and thus truly meaningful our experience of reality must correspond in some way and to a significant degree to that which really is. Work both is and must be something other than only an instrumental activity, and it must be experienced as such if it is to be truly human and truly Christian in the fullest sense.

A second response to the question of why it is essential to construe work as more than an instrumental activity is that the theological evidence from this research suggests that it is. Of course this is not a proof, but it does address the question. As I have studied theology and the Church's theological reflections on work it has become clear to me, whether or not it was clear to those offering the reflections, that there is more by definition to work than only its results.

What however, do I mean by each of the three categories; instrumental, relational and ontological?

The instrumental aspect of work is the most readily perceived, and it has been suggested that it is the aspect of work emphasized by John Locke, Adam Smith, Max Weber and almost all Americans.[12] Instrumentally, work is seen as a means to some end whether that be mundane, or, as is often the case in theology, spiritual. Instrumental in the mundane sense refers to work as a means to continued survival; that is, the provision of sustenance for ourselves, our dependants or other co-creatures. It also refers to work as a means for further economic expansion and growth. Here the focus is not on work, but rather its product used directly or indirectly as a way of securing more of life's necessi-

---

[11] This critique of work as only a means-to-some-end is similar to Karl Marx's conclusions concerning 'work as a means' which will be considered shortly.

[12] Raines, (1993), p.624.

ties or wants.

Instrumentality in the spiritual sense refers to work as useful for some end in the maturing spiritual life. For example, the discipline that comes through working can be character building and thus a part of one's spiritual development. Further, by working one meets the needs of one's fellow creatures and / or acquires the means necessary for acts of charity, the performance of which lessens the suffering of others and also contributes to one's own spiritual growth. Work as instrumental in the spiritual life also becomes important as a platform and means for spreading the message of the Gospel, the message of faith. In as much as we grow spiritually through our obedient witness, work becomes a means to this spiritual end. In these respects work instrumentally involves more than mundane sustenance or raw economic growth. It becomes also a means or occasion for one's process of religious discipleship.

As distinguished from the instrumental, the relational aspect of work refers to work's aim toward appropriate social relationships and / or to some form of human existential realization and fulfillment. By social relationships I mean the way we humans organise work, and its effect on our social order or structures. Here work is viewed as critical for establishing right relationships in society. Right relationships could refer to equality or justice (however these are conceived) on a broad level, or to the interpersonal interaction between workers.

The existential realization and fulfillment of persons referred to here points to an aspect of work that allows the worker to creatively explore and express herself. It relates to her being productive and making a contribution to the world. It relates to the realization of her potential as a human. This humanization involves her sense of satisfaction in and through work, and is necessarily linked with her very process of becoming. Herein lies the existential aspect of work; a person finds, or contributes to who they are and will be (as well as what the world is and will be) in the process of working.[13]

Of course the relational aspect of work thus explained might be considered merely a sub-category of the instrumental. Moreover, in contemporary reflections the relational aspect has received special attention and emphasis. It has of late been elevated to 'a' if not 'the' primary aspect of work. Since it has come to be treated separately and does highlight distinct aspects of work particularly needing attention in a theology and ethics of work, I will treat it as separate but not dissimilar to the category of instrumentality.[14]

---

[13] See Piper, (1957), p.178. Here Piper argues that Hegel introduced (as distinct from work's general usefulness) the idea that through work a person becomes truly human.
[14] For an example of the contemporary importance of the relational aspect of work see: Nash, (1986), pp.23-27.

The Ontology of Work

Admittedly, the ontological aspect of work being developed in this project is rather more difficult to envision than the other two aspects. Strictly speaking however, I have invented neither the term 'ontological' to describe the nature of work, nor the ontology of work concept itself.[15] Indeed, part of my argument is that something akin to my description of an ontology of work can be perceived in most theological (and philosophical) construals of work. The unique contribution of this project then, is not in the wider suggestion or even naming of the concept (although I have contributed here), but rather, it is that in this book I undertake a more sustained examination, and consequently offer a more comprehensive and coherent development of the idea from systematic theology than has yet been provided.

Before suggesting the contours of my own theological understanding of the ontology of work it will be helpful to pause, and for the purpose of comparison and contrast, to consider briefly another's construal of an 'ontology' of work. Here it is Karl Marx's conception of work that I will be considering, for in some ways it is similar to the construct that I will be developing.

KARL MARX ON WORK

On issues dealing with political economy Karl Marx has beyond question been one of the most important figures in the contemporary world. Equally important have been his related reflections, developed within his anthropology, on the nature and essence of the phenomenon of human work. One does not need to look long in most contemporary philosophical or theological reflections on work to find either a negative or positive interaction with ideas which are essentially his.

Why may Marx's understanding of work be termed ontological? Marx saw work as more than simply a means to an economic end. He does not deny this instrumental aspect of work, but throughout his writings he argues that work is also about human social development and our self-realization as individuals and as a species.[16] Therefore for Marx, work's ultimate significance lies in its

---

[15] For example, John C. Raines uses the term to describe how Karl Marx understood work. 'Marx saw human work not as an instrument to gain something else –wealth or social status (as John Locke, Adam Smith, Max Weber and almost all Americans view work) – but as ontological. Specifically, for Marx, work is our species' specific way of establishing and transforming ourselves, not just biologically and socially but also in terms of our self-understanding. For most Americans such a view of work is dangerous... Work it seems to us, is about productivity, wealth, and self-interest, not about the continuing evolution of the species.' Raines, (1993), p.624.

[16] Central to Marx's concern are issues of a just social order which he argues will be achieved through work when labor is properly ordered to capital. His discussions of 'alienation' in both the earlier *Economic and Philosophic Manuscripts of 1844*, (*Karl*

being a specifically human creative activity through which we realize ourselves and contribute to our own evolution, and, through which we create a human world. For Marx (and many who have since followed his reasoning) what I am calling the relational aspect points to work's greater meaning and significance.

Yet, even with these deeper ethical concerns Marx is not yet presenting a view of work as ontological. Work is still only an instrument, a means to an end, albeit an instrument which has far more significance than simply economic usefulness. In what way then can we say that Marx understood work to be ontological? To build the case we must look to Marx's anthropology.[17] The degree to which Marx offers a unified and / or normative view of man and human nature is debatable. This important broader discussion notwithstanding, Marx nonetheless offers specific anthropological observations. Herein lies his conception of work that I have labeled ontological. How so?

First, I return briefly to the idea of work as a means-to-an-end. I have already stated that for Marx work should not be understood as only a means to an economic end. This is because such work, a feature of capitalist societies, will necessarily lead to alienation and will destroy the human. Interestingly, according to Marx's logic such a critique would apply any time work is construed as only a means to an end. His observations and critiques of work-as-a-means, even though offered in the context of his broader discussions of alienation and work / forced labor and the division of labor in a capitalist economic system, would apply in any economic system whether the end to which work is directed is economic or something else. (If work were simply a means to spiritual ends, or to relational ends it would likewise lead to destructive alienation).

According to Marx, to avoid alienation, work itself must be more than only a means to an end. When it is only a means (whatever the end), man, the species-being who is characterized by work, becomes alienated from 'his own body', 'nature outside him', his 'spiritual / *human* being' and other men.[18] Marx's argument might seem strange to us, yet once grasped it becomes quite persuasive. Work construed or experienced only as a means (a belief and experience which he believes to be bound up with 'political economies') is in direct opposition to

---

Marx, Frederick Engels: Collected Works. Vol. 3. pp.270-282.) as well as his later discussion of alienation in *Grundrisse* (McLellan, *Marx's Grundrisse.* (1971) pp.96-102.) illustrate this well.

Marx also believes that humanity's self-creation and self-realization will be achieved through work. In his earlier *Third Manuscript*, within his general critique of Hegel, Marx cites Hegel approvingly with reference to man's 'self-creation' through work. (*Marx, and Engels Works*, Vol. 3. pp.332-333.) Also in *Grundrisse* a later work, he discusses labor's role in man's self-realization. (Marx, *Grundrisse.* (1973), pp.610-616.)

[17] For good studies of Marx's anthropology see: Fromm, (1961), Ollman, (1971), and Plamenatz, (1975). See also: Bottomore, (1983), pp.214-217.

[18] Kamenka, (1983), p.140. From *Economico-Philosophical Manuscripts of 1844*, First Manuscript - 'Alienated Labour'.

what he calls our species-being; that is, to our very humanness.

> Labor, *life activity* and *productive life*, indeed, first appear to man only as a *means* to satisfy a need, the need of maintaining physical existence. Productive life, however, is species-life. It is life-begetting life. The whole character of a species – its species-character – is contained in the character of its life activity; and free conscious activity is the species-character of man. Life itself appears only as a *means* to life.

> The animal is immediately one with its life activity. It does not distinguish itself from it. The animal is *its life activity*. Man makes his life activity itself into an object of his will and of his consciousness. He has conscious life activity. It is not a determination with which he merges directly. Conscious life activity distinguishes man directly from the life activity of the animal. It is only thereby that he is a species-being. Or rather he is only a conscious being – that is, his own life is an object for him – precisely because he is a species-being. Only for that reason is his activity free activity. Alienated labor reverses this relationship in such a way that man, just because he is a conscious being, makes his life activity, his *essence*, a mere means for his *existence*.[19]

For Marx, whenever work is only a means to an end and not something more, it becomes alienating and therefore something less than human.

I now move to a second related point with reference to Marx's anthropology that indicates he understood work to be in some way 'ontological'. It has been observed that for Marx work constitutes our human essence.[20] The idea is that man is a species-being and it is work, man's 'productive, creative activity' as a combination of his physical and mental capacities applied to nature which distinguishes him from animals and specifically makes him human.[21] As Marx's later writing illustrates,

> We presuppose labour in a form that stamps it as exclusively human. A spider conducts operations that resemble those of a weaver, and a bee puts to shame many an architect in the construction of her cells. But what distinguishes the worst architect from the best of bees is this, that the architect raises his structure in imagination before he erects it in reality. At the end of every labour process, we get a result that already existed in the imagination of the labourer at its commencement.[22]

---

[19] Ibid., pp.138-139.

[20] Volf, (1991), p.59.

[21] Marx, *Grundrisse* (1973.) p.614. For a general discussion of work as that which distinguishes man from animals see: *Karl Marx, Frederick Engels: Collected Works.* Vol. 3. pp.275-277.

[22] *Capital* vol. 1 (*Karl Marx, Frederick Engels: Collected Works.* Vol. 35.), p.188.

Work is for humans a species-specific activity bound up with and providing the necessary basis for what it means for us to live as humans. That is, work is essentially our way of being humans rather than simply animals in the world. It is a useful activity but more than this because it is our starting point for a human rather than animal existence. It is a way of being which constitutes our humanness. Hence, it is the ontological condition and not simply the result of our humanness.

Marx clearly expresses this idea in yet another context when discussing the 'simple' nature of work as a 'human action with a view to the production of use value'. Here he assumes the instrumental value of work, (use value) but suggests that more fundamentally the labor process,

> is the everlasting Nature-imposed condition of human existence, and therefore is independent of every social phase of that existence, or rather, is common to every such phase.[23]

It could not be stated more succinctly. The concept 'Nature-imposed' (with an upper case 'N') is the significant idea to notice here. A Christian might argue that prior to our historically developing existence God created us to be workers in nature. Marx however, in a move reminiscent of this idea suggests that 'in the beginning', prior to our socially and historically specific working experience, 'Nature' created us to be workers, or has built into man the condition of work.[24] Work is thus understood as an a-priori and thus universal ground of man. It is a 'thing' which contributes to man's very constitution as man. Work is not simply an activity undertaken by man out of necessity. Rather, it is an activity without which he could not be human. Here we find Marx's concept of work as ontological. It is the 'Nature-imposed condition of human existence.'

Because of these anthropological assessments it is not surprising that Marx was able to identify and sustain discussions on what I have called work's relational aspect. If work is ontological in the way that he has suggested, if it is the natural condition of human existence, it follows that its significance and meaning must ultimately lie in its relationship to human social and existential existence and not simply be bound up with its economic usefulness. Ultimately for Marx, work is conceived of practically as a hierarchical construct. The ontology of work (derived solely from natural or evolutionary anthropology) forms the basis for work's relationality, and its economic nature, while not denied, is interpreted more restrictively in the light of its relationality. A descending hierarchical construct is established which carries with it many ethical implications.

Now, I am not here adopting Marx's particulars with respect to an ontology of work. Nor however, am I totally rejecting them out of hand. Of course my

---

[23] Ibid., p.194.
[24] Ibid., pp.193-194.

own construct will differ from Marx's since I am building it specifically within and upon a Christian theology and anthropology. However, this does not mean that I will necessarily oppose Marx's, or anyone else's, similar observations. If a theological ontology of work is true as I am suggesting, one would expect others to have observed the reality to which the construct points even if their own formulations of it vary because of their different worldviews. Although I believe that my own position will better account for reality, and will therefore prove more true than Marx's, I do not deny that there will be similarities between my unfolding construct and his.

For example, I recognize the logic of Marx's hierarchical construal of work – ontological to relational to economic. However, I do not ultimately find it satisfying as he has left it. I suggest as he does that the ontology of work does initially provide the basis for work's relational aspect, which in turn determines its instrumental aspect. Yet I suggest that it does so without then necessitating a hierarchy. I argue that the nature of the ontology of work is such that it places both the relational and instrumental aspects on an equal, mutually restricting plane while it also places itself on that same level. Thus, I might begin as he does, but rather than ending with a hierarchy, I suggest hypothetically that the three aspects of work must ultimately be seen as mutually interdependent. This is so even if the ontological aspect has a specific role that is logically prior to the others.

THE ONTOLOGY OF WORK IN THIS BOOK

Having here begun to explain my own understanding of the ontology of work, I now return to what I mean specifically by a theological formulation of an ontology of work. An exhaustive description of it is what remains to be done throughout the project. I offer here the contours of a theological ontology of work as I will be developing it.

By the term 'ontological' with reference to work I mean that work in its broadest richness is considered to be more than, or its fuller meaning is understood to incorporate but to transcend, both its instrumental and relational functions. By defining it as ontological, I speak of work as a thing in itself with its own intrinsic value apart from but of course related to these functions. Rather than simply seeing work's combined practical uses as constituent of its essence, I understand work's essential nature to be derived ontologically from its having been built into the fabric of creation by God. The person is a worker, not as an accident of nature but because God first is a worker and persons are created in his image. Humanity's work however, is not identical to God's but is specific to our created existence. Thus, to best understand humanity's work it is essential to look specifically at theological anthropology and not just to God's work.

In summary, it is this ontological dimension of work along with its instrumental and relational functions that ultimately gives work its definition and meaningful role in human life. Work includes but is more than the sum total of its functional parts. Work is not simply to be defined descriptively from within a given culture, nor is its value merely to be determined by its practical functions therein. Rather, work is understood to be more fundamental to created existence, an ontological reality, built by God into the very structures of human nature and as a result, the natural order. Work, in as much as it is fundamental to humanness, 'is' an end in itself. It is ontological.

Having here outlined the beginnings of what I mean by work's instrumental, relational and ontological aspects I conclude this introduction. As I move into the first section of the project the main questions become how the Church in its diversity of traditions understands work, and whether my threefold understanding of it is an acceptable way to describe what needs to be said.

CHAPTER 2

Modern Roman Catholic Social Teaching and Work

Developments in Official Catholic Teaching on Work: 1891-1981

Until the nineteenth century Roman Catholic teaching on work was mostly a continuation of the tradition established by the Medieval Church. Then, during the 1800's Catholic social thought in general and its view of work in particular began to change significantly. A. R. Vidler in his classic study *A Century of Social Catholicism 1820-1920* demonstrates that in Europe throughout the nineteenth century Catholicism was starting to develop what by modern standards could be called a social awareness. Gradually surfacing in Catholicism during this century was a belief that 'it was possible and a matter of moral obligation to improve the social structures as well as bring charitable relief to the victims of industrialism'. (Vidler, p.xii.) According to Vidler, toward the end of the century, and as a specific result of both the Industrial Revolution and the liberal doctrine of *laissez faire* economics, the expression 'social Catholicism' came into use. (Vidler, pp.ix-xii.)

The culmination of this growing awareness and concern for broader social-structural problems was the publication in 1891 of Pope Leo XIII's encyclical *Rerum Novarum* (the worker's charter). It is generally agreed that with this document a new era in Catholic social thought had officially begun.

Rerum Novarum is primarily a response by the Church critiquing the social and political liberalism which had spread throughout Europe during the 1800's. Generally, it is an economically and politically conservative document, the main thrust of which is to examine the plight of the working class poor in the light of expanding technology, urbanization and industrialization. Its primary concerns include the affirmation of the right of persons to private property (against socialism) and the limiting of state intervention in working and economic life.

Vidler underscores the fact that part of Leo XIII's motivation with *Rerum Novarum* was 'to change the inward-looking, citadel mentality that Pius IX had fostered in the Church.' (Vidler, p.127.) After the Reformation, the Catholic Church had become preoccupied both with its own survival and with reasserting its power and influence in Europe. With *Rerum Novarum* however, Leo XIII opened the door and redirected Catholic concern in such a way that broader social-ethical questions which transcend those more preservationist concerns could emerge.

Further, by broadening Catholics' horizons to include social questions which by definition address more than simply the eternal condition of an individual's 'soul', Catholicism's overemphasis on the contemplative life over and against the active was subtly challenged, even if not completely overcome. The Church's historic preoccupation with the 'soul' (narrowly conceived) was re-cast so that the problems faced by the person in his or her active social relationships could likewise become important.

This shift is particularly important for the emerging Catholic understanding of work. Work, a central theme in *Rerum Novarum,* is no longer discussed only as instrumental to personal sustenance and spiritual achievement. Throughout the encyclical, work's instrumental nature is taken for granted, and its functions in providing sustenance, and in individual spiritual development are simply not the focus. Rather, the advancement this encyclical makes in Catholic social teaching on work is found in the direction and impetus it gives for exploring work's relational dimensions and potentialities. (*RN,* n.27, 34.) The issues addressed in *Rerum Novarum* examine what the structures of work do to the workers as individuals and to the societies in which they live.

This, it must be emphasized, was a new direction for Catholics. Although *Rerum Novarum's* suggestions may seem obvious to those of us living in the beginning of the twenty-first century, for Catholics in the late 1800's it was a radical departure from the norm. With this encyclical then, work was coming to be more fully understood as an important component in the overall structuring of human social life. Further, work was beginning to be seen as an indispensable factor in shaping a person's broader social and individual identity.

By implication, the encyclical may be read as the Catholic Church's official affirmation of the legitimacy of ordinary life and work. In this respect we see tendencies developing in the Catholic Church which correspond to the relational dimensions of work presented by both Luther and Calvin.[1]

The next significant development in the Catholic social teaching generally came with the encyclical *Quadragesimo Anno* (The Social Order) which was published in 1931 by Pope Pius XI. This encyclical was written to trace the results and benefits of *Rerum Novarum* and to further vindicate and explain its teachings. It commented on the economic realities of its day and addressed the problem of translating *Rerum Novarum's* teachings into social policy. Interestingly, in this document one detects what appears to be a conscious shift politically and economically. Its tone is decidedly both more radical and 'liberal'

---

[1] Compare for example *Rerum Novarum* 19 with Luther's emphasis on work as primarily for the benefit of others, and 45 with Luther's views on the stations. Also compare 14 with Calvin's views on inequality and differentiation based on the application of the New Testament 'body' concept to the broader society.

than the first encyclical's.[2] In the section on the 'Emancipation of the Proletariat' for example, it uses explicitly Marxist terminology, concepts and analysis. (*QA,* 59-62.) Further, it calls for significantly more state intervention than did *Rerum Novarum.*

With regard to work specifically, this encyclical does not take us much beyond the teachings of *Rerum Novarum.* This is understandable considering that its emphasis is on economics rather than on work itself. However, one should not fail to see the continued emphasis on the relational aspects of work. The social use of work's fruits or products remains the central concern of this encyclical. *Quadragesimo Anno,* although not a commentary on work itself, is nonetheless an attempt to suggest how the view of work offered in *Rerum Novarum* should be implemented in society.

Next, toward the end of the Second World War, we find a flourishing of creative explorations in Catholic social theory. We are not here concerned with an encyclical or Papal pronouncement, but rather with certain undercurrents or movements which were taking place elsewhere within the Catholic Church.

Among these movements were the developments in theological reflection which led to the emergence of 'genitive' theologies. 'Theologies of secular realities' and hence 'theologies of work' were being explored by several continental Catholic thinkers. Particularly important was M.-D. Chenu. Chenu's reapplication of the Thomist tradition to the problem of work's nature and meaning introduced into Catholicism a new paradigm for thinking theologically about work. Although by late twentieth century standards his conclusions are probably both too optimistic concerning what we can expect humans to achieve through their work, and too environmentally unfriendly, Chenu's new model, a theology of work, was nevertheless ground-breaking and its significance and value therefore should not be underrated.

However, those working on theologies of work were not the only ones in Catholicism in the middle of the century exploring the meaning and role of work in the life of the individual and society. Other initiatives also shaped Catholicism's emerging understanding of work. There were for example, the Worker Priest movement in France (Mission de France), the Little Sisters / Little Brothers of Jesus movement, Jeunesse Ouviere Chretienne and Opus Dei.[3]

Importantly, Catholics not directly a part of either the developments in genitive theologies or these experimental lifestyle movements began to consider the contributions from these trends. By 1960 in Great Britain a symposium specifically on work had been held which involved several prominent English Catholic scholars and 'working' persons. Several participants produced essays which

---

[2] The social vision in this encyclical is similar to the version of corporatism which was exemplified by Mussolini's idea in Italy to organise people in blocks similar to the Mediaeval guilds.

[3] Todd, pp.113-119, and Illanes, *On the Theology of Work* (1967).

were published in a book edited by John Todd called *Work: Christian Thought and Practice*. The content of the book suggests how influential each of the above mentioned developments had become. The English participants had come to discuss work using the very language and categories which these initiatives had established. For example, the closing section of the book (which functions as a summary and call for further reflection) adopts the genitive 'theology of work' motif. It uses this motif rather than the 'vocation' model standardized by the Reformers and still in use by most Protestants. Moreover, the suggestions in this section, particularly in the chapter by Herbert McCabe O.P., in many ways reflect those presented first by Chenu. McCabe uses similar categories and terminology, and indicates that he is working with a Thomist framework (similar to that used by Chenu).[4]

The important observation from these trends is that the Catholic Church had finally come up with a motif, or model, with which to develop its own reflections specifically on the nature and meaning of work. Further, the broader impact of this model can be seen from the fact that its influence has now spread even beyond its originally Catholic context. As a methodology it has recently been adopted for Protestant theological reflections on work. Volf for example, chooses the theology of work motif rather than the vocational model.

The currents and trends to which we have been referring were certainly among those which lead to and heavily influenced the Catholic Church as it moved into Vatican II. This series of meetings was to make official a host of developments in theology, ecclesiology and social thought which were already underway within the Church. The topic of work, as we have seen, was integral and closely tied to these broader developments. Based on work's prominence in previous encyclicals and due particularly to the post war emphasis it received, it can be argued that the theological reflection on work was one of the underlying (if not initially expressed) concerns leading to Vatican II's re-shaping of modern Catholicism.

For current purposes, when referring to the Vatican II period I will look only at the 1961 encyclical *Mater et Magistra* by Pope John XXIII and the Vatican II document *Gaudium et Spes*. These are not the only Vatican II period documents central to the continued story of developing Catholic social thought, but they are the ones particularly relevant with reference to work.[5]

Mater et Magistra aims at being a further explication of *Rerum Novarum* as it attempts to reevaluate the 'social problem' in the light of Christian teaching. 'Justice', closely linked with 'equity', between the different branches in the economy is the new aspect of the social question it introduces. The need for just

---

[4] Todd, pp.211-221.

[5] Another important encyclical of this period, but not one which contributes significantly beyond those we are considering to the question of work is Pope Paul VI's encyclical of 1967, *Populorum Progressio*.

relationships between such branches as agriculture, public services, and taxation are highlighted. Interestingly, agriculture becomes a key issue throughout the document.[6]

Although in the tradition of *Rerum Novarum*, *Mater et Magistra* moves even further away from *Rerum Novarum* in its social and political outlook. Pope John XXIII argues specifically for state intervention in economic planning and positively affirms our evolution to a welfare state. (*MM*, 20.)

We also find introduced in this encyclical however, a new area for consideration. In line with the ethos of Vatican II, we find more prominence placed on the need for Christian education, and a higher priority given to lay persons and lay ministry in the Church. Therefore, it is not surprising that the specific topic of work the universal activity of the laity would become prominent in the document. It is noteworthy that the understanding of work presented in *Mater et Magistra* closely corresponds with the idea of the priority of the human (labor) over the material (capital) which later becomes the foundation for the theology of work found in *Laborem Exercens*. Two quotes suffice to illustrate this emerging understanding of the nature of work.

First, work 'must be regarded not merely as a commodity, but as a specifically human activity. In the majority of cases a man's work is his sole means of livelihood. Its remuneration, therefore, cannot be made to depend on the state of the market.' (*MM*, 18.) Second, it is suggested that 'work, which is the immediate expression of a human personality, must always be rated higher than the possession of external goods which of their very nature are merely instrumental.' (*MM*, 107.) Notice here the defining characteristics of work. It is a 'specifically human activity', and it is an 'immediate expression of a human personality'. Other aspects which might contribute to work's essential nature are minimized. Its nature as a commodity is so depicted that it is in effect denied or at best presented to be a negative. Further, the work act is argued to have priority over that which work produces. The implication is that the act of working is what is important rather than its product.

Four years after *Mater et Magistra* another document reflecting further developments in Catholic social thought was published; this was *Gaudium et Spes*. It was the product of Vatican II's far ranging attempts to reform the Church and reflects an unprecedented openness to non-Catholics, even more emphasis on lay activity, and a marked return to Biblical theology as the basis for Church practice. Its themes include an emphasis on human dignity as the theological basis for social ethics, and an emphasis on humanity's general purpose to advance the works of God in creation.

Not surprisingly, the topic of work also surfaces several times in this document. Two points demonstrate its continuity with developing Catholic social

---

[6] Agriculture became important because the massive pressure placed on Vatican II by third world Bishops from Africa, Asia and Latin America.

thought with respect to work. First, as with Chenu, McCabe and the revised Thomist tradition which they represent (with the focus on teleology), the discussions of human purpose in *Gaudium et Spes* securely place work constitutionally (or ontologically) within God's desired plans for humanity. Here work's importance goes far beyond its instrumental function for survival or spiritual advancement. (*GS*, 20, 40.) Strategically, by highlighting that human labor was intended by God as part of humanity's purpose, work was endowed with its own value and worth.

A second point however, is that by so emphasizing work's relational aspects both social-structural and existential, the specifically 'human' dimensions of work begin to overshadow its other instrumental and ontological aspects. (*GS*, 9, 33, 34, 35.) This results in further embedding into Catholic social tradition the concept of the priority of the acts of labor over its products, material consequences or benefits. A quote toward the end of the document is telling on this point. 'Human labour, employed in the production and exchange of goods and in supplying economic services, is the chief element in economic life - all else is instrumental.' (*GS*, 67.)

Laborem Exercens

The next and final development in Catholic social thought to be considered is the 1981 publication by Pope John Paul II of the encyclical *Laborem Exercens* (On Human Work).[7] With this document official Catholic social teaching reaches its culmination with respect to work. Thus, we here turn our attention to a more careful evaluation of it.[8]

Simply described, *Laborem Exercens* is another in the line of papal encycli-

---

[7] *Laborem Exercens* (1981), in Baum, *The Priority of Labor*, pp.95-152. (1982.) We should mention here that in this text Baum offers a quite interesting socialist reading of this encyclical. However, as my analysis will show, such a reading is not ultimately sustainable.

Also, between the early period in theology of work development (represented by Chenu and then McCabe), and the publication of *Laborem Exercens*, there was in Catholicism outside of the Vatican additional probing for possibilities and further exploration into the theological basis for understandings of work. Part of this search, focusing on the questions of work's relation to eternal salvation and the relationship between nature and grace can be traced in: Reck, (1964), pp.228-39. See also for a more developed alternative approach at a Catholic theology of work: Davies, (1968), pp.93-116.

[8] Of course, Pope John Paul II has published several social encyclicals subsequent to *Laborem Exercens* and the importance of these documents to the developing tradition of Catholic social thought in general is beyond question. However, given that my concern in this book is with Catholic social teaching on work, I will not comment on these encyclicals. This is because on the question of work, these subsequent encyclicals stand in continuity with *Laborem Exercens* and do not make further contributions to it.

cals outlining the social teaching of the Catholic Church, or, addressing the
'social question'. It was occasioned by the ninetieth anniversary of Pope Leo
XIII's publication of the first social encyclical *Rerum Novarum.*

Laborem exercens is quite unique however compared to other encyclicals. It
is a highly theological document, yet it also has a quite narrow focus. While
other encyclicals range broadly over a host of social issues, *Laborem Exercens*
focuses primarily on one aspect of the social question, that of human work. As
Pope John Paul II explains, 'I wish to devote this document to human work,
and even more, to man in the vast context of the reality of work.' (*LE, 1.*) For
Pope John Paul II it is important to focus this letter, 'perhaps more than has
been done before', on human work when dealing with the social question, for
human work is the 'key, probably the essential key, to the whole social question'. (*LE, 3.*) Why so?

> And if the solution – or rather the gradual solution – of the social question, which
> keeps coming up and becomes ever more complex, must be sought in the direction
> of 'making life more human,' then the key, namely human work, acquires funda-
> mental and decisive importance. (*LE, 3.*)

Now this peculiar elevation of one aspect of the social question – work – to
the level of prime importance is not intended to be seen as incongruous with the
developing trajectory of the tradition as found in the previous encyclicals. Pope
John Paul II is clear that this encyclical is 'not intended to follow a different
line, but rather to be in organic connection with the whole tradition of this
teaching and activity.' (*LE,*2.) Indeed, in keeping with what has already been
seen in the broader survey of Catholic teaching, he points out that throughout
the

> Church's teaching in the sphere of the complex and many-sided social question –
> the question of human work naturally appears many times. This issue is, in a way,
> a constant factor both of social life and of the Church's teaching. (*LE, 3.*)

This emphasis on continuity with the tradition however, does not mean that
this Pope's specific conclusions on work in *Laborem Exercens* are simply re-
statements of what has been said previously in the Catholic tradition or elsewhere in the Christian Church. On the contrary, although it is thoroughly
Catholic theologically and ethically, and even though there are important points
where its teachings converge with wider ecumenical understandings of work, in
this document we nevertheless find a creative and original theological and ethical reflection on work. The uniqueness of this reflection largely stems from the
sources which have gone into producing it. Specifically, I shall be highlighting
three primary sources which the Pope has drawn upon, consciously or uncon-
sciously to formulate both the character and content of this letter. One of these
sources is Scripture itself. Another is a corporatist social tradition associated
with Catholic Europe. The other, more idiosyncratic source, is Pope John Paul

II's own personalist philosophical tradition.

Having made these general introductory points however, and before entering into a discussion of the letter's content, I want to comment briefly on what exactly I understand this encyclical's theological genre to be. This is necessary, as conclusions here will affect the directions and limits, and thus kind of analysis which I shall offer.

Firstly, this letter is written as a papal social encyclical and as such it is by design a succinct theological statement on work and an application of this statement to specific social conditions. It is not primarily a detailed thesis or abstract argument about the nature of work even if it implies one. Hence, we will need to be cautious and not demand from the letter the amount or kind of detail that we might expect find in other types of writings.

Secondly, and related to this, *Laborem Exercens* has been called a 'theology of work'.[9] Undeniably the letter is a theological reflection devoted specifically to human work. However, I do not believe that it is appropriate to classify the letter, an encyclical, as a theology of work. It simply is not structured as a comprehensive theological reflection on work. Rather, given its form and the concrete issues which it covers, it is better to read the document more restrictively as a theological ethics of work and not as a theology of work proper. This means that I will not be evaluating the content of the encyclical or its methodology according to the criteria outlined for a more fully developed theology of work. Such criticism would not be entirely fair to the nature of the document we have and would serve no broader purpose.

In what follows my purpose is twofold. Initially, without going into great detail, I shall outline how work in *Laborem Exercens* can be perceived as instrumental, relational, and, in some ways, ontological. (This will further demonstrate the appropriateness of the overall hypothesis.) More importantly however, I will then demonstrate how in this encyclical these three aspects function hierarchically in relationship to each other, and in so doing I will argue that this ordering, (which I believe to be flawed) is largely a result of an underdeveloped and thus inadequate ontological aspect of work.

The Instrumental Aspect of Work

Appearing quite prominently throughout this encyclical one finds what I have labeled the instrumental aspect of work. Both in relation to basic human sustenance and economics, and in relation to the developing spiritual life, work in *Laborem Exercens* is clearly depicted as a means to an end.

The instrumentality of work for human sustenance is highlighted throughout the letter. The opening words of the preface indicate that work is initially about man earning his daily bread. (*LE*, preface.) Later, Pope John Paul II talks about

---

[9] West, (1986), 'Cruciform Labour' pp.9-15.

the importance of this sustenance aspect of work in relation to family formation. Work, he says, 'is a condition for making it possible to found a family, since the family requires the means of subsistence which man normally gains through work.' (*LE*, 10.) Again, near the end of the encyclical we are reminded that work necessarily involves humans 'providing the substance of life for themselves and their families'. (*LE*, 25.)

Likewise, as a result of this concern for subsistence, the instrumental importance of human work in the sphere of economics is given prominence. Section IV, which addresses various issues concerning the rights of workers, is essentially an ethical discussion of specific work-related issues imbedded in and affected by economic considerations. The discussions of the direct and indirect employer (17.), the employment issue (18.), and wages (19.) all deal with work as a means to an end in the economic arena.

Work in *Laborem Exercens* is also construed as instrumental in the developing spiritual life. It is commanded by God, is God's will for man, and is a part of 'the salvation process' (understood here with reference to sanctification rather than justification). (*LE*, 16, 25, 24) Indeed, the importance of work for human spiritual development is most importantly highlighted by the fact that Pope John Paul II devotes the entire concluding section (V) to the elements of a spirituality of work.

Instrumentally then, work is not simply concerned with sustenance or economics. It is also about helping people 'come closer... to God, the Creator and Redeemer', and participating in 'his salvific plan for man and the world', and deepening our 'friendship with Christ'. (*LE*, 24.)

The Relational Aspect of Work

When considering work as a means to an end, however, *Laborem Exercens* does not limit its focus to the instrumental aspects of work. Indeed, prominent throughout the letter, and of more social ethical significance, is the concern for what I have called the relational aspect of work. What I have described as the social and existential dimensions of the relational aspect surface repeatedly throughout the document.

In the preface and to the opening sentence of the encyclical we find emphasized, beside the concern for earning one's daily bread, the relational / social aspect of work. Here work is understood to be centrally important to the continual advancement of humanity as a whole, including our corporate scientific and technological, and cultural and moral advancement. (*LE*, preface.) This idea is expressed repeatedly through the letter and as Pope John Paul II summarizes,

It is characteristic of work that it first and foremost unites people. In this consists its social power: the power to build a community. (*LE*, 20.)

We find then, that work is primarily characterized by its interpersonal / relational higher human dimension. As important as its economic or even basic subsistence value is, its greater ethical significance lies in its ability to create community.

However, this emphasis on the relational / social dimension of work should not be understood as essentially different than, or as minimizing, work's related ethical importance in the relational / existential realm. As the basis for social development, man has a 'tendency to self-realization' and work must 'serve to realize his humanity, to fulfill the calling to be a person that is his by reason of his very humanity.' (*LE*, 6.) What though, does self-realization through work mean? It means that man 'achieves that "domination" which is proper to him over the visible world'. (*LE*, 9.) It means that man 'not only transforms nature, adapting it to his own needs, but he also achieves fulfillment as a human being and indeed in a sense becomes "more a human being"' through work. (*LE*, 9.) Man therefore, needs work so that his own humanity (corporately and individually) may be both 'maintained and developed'. (*LE*, 16.) 'For when a man works he not only alters things and society, he develops himself as well.' (*LE*, 26.)

The Ontological Aspect of Work

Pope John Paul II however, does not conceive of, and thus does not develop work's instrumental and relational aspects independent of a theological foundation for work, or, what may rightly be understood to be an ontology of work. Work, for him, is more fundamental to created existence than simply its usefulness.

Again we begin in the preface with the initial lines of the encyclical. Here we find that man is 'predisposed by his very nature, by virtue of humanity itself' to work. Work is 'one of the characteristics that distinguish man from the rest of creatures'. Work, subduing the earth, is thus very closely linked with what it means to be created in the image and likeness of God. (*LE*, preface.) It is a 'basic dimension of human existence.' (*LE*, 1.) It is a 'fundamental dimension of man's existence on earth' as taught by the 'first pages of the Book of Genesis'. (*LE*, 4.)

In fact, work is so fundamental to man's existence that not surprisingly, it also 'enters into the salvation process'. (*LE*, 25.) In the first place, when humans work 'they are unfolding the Creator's work', that is, they are as image bearers sharing in the activity of the creator. (*LE*, 25.) However, work is even more closely tied to the salvation process than this. It is a participation in the cross and resurrection of Christ. In this sense, work has an eschatological thrust. It provides 'an announcement of "the new heavens and the new earth" in which man and the world participate precisely through the toil that goes with work.' (*LE*, 27.)

Do these points however, indicate that Pope John Paul II understands work to be in any way 'ontological'? Whether consciously or not, when he talks about work as being fundamental to human existence (and not merely an instrument to it), when he talks about work as a given in creation, when he speaks of work as part of the salvation process, when he offers these ideas as the theological and ethical foundations for the working life, he is suggesting an ontology of work. This does not mean that he has fully developed an ontology of work but it does mean that he sees the need for one and has made significant strides toward offering one.

Having established however, that *Laborem Exercens* offers a vision of work as instrumental, relational and ontological, the more interesting question becomes, in what way are these three aspects understood to be related to each other? How does one aspect effect the other, and what kind of an ethical picture of work do all three together produce?

In as much as they are, or can be said to be interrelated, the picture of work which emerges in *Laborem Exercens* is one of a strict hierarchical-subordinational ordering of our three aspects of work, rather than a mutual interdependent and 'egalitarian' relationship existing between the three. All three aspects of work are understood as necessary and important and none can be subordinated to the other so as to make any redundant. However, the instrumental aspect of work (here primarily referring to economic function) is subordinated (metaphysically and ethically) to the relational or 'human' aspect, while the relational, although ethically primary in the broadest sense, is nonetheless metaphysically subordinate to the ontological, in the sense that it has its source solely in the ontological.

What this means practically is that to resolve the ethical dilemmas when there is conflict in the area of work, the relational (because of the nature of the ontological) is granted priority over and allowed to limit and dictate parameters to the instrumental (and this must never happen in reverse order - instrumental to relational). The ontological here, does not bring the instrumental and relational together into a mutually defining and equally valuing give-and-take relationship, (nor does it allow itself to be further defined, 'located', or balanced by the other two). Rather, the ontological aspect guarantees the complete subordination of the former to the latter while itself remaining 'on the sidelines' and thus staying hierarchically prior to, and in reality unaffected by the other aspects. Thus, because of the ontological (as it is here depicted) the relational must have the priority. Because of the ontological the relational effects and results of work are given a strict priority over the objective products of work. The relational, human / spiritual are given priority over the instrumental / material elements of work.

In the analysis that follows I will substantiate these conclusions from *Laborem Exercens,* and will further develop them where necessary. I will likewise offer a critique of this hierarchical understanding of work and will suggest, foreshadowing the second half of this book, that a more adequately developed ontology of work would present a quite different non-hierarchical picture of work.

After an introductory section, Pope John Paul II begins to develop his understanding of work, a fundamental dimension of human existence, by using Scripture. That is, he begins his discussion of work in the Book of Genesis. This,
combined with a discussion of the spirituality of work at the end of the encyclical similarly appealing primarily to Scripture reveals that the foundations for an
adequate understanding of work are perceived to be primarily theological.
Structurally, it is interesting to note that the theological, here properly expressed as ontological, understanding of the nature of work becomes the beginning and concluding concern for that which must be said about work. The theological / ontological provides, therefore, the foundational parameters for an
understanding of what work should be both theoretically and practically. With
this structure, the primary element (the ontological) in work's hierarchical
structure has been laid down if not fully developed. That is, as a result of creation and salvation, work becomes a fundamental part of *man's* existence on
earth.

It should be noticed however, that while affirming that man's work must be
seen as a reflection of God's work, ultimately work is ethically and theologically defined mostly with reference to the human. Work's ontology stems from
man's reality. The bulk of the theological argumentation in the encyclical is
intended to demonstrate that work is 'transitive', an 'activity beginning in the
human subject and directed toward an external object'. (*LE*, 4.) As such, anthropology (theological anthropology) becomes the dominant and determining
source discipline for construing work's essential nature, rather than the doctrines of God or eschatology. The latter are affirmed in section V but appear as
additions rather than as essential to the developed argument. Therefore, they are
not, like anthropology, of the same determinative value.

Further, the development of work almost exclusively from anthropology
leads Pope John Paul II to the eventual conclusion that work cannot be seen as
something existing beside humanity in any way (as if it were a thing in itself,
intrinsically ordered also to itself). Rather, given its source in humanity, it ultimately needs always to be subordinated to humanity if it is to be theologically
and ethically viable. 'In the first place work is "for man" and not man "for
work"'. (*LE*, 6.)

It is instructive to probe how and why Pope John Paul II reaches such a hierarchical conclusion. Concerning the 'why', we begin to see another source for
his thought emerge (in addition to the Bible); namely, his personalist philosophy.[10] Concerning the 'how', Pope John Paul II finds it necessary to propose

---

[10] I will not be providing a detailed account of Pope John Paul II's personalist philosophy. For my purposes, the important effects of it emerge naturally in *Laborem Exercens*
and it will be sufficient to simply point out some of these connections as they arise. The

two senses of work. He develops the idea that there is both the objective and subjective sense of work.

By objective, he means that sense of work which focuses upon what humans produce through their work. This is most often talked about in economic terms as a material or technological product of working. (*LE*, 5.) When referring to the subjective sense of work, he is asserting that man is always the subject of work. (*LE*, 6.)

When Pope John Paul II speaks of these two senses of work together, it is a person who is doing the work, the subject, which must be seen as primary. 'The sources of the dignity of work are to be sought primarily in the subjective dimension, not in the objective one.' (*LE*, 6.) Thus, the 'primary basis of the value of work is man himself, who is its subject,' and not the product or object of work. (*LE*, 6.) Further, 'through this conclusion one rightly comes to recognize the preeminence of the subjective meaning of work over the objective one.' (*LE*, 6.)

With this section, Pope John Paul II is laying the foundations for his later argument and ethical principle which will assert the priority of labor over capital, or the subordination of that which work produces to the needs of labor. (I will return to this point shortly.) Here however, in personalist fashion, he is simply arguing that the person is more important than what he produces. As he will later state, the subjective dimension, or 'the concrete reality of the worker, takes precedence over the objective dimension.' (*LE*, 10.)

This point is so central to his argument that Pope John Paul II adds a section (7) to make sure that these values are kept in proper hierarchical order. His fear is that we regularly undermine human / spiritual values and replace them with materialistic or economistic ones. We do this by giving the 'prime importance to the objective dimension of work, while the subjective dimension – every thing in direct or indirect relationship with the subject of work – remains on a secondary level.' (*LE*, 7.) He argues however, that this hierarchical relationship (objective over subjective) is the reversal of the order laid down in Genesis and that it is precisely this reversal of order which has led to the error of capitalism.

Lest we get too far ahead of ourselves, I shall momentarily look ahead in the text, for this same argument is later taken up and more fully developed in section III, 13. There Pope John Paul II focuses his attention on the fundamental

---

point here is simply to draw attention to another of the important sources for the ideas in *Laborem Exercens*.

For a detailed understanding of Pope John Paul II's personalism, particularly as it deals with the nature of society, one should see: Emmanuel Mounier, and Jacques Maritain (specifically Maritain's *The Person and the Common Good* and *True Humanism*). Additionally, to understand more specifically Pope John Paul II's action (work) oriented anthropology one should see his book, *The Acting Person*. (1979) (published as Karol Wojtyla). This book grew out of his interaction with Max Scheler.

error, as he sees it, of the economistic perspective. (We can see here the emergence of his commitment to an economic middle way somewhere between capitalism and socialism; a personalist vision grounded in corporatist thinking.) According to Pope John Paul II, the error is

> that of considering human labor solely according to its economic purpose. This fundamental error of thought can and must be called an error of materialism, in that economism directly or indirectly includes a conviction of the primacy and superiority of the material, and directly or indirectly places the spiritual and the personal (man's activity, moral values and such matters) in a position of subordination to material reality. (*LE,* 13.)

I do not here want go into great detail critiquing this challenge to both capitalism and communism. It is interesting however, to notice briefly the options given and the 'either-or' way that they are presented. Hierarchy here has been assumed. It is a given, and as such, one, either the personal / spiritual or the material, will need to be on top. Given these options as ordered, Pope John Paul II's conclusions do follow. However, my contention (which I will be developing in the second part of this book) is that there does not need to be a hierarchy at all. The personal and material are, and thus can be, related and valued in a non-hierarchical manner so that neither must be subordinated to the other.

Such a suggestion would not satisfy Pope John Paul II. His concern is not simply the subordination of the subjective to the objective. For him it would be equally problematic to value the material on the same or similar level as the human. He is clear, returning to section II, 7 that 'the error of early capitalism can be repeated whenever man is in a way treated on the same level as the whole complex of the material means of production'. (*LE,* 7.) Stated simply, whenever man as the subject is treated equally with the material which is necessarily object, (specifically here the material object which he produces) one is in error.

Is this not simply a new version of an old Catholic (and Platonic) hierarchy where the soul, or 'spirit' is seen as superior to, or valued over, matter? According to his construct, matter, either in its raw God created form or as further shaped by humans, can never be valued as equal to spirit (or person / souls). Pope John Paul II clearly states this in his first encyclical *Redemptor Hominis* (1979). Here, explaining the Second Vatican Council's understanding of man's kingship he states,

> The essential meaning of this 'kingship' and 'dominion' of man over the visible world, which the Creator himself gave man for his task, consists in the priority of ethics over technology, in the primacy of the person over things, and in the superiority of spirit over matter. (*RH,* 16.)

What is essential here to see is that not only can work's subjective sense never be subordinated to its objective sense, but that fundamentally, these two senses cannot be treated or valued equally. We never have two 'subjects' which can make equally limiting demands upon the other when it might seem necessary. A hierarchy must always be maintained, and the order of this must be the subordination of the objective sense of work to the subjective sense of work, the material to the human, matter to spirit. The principle, which will be later stated, is 'the primacy of the person over things'. (*LE,* 13.) Ultimately therefore, as we shall see, this principle leads to the further principle of the subordination of capital to labor.

Returning to the flow of the encyclical, that which follows in Pope John Paul II's reasoning is largely an outworking and further defining of the principles which he has so far presented. Beginning with section III paragraph 11, he builds his defense and application of these principles in a context of conflict between the subject and object of work, between labor and capital. His point throughout this section however, is that there is no conflict, nor does there need to be a conflict, *so long as* the subject and object, labor and capital, the human and things, spirit and matter, are kept in a proper hierarchical relationship to each other. 'The principle', he argues, the one which the Church has always taught, is 'of the priority of labor over capital', the 'substantial and real priority of labor'. (*LE,* 12, 13.) Expressed similarly, the commitment is to the 'primacy of man over things.' (*LE,* 12.) Things, the objects and products of work, are simply a 'collection of instruments' and 'are only a mere instrument subordinate to human labor.' (*LE,* 12.) Things can never also be 'an impersonal "subject" putting man and man's work into a position of dependence.' (*LE,* 13.) Here we find again that things, nature either in its raw form or its further-shaped-by-human form, can never be in a subject to subject relationship with man. Man is always the dominating subject and nature the responsive object. Importantly, this principle of hierarchy and subordination is paradigmatic for the whole of Pope John Paul II's, and thus *Laborem Exercens'* social ethics. 'The principle of the priority of labor over capital is a postulate of the order of social morality.' (*LE,* 15.)

Thus, we arrive where we began. Because of the ontological commitment that the objective aspect of work must always be subordinate to work's subject, it necessarily follows that work's instrumental aspect (here its economic and material value) must be hierarchically subordinated to its relational aspect (its social and existential function). It could be no other way. What this demonstrates is that our earlier conclusion was valid. In *Laborem Exercens* work is strictly a hierarchical construct.

Now, pointing ahead to what will follow in the second half of the book, I want to briefly sketch why this approach to work's threefold nature is inadequate. I find the hierarchical-subordinational understanding of work as offered in *Laborem Exercens,* where the instrumental is always subordinated to the relational because of the ontological, to be unacceptable for several reasons. Practically, it would ultimately be impossible to consistently live with such an approach. In the real world, and for the ethical sake of whole communities, there are times when broader economic considerations (markets) must be placed before, for example, the commitment to total employment. Rather than always trying to subordinate the former to the latter in a moralist fashion, it is actually both more realistic and ethically superior to judge each situation independently and determine ways forward at a given time and place. Here both the object and the subject of work will be allowed to make their respective legitimate demands. This will only be possible however, according to moral theory if the instrumental and relational aspects of work are related to each other metaphysically in some kind of reciprocal rather than hierarchical manner. In some way, both need to become subjects.

This practical critique however, is simply an indication that there is something wrong with the theory itself. Therefore, it is to this theoretical evaluation of work in *Laborem Exercens* that we now turn our attention.

To begin with, I do not want to deny the appropriateness of seeking to derive the essential nature of work from theological anthropology. Indeed, I shall be taking an approach similar to this in the second part of this book. However, unlike *Laborem Exercens,* which for all practical purposes when discussing work appends the doctrines of God and eschatology to the end of an already developed anthropology (under the heading of a spirituality of work), my approach will be to integrate these, and other doctrines as necessary, into a theological anthropology.

This will result in what I believe to be a more adequately developed ontology of work, one superior to that which is offered in *Laborem Exercens.* This then, becomes my main criticism of the hierarchical-subordinational understanding of work presented in the encyclical. It has an underdeveloped and thus inadequate ontology of work at its foundation. By not integrating other doctrines more explicitly and directly into its anthropology, the ontology of work offered here suffers as an unfinished and out of balance foundation.

A more adequately developed ontology of work will need to pay more attention, for example, to the theology of nature even if this is offered (as I shall do) within a discussion of anthropology. What nature's eschatological *telos* proves to be, becomes important for if nature is seen as having its own *telos* and ordering to God, related to but also distinct from its ordering to humanity, then the exclusive hierarchical ordering of the subject of work to the object of work, man to material, labor to capital proves to be inadequate. If nature too has its own ordering to God, then it too becomes in some respects a subject. Thus, the instrumental and the relational aspects of work can be seen to be mutually related to each other, subject to subject. The former need not necessarily and always be subordinated to the latter.

Likewise, if man proves first to be a part of nature and only then is secondarily distinguished from it, then his dominion of nature, while not necessarily denied, will necessarily be of a different kind than if he were first distinct from and set over and opposed to nature. If it is affirmed that man is firstly a unity in nature, then again a hierarchy dissipates. Matter cannot be subordinate to man for it is essential to man that he is matter. Here it would make little sense to speak of man (material) subordinated to man (person). Such a dualism would be redundant.

Related to these types of enquiries, to develop an adequate ontology of work it will also be essential to consider more specifically what eschatology, or the resurrection of Jesus, and then nature's and our resurrection at the end of time, mean to work in the context of a natural humanity. If the material products or objects of work are included in nature and thus in the resurrection in any way, (and therefore are included in the new heavens and new earth) then work again objectively develops a value unique to itself. It ceases to be simply 'for man' in the way described in *Laborem Exercens*. Objective work (matter) ceases to be an object in the sense that Pope John Paul II describes it. It becomes also and equally a subject. In this scenario, humans and things can be placed beside each other and theoretically both can be valued equally and non-hierarchically. There may be times when one or the other must take the practical priority for instance, when either ecology or human development becomes the primary problem. This, however, can be decided upon the merits of each case and it will not necessitate a predetermined subordination of the one to the other. Thus, both work's instrumental and relational aspects will be allowed to mutually balance and even define each other.

Likewise, when the ontology of work is fully developed along the lines out-lined above, it too forfeits its insularity. It will still be initially foundational in the overall work construct (instrumental, relational and ontological). However, when it is developed as suggested above, it will, as it were, enter into the game. No longer will it simply be on the sidelines dictating what the relational, or instrumental, aspects must be. Rather, it too will allow both the instrumental and relational aspects a type of subjective role in defining and locating it. That is, it will cease to be the only subject in the construct. The ontological aspect of work will become a part of work in such a way that it will allow itself to be shaped by what is objectively both its instrumental and relational function.

Taking all of this into account I am suggesting that what *Laborem Exercens* needs is a more adequately developed ontology of work. Once this is provided, a hierarchical-subordinational understanding of the three aspects of work will be undermined and there will emerge a vision of work at once more theoreti-cally sound and more practical. Providing this better developed ontology of work as stated becomes the task in the second part of this project.

CHAPTER 3

Modern Protestant Understandings of Work

During the Reformation those Christians who identified with the Protestant movement were challenged to conceive of their ordinary daily work as an ordained calling or vocation from God. This understanding of the doctrine of vocation has by and large persisted to the present and has become for Protestants the primary motif or model used to explain the spiritual place of work in human life. Broadly speaking the vocational model outlines the spiritual meaning of work as twofold; as acts of personal obedience to God/God's call, and, as outward service to others as God's means for meeting their physical needs. As I will show, this particularly Protestant approach to work as vocation has continued to be influential in twentieth century Protestant theological reflection on work. Despite several critiques and attempts by some to leave it behind, for many Protestants seeking to understand the nature and meaning of human work the doctrine of vocation has continued to provide the foundation or superstructure.

This does not mean however that there is or has been only one Protestant approach to and understanding of work set forth during the twentieth century (or that the vocational model is the only one appropriate to Protestantism). On the contrary, Protestant theological understandings of work have become as diversified as Protestantism itself. Therefore what follows is necessarily an interpretation of twentieth century Protestant construals of work that both reflects the enduring influence of the vocational model and also emphasizes where the substantial differences in approach and understanding have developed.

Classifying the Literary Sources

The initial methodological challenge lies in identifying and classifying the variety of twentieth century Protestant sources addressing work. Basically there are three different types of literature available, each offering a distinctive approach to thinking theologically about work. There are: reflections on work that are offered secondarily within more general systematic theological explorations, studies that are narrowly focused on exploring work *qua* work, and there is ethical or contextual literature that deals with work indirectly while offering specific ethical reflection on some other issue.

Systematic Theology

It is not uncommon to find in a systematic theology or in substantial doctrinal expositions specific reflections on the nature and meaning of human work. Theologians such as Barth, Brunner, Bonhoeffer and Moltmann each offer reflections on work within their more comprehensive theological treatises. However they offer these in the context of exploring a major doctrine or while discussing other points of doctrine. Work is addressed from a theological perspective, yet work is not primarily (in and for itself) what is being explored, nor is work being addressed comprehensively. Rather, a particular doctrinal point is being explored and work is discussed as it relates to this doctrine.

Of course there are both advantages and disadvantages to using this type of theological literature to explore the theological meaning of work. On the positive side, when construed within an overall systematic theology, work does find its own 'place', meaning that work is perceived as a proper object for theological reflection and that work can be located or understood in relationship to broader theological truth. An advantage of this is that 'tunnel vision', or the temptation to overestimate work's theological place, is kept in check. Work is understood as an implication or application of some more foundational or first order doctrine. Work is not depicted as the be all and end all of human existence, nor the centerpiece around which to organize all theology. On the negative side however, in a systematic theology it is obviously not work *qua* work that is the primary question. Therefore, it is virtually unavoidable that some important considerations and angles will be overlooked in the discussion.

Focused Studies

Another type of literature providing theological reflection on work are those books or articles that take the question of work as the starting point. That is, this literature makes work itself the primary object of exploration. This literature might focus on a theological, Biblical, pastoral, or sociological analysis of work, but most are attempts to probe each of these areas en route to proposing a more comprehensive Christian picture of work. Of course, there are strengths and weaknesses arising from this type of literature. Negatively, when focusing primarily on the phenomenon of work it is easy to lose perspective and fail to recognize that work is only a part (albeit a fundamental part) of our life as humans. The danger when attempting to consider work from all angles is that our vision can become myopic. The temptation is to see everything in life and theology as leading to and from work, as if all life and theology were a subcategory of work. Positively, however, this approach does allow for a more comprehensive reflection on work and a deeper exploration into important themes that often greatly enhance our understanding of both work and the Christian theology within which it is being evaluated.

Ethical / Contextual Studies

A third type of theological literature reflecting on work might be called ethical or contextual. This is a body of literature that although reflecting on work, does so only indirectly while attempting to explore or resolve other pressing ethical issues. The fundamental concerns in this literature might be issues such as the exploitation of nature, unemployment, the exploitation of the poor, racial and sexual discrimination at work, basic human rights, or redressing the problems of power and authority relationships in the workplace. In as much as work itself is related to these ethical concerns, it is explored theologically.

Like the other two types of literature, these ethical or contextual writings also bring with them methodological strengths and weaknesses. On the positive side, these approaches are usually grounded in concrete reality and are often based on some social analysis, with genuine human, and even non-human, need at the forefront. As such, their conclusions tend to be practical (or applied) and tend to avoid the often abstract and detached theoretical pronouncements sometimes associated with research narrowly focused on work itself. Negatively, however, there are limitations to this approach. The most significant is that when trying to make a related ethical point, it becomes all too easy to distort work's nature and meaning by over emphasizing one or another of its important aspects (e.g. instrumental or relational). Here the final vision of work either directly or indirectly offered often becomes ideologically driven and less than comprehensive, and thus, inadequate.

There are then basically three 'genres' or types of contemporary Protestant theological literature exploring work, and each methodologically carries with it both strengths and weakness. All genres are valuable in that each in its own way can reveal certain aspects or questions related to work that must be seriously considered. In attempting a theology or ethics of work, methodologically it will prove invaluable to identify these different types of literature, interpreting each methodologically according to its genre and thus uncovering what it is attempting to offer. In this way, each type of literature will make its own unique offering.

Directions Old and New: Methodologies Considered

Growing out of and related to the type of literature available, in the twentieth century there emerged several often divergent Protestant ways of thinking theologically about work. Yet, methodologically speaking most Protestant constructs bear some family resemblance. The heritage of vocational theology has left certain marks on most of these constructs regardless of whether they are reappropriations of the vocational model or attempts to move beyond it. In what follows I will differentiate between contemporary reformulations of the vocational model and new models (or directions) that Protestants have found to be promising. I will, however, also highlight where the continuing influence of vocational theology can be seen even in those approaches which have set the model aside.

Re-appropriations of the Vocational Model

Vocation as the Paradigm. It is almost instinctive for Protestants to interpret a person's work as in some way a calling or vocation.[1] By and large, Protestants have either simply assumed that this model is the starting point for reflection, or argued that it can be the starting point. The latter, although recognizing the question, argue that there is still mileage left in the model provided that it is further developed to account for modern social realities, and provided that it is rooted more satisfactorily in biblical / theological thinking. Indeed, in line with Luther and Calvin most Protestants writing on the subject (excluding possibly Jacques Ellul) have continued to argue that work is a vocation from God and thus that the active working life is positively a part of one's continued spiritual life. Obedience to God in one's daily activities (or to God's 'call' to work), and a motivation to meet the needs of others through work continue to be Reformational emphases that most Protestants have wanted to retain in some form.

Many European Protestants in the aftermath of World War II turned their theological attention to the problem of work. While Catholics were exploring 'theologies of work', most of these Protestants turned to their own tradition's vocation motif.[2] By the middle of the century, Protestants had come to believe that, though still applicable, the doctrine of vocation needed to be revitalized and reinterpreted. With the end of the war tremendous changes had taken place in the world in general and, in the world of work in particular. Given the effects of industrialization and the global economic depression earlier in the century, the influence of expanding markets with the unstable workforce and unemployment which this brings, the growing influence of socialism, the appeal of the welfare state, and the realisations of both the negative as well as positive effects of technology, many Protestants felt compelled to reexamine their own theological understandings of vocation and work and to bring them more into line with these contemporary realities. Additionally, common critiques of the traditional understanding of vocation were: that it was too inwardly oriented and individualistic, that there was not enough concern about social / structural questions related to work, that it was too closely aligned with the spirit of capi-

---

[1] Even for those who have chosen to understand work theologically according to alternative models, vocation remains the backdrop against which they are developing their proposals, or often, the dialogue partner with which they are arguing.

[2] One notable exception here is A. Richardson, a prominent figure in the World Council of Churches. In *The Biblical Doctrine of Work* (1952) he attempted to consider afresh the nature and meaning of work but Richardson criticizes and sets aside the vocational understanding of work. See: pp.35-39.

talism, and, that it was dependant on, and encouraged, a far too static form of society.

These critiques may or may not be judged as substantial at the dawn of the twenty-first century, especially given a more careful reading of what the Reformers actually taught concerning vocation. Doubtless however, the concerns behind the critiques are legitimate and were appropriate at that time. Nevertheless, the point is that by the middle of the century these perceived needs led many Protestants to look afresh at and to reformulate their theological understanding of work and vocation. Examples of those attempting to re-appropriate the vocational model include O. Nelson *Work and Vocation,* (1954), and W. R. Forrester *Christian Vocation,* (1951).

Toward the end of the century Protestants again took up the discussion on the vocational model for interpreting work. Some like Miroslav Volf have been critical, calling Protestants to move further away from the tradition. Others have at least called for a serious recasting of it.[3] Still others, mostly from Reformed / evangelical traditions have appealed for a more direct and only slightly refined return to and rediscovery of the Reformation and Puritan doctrines of vocation. Three articles by Ian Hart (1995), and the books by Lee Hardy *The Fabric of This World,* (1990), and Lyland Ryken *Work and Leisure in Christian Perspective,* (1987), are fine examples of this.

This sampling shows us that during the twentieth century a vocational understanding of work remained influential in Protestant theology. Although no longer the only voice, it is nonetheless an enduring one. Since the model has received such ongoing support, and shown its ability to be reformed, and since many can demonstrate that it is still able to offer important contributions to our understanding of work's nature and meaning, any contemporary theological reflection on work would do well to engage reflectively with it and at least to come through it, rather than simply writing it off. In terms of my hypothesis, the vocational model emphasises particularly the importance of work's instrumental aspect (especially with respect to human obedience / sanctification) and its relational aspect (concerning how our work can contribute toward meeting the needs of others and the broader society).

A FOCUS ON THE INITIAL CREATION

When theologically exploring work, a common feature among Protestants generally and also among those particularly viewing work as vocation is a strong appeal to and dependence on the various doctrines surrounding the initial creation, or, protology. During the twentieth century the doctrines of creation order/ordinances, creation mandates, the image of God in humanity, and the Fall have been given considerable attention both in biblical and systematic theology. Often, the topic of human work has emerged from discussion of these themes.

---

[3] See for example the call to rework the entire tradition: Shriver, (1995), pp.538-545.

The idea that the initial creation is the theological and ethical starting point for reflection on work has persisted in all but a few of the most recent writers. Emil Brunner for example, construed work as a command grounded in the initial creation. That is, as a creation 'ordinance'.[4] Dietrich Bonhoeffer, uncomfortable with the concept of 'ordinance' due in part to its ideological abuse by the Nazis, nonetheless considers work primarily as a creation 'mandate'.[5] Likewise, many in the Evangelical tradition following Dutch Calvinism are also keen to construe work as first and foremost a creation mandate issued directly by God.[6] Even Karl Barth with his distrust of natural theology as seen in his argument with Brunner concerning 'creation ordinances' with his critique of the vocational approach to work and his replacement of it with a 'Sabbath' model, - even Barth finally theologizes on work at the end of his doctrine of the initial creation. While not referring to it as a creation ordinance or mandate, he does consider it to be a necessary 'relationship of creation'.[7]

This focus on protology as the doctrine in which to explore work suggests that modern Protestant theology, explicitly or not, has been probing for and moving in the direction of developing an ontological dimension of work. The desire to locate and secure work's nature and meaning in the very structure of the created world suggests that work has been perceived to be more than simply an instrumental activity. This possibility of developing an ontology of work, a central concern of my hypothesis, will not I believe be fully possible until Christological / eschatological doctrines are also considered in relationship to the doctrines of the initial creation. Nevertheless, the explorations in protology provide necessary resources for a good part of this task.

Departures from the Vocation Tradition

As stated, the vocational model, with its close dependence on protology, has not been the only Protestant model of work in the twentieth century. As I shall now outline, some have been searching for other models and ways to theologically understand work to get beyond the weaknesses and potentially oppressive misuses of the vocational motif. What is apparent however, is that very few of these Protestant writers completely skirt the themes common in vocational

---

[4] Brunner, (1937), pp.384-394.

[5] Bonhoeffer, (1955), pp.179-184.

[6] See for example the writings of Paul Marshall: "Work and Vocation", (1980), "Calling, Work, and Rest", (1988), *Thine is the Kingdom: A Biblical Perspective on the Nature of Government and Politics Today*, (1984). See also: Scanzoni, (1974)., and Scotchmer, (1980).

[7] Barth, *Church Dogmatics*, III 4. (1961). Whether Barth would have returned to a discussion of work with reference to the new creation, had he lived long enough to produce his volume on eschatology, is simply a matter for speculation.

thinking. The majority indeed seem, in some modified form, to have re-appropriated many of its contributions. This should not be surprising given that many of its themes are quite biblical. What I am suggesting however, is that these Protestants have come 'through' vocational thinking even if they have not retained it as a model.

This suggestion of continuity should not draw attention away from the genuine innovations that some Protestants have made. Of those critical of the vocational model, some have moved to more 'contextual' methodologies. Others have borrowed the 'theology of work' motif from Catholic thinking, and still others have let their own system of theology guide their construals of work. I will now classify several of these writers and will pay special attention to how these developments have pushed forward the entire enterprise of theologically construing work.

CONTEXTUAL METHODOLOGIES

The first alternative models that I will mention can broadly be called contextual. Here, certain concrete ethical concerns have determined the agenda within which work will be considered, the materials which will be selected to inform the discussion on work, and, the particular slant given to the arguments about work. I have in mind, for instance, the attempts by politically, economically, or racially oppressed peoples to suggest theological understandings of work that are particularly directed toward their points of conflict. With these types of writings, the emphasis with reference to work usually has to do with liberation and economic equality. Good examples of this contextual approach are found in Cochrane and West's *The Three-Fold Cord: Theology, Work and Labour* (1991). We find among other offerings a specifically black theology of work and also a theology of work for 'workers'.[8]

Not surprisingly, feminist theological models for depicting work have also emerged. Dorothee Soelle's *To Work and to Love* (1984) is one example, Elizabeth J. Nash's article 'A New Model for a Theology of Work.' (1986) is another. Yet another, which combines both feminist and black perspectives, is offered by Nondyebo Taki.[9] Two common threads in most feminist models are the achievement of the human being's personal self-end through work, and a sustained focus on the interpersonal / relational dimension of work.

Feminists are not the only ones to be concerned with the existential ideas of fulfillment, personal development, and interpersonal relationality in and through work. Others have also recently taken this approach, usually combining these personal and relational concerns with additional explorations related to broader social relationships, politics and economics. Jürgen Moltmann, Douglas Meeks, Timothy Gorringe, and John Scanzoni are only a few examples

---

[8] Cochrane, (1991), pp.142-154, and 160-168.
[9] Cochrane. (1991), pp.169-176.

here.[10] Similarly, Jacques Ellul also shares these concerns, although his reflections are critical, warning that work and its technological products are actually damaging to human development and human relationships.[11]

On the other end of the ideological spectrum, several have written theological enquiries relating to work that are meant to support their own particularly conservative theories of politics and economics. Michael Novak's writings and several articles in Richard Chewning's 'Christians in the Marketplace Series' are examples of this.[12] Here work's instrumental value in providing one's basic needs is in focus, and work is construed as if it were mostly a sub-division of economics.

Still others, including Jürgen Moltmann and Rosemary Radford Ruether have discussed work with particular attention to how it relates (usually negatively) to the current ecological crisis.[13] These primarily negative pronouncements on work do nonetheless offer valuable resources that are important for any theologically positive evaluation of work.

What these contextual approaches demonstrate is that any contemporary theological construal of work that hopes to be comprehensive, must broaden the range of its theological reflection beyond simply doctrinal explorations so as to guarantee that concrete concerns are adequately addressed. In terms of my hypothesis, this means that any contemporary theology of work must include considerations of: work's instrumentality concerning economic survival, its role relationally in personal existential and interpersonal development, its relational role in social reoganisation and social service in light of the effects of technology on individuals and society, and its relationship to and effect on the environment. This means that the instrumental and relational aspects of work, as I have called them, must be reckoned with in concrete terms.

SABBATH NOT VOCATION

During the twentieth century, prominent Protestant theologians like Karl Barth began to criticize the adequacy of the vocational model of work on Biblical / theological, and not simply on ethical grounds. Barth, critical of natural theol-

---

[10] See: Moltmann, *On Human Dignity*, (1984), Meeks, 'God and Work.' in *God the Economist* (1989), Gorringe, 'Work Leisure and Human Fulfillment.' in *Capital and the Kingdom*: (1994), and Scanzoni, 'The Christian View of Work.' (1974).

[11] Ellul, (1972).

[12] See Novak's articles in *Co-Creation and Capitalism: John Paul II's 'Laborum Exercens'*, eds. Houck and Williams. (1983), Novak, *The Spirit of Democratic Capitalism*, (1982). Also see: Chewning, ed. *Biblical Principles & Business. Vol. 1.* (1989), and *Biblical Principles & Economics. Vol. 2.* (1989).

[13] See, Moltmann, *On Human Dignity*, (1984), *God in Creation*, (1985), and Ruether, *Liberation Theology: Human Hope Confronts Christian History and American Power.* (1972), *To Change the World: Christology and Cultural Criticism.* (1981), and *Sexism and God Talk: Toward a Feminist Theology.* (1983).

ogy and of Luther's exegesis concerning 'klesis', offered Protestants a new model and a new theological place for work beginning with the principle of 'sabbath' rather than vocation. Barth still addressed work within protology, but rather than starting with a calling to human activity he took the sabbath to be the logical and conceptual theological starting point. This approach to work retained many of the traditional emphases of the vocational model, such as the importance of human obedience to the call of God, and the importance of work as a service to God and others. At the same time it challenged and relativized the modern, almost 'deified' understanding of human work in a way that the traditional Reformation model presumably could not.

Of course, the Reformers and Puritans emphasized the sabbath and took it seriously. However, in their teachings, the sabbath relativised human work simply by being a complementary command beside it; that is, a type of additional duty to be observed. In Barth however, sabbath becomes paradigmatic and is meant to be a principle that permeates and transforms the entire nature and structure of work, and thus its meaning. It is not simply meant to keep work in balance or in check in a person's life.

The particulars of Barth's innovative teaching on work have largely been neglected in subsequent theological reflections on work.[14] However, broadly speaking his influence can be seen in more recent theological construals of work that attempt to integrate the sabbath and related concepts into the understanding of work itself (rather than to have it function simply as a parallel idea and limitation to it). Although Jürgen Moltmann himself does not draw specifically on Barth's view of sabbath when commenting on human action and work, one can nevertheless detect Barth's influence in his writings. Moltmann's view that our human *telos* involves a participation in God's sabbath (or the divine shekinah as he eventually calls its eschatological fulfillment) does bear striking similarities to Barth's view.

Douglas Meeks' chapter 'God and Work' in *God the Economist* reflects elements of Barth's sabbath principle, (although it is questionable whether this emphasis is drawn more directly from Moltmann rather than Barth).[15] In either case, Barth's lasting influence on theological understandings of work is his idea that work is not the opposite of sabbath, but rather, that sabbath rest should be a characteristic of all human activity and thus also of work.

ESCHATOLOGY NOT PROTOLOGY

In contemporary Protestant theology's attempt to reinterpret work, a recent trend is the reconstruction of theological models of work based upon eschato-

---

[14] However, for examples of attempts to probe and build upon Barth see: Atkinson, (1994), pp.104-11., and West, 'Karl Barth's Theology of Work: A Resource for the Late 1980s', (1988).

[15] Meeks, (1989), pp.127-155.

logical rather than strictly protological foundations. Both Jürgen Moltmann (as I shall shortly examine) and Miroslav Volf (in *Work in the Spirit*, (1991)) are the primary theologians leading in this direction. Here again, we find a departure from the vocational motif. More significant however, is that for the first time some within Protestantism have made a decided move away from protology as work's theological orientation point. This is not to say that these theologians have ignored protology or its importance in understanding work. Rather, their eschatological orientation means that from protology, work is perceived as teleologically directed and oriented forward toward the future new creation rather than backward toward the restoration of the initial creation. It would not be inappropriate to claim therefore, that with this 'new creation' orientation, work becomes a type of eschatological mandate rather than simply a creation mandate. Herein lies a significant shift in ethics.

To sum up, what we have seen from this interpretive survey of twentieth century Protestant theological understandings of work is that the vocational model is still both influential and helpful, even if it is no longer the only possible or fruitful model available to Protestants. With the re-appropriation of vocation as a methodology, we find preserved in some form the Reformation's accent on personal obedience to God in work, and meeting the needs of others through work. In terms of my hypothesis, this suggests that the instrumental and relational / social aspects of work continue to be important.

Further, the variety of contextual and new approaches mentioned have suggested that work plays an important role in human, or 'personal' development and fulfillment. These approaches have likewise highlighted further the importance of social, structural, and even ecological concerns associated with human work and its economic (and technological) products. In terms of my hypothesis, this further suggests that the relational aspect of work, (both existential and social), must not be neglected. Any attempt at a comprehensive theology of work will need to explore carefully the personal, social and environmental issues related to work.

Finally, the doctrinal foundations for the vocational model, as well as the theological probing undertaken by the new models of work suggest that there is more to work than simply its instrumental or relational value. The various construals of work, whether protological or eschatological, suggest that work is in some way fundamental to divine, human and the broader created reality. In terms of my hypothesis this means that there is, whether consciously or not, a groping towards an ontology of work which will carry it beyond its purely resultant functioning.

What remains to be done in Protestant theology is to articulate consistently and coherently this theological ontology of work. The recent eschatological models for understanding work suggest that this ontology will need to appropriate 'new creation' insights as well as those gleaned from protology. In order to see what this might look like I now turn to consider in more detail one of these approaches, the one offered by Jürgen Moltmann.

Jürgen Moltmann on Work

Jürgen Moltmann writing in the latter half of the twentieth century is one of the more influential theologians to have made an important contribution to a Protestant theological understanding of work. His reflections on work's nature and meaning are primarily found in two essays. The first, 'The First Liberated Men in Creation' was published as a book entitled *Theology of Play* (1972).[16] The second, 'The Right to Meaningful Work' appears in the volume of essays on political theology and ethics titled *On Human Dignity* (1984).[17] Here I offer an analysis and critique of these essays and consider whether Moltmann's theological understanding of work might provide the basis for a further, more comprehensive attempt at a theology of work.

Work Begins with Play

I shall begin my analysis of Moltmann's conception of work by looking at his discussion of play. I do this primarily because in his later essay 'The Right to Meaningful Work' Moltmann, referring the reader back to his earlier publication *Theology of Play,* shows that his basic understanding of work's nature and meaning is developed in those earlier more detailed discussions of play / work. (*HD*, p.41. note 7.)

A central concern in 'The Right to Meaningful Work' is that joy, freedom, and playfulness be a fundamental part of work's nature and meaning. (*HD*, p.41.) However, Moltmann first explored these concepts in depth in 'The First Liberated Men in Creation' and it is in this essay that their meaning and relationship to each other are made clear.

At the beginning of this earlier essay Moltmann suggests that fundamentally people are oriented toward happiness and enjoyment. To be happy however, we must above all be free. When we are free the result in our daily lives is that 'we gain distance from ourselves and our plans move forward in a natural, unforced way.' (*TP*, p.1.) These plans referred to here include our projects in life, or our work. Moltmann's vision is that when our activities, our work, are characterized by freedom, rejoicing, and laughing, then we can 'find it easy to cope with other men and circumstances.' (*TP*, p.1.) Then we can be happy.

To explore this understanding of freedom which results in happiness, Moltmann begins to discuss the aesthetic category of play. He begins an inquiry into

---

[16] Hereafter referred to as *TP*.

The English translation of this essay was first published in America in: *Theology of Play,* (1972). This same essay later appeared in the United Kingdom published as *Theology and Joy,* (1973). The essay itself, entitled 'The First Liberated Men in Creation' ('Die Ersten Freigelassenen Der Schopfung'), was first published in German in 1971 by Chr. Kaiser Verlag, München.

[17] Hereafter referred to as *HD*.

critical game theory and starts the discussion arguing that play has been degraded in modern industrial society. Again, the concept of work (here understood as labor which is 'forced' and necessary for basic survival) is lurking at the corners. Play has become a 'theoretical problem' only as a result of rationalized, industrial labor which has banned playfulness as mere foolishness. (*TP*, p.4.) Forced labor, at least in an industrialized society, is the culprit. It undermines play and thus happiness.

What does game theory itself suggest about play? Moltmann states, 'All theories about play make the point that a game is meaningful within itself but that it must appear useless and purposeless from an outside point of view.' (*TP*, p.5.) On this view, we cannot therefore enquire about the purpose of a game or we become spoilsports. Moltmann suggests that rather than asking what the purpose of a game is, we should be asking whom does it serve? 'Of course this may sound like the miserable mood of a spoilsport, but the question really serves only to unmask those who cheat at the game.' (*TP*, p.6.) Who are these cheaters? They are those who try to construe play in relationship to work. They consider play essentially to be a useful diversion which is necessary so that work can be resumed more effectively or productively. Moltmann argues that this 'common view' is the ideological abuse of play which is used by the culture of work as a tool for oppressing the masses of workers.

Rather than serving the oppressors, who support the culture of work, play should be construed so as to support the oppressed. Play, not work, should have conceptual priority. Work should be understood in the light of play and not vice versa. In this way, play becomes linked with liberation. Games become meaningful, and even useful in a non-ideological way, as games of liberation. (*TP*, pp.10-14.) A game, or play, is meaningful when it is a game of freedom which prepares men for a more liberated society. (*TP*, p.12.) Play should be an anticipation of, and an experiment in, liberation. This liberation or freedom is characterized by a lack of fear; that is, by a lack of necessity or compulsion. Play, not labor, is where human activity becomes meaningful.[18]

So how does Moltmann's modified version of game theory relate to theology? He begins his section on 'Theological Play of the Good Will of God' arguing that currently theology has little use for aesthetic categories. Faith is no longer interested in play but only in utility. Everything must be useful and used. Ethics is everything.

This emphasis on utility naturally leads to the question; why did God create the world? Moltmann is critical of this question for the very reason that it is bound to utility. To Moltmann it is a wrong or misdirected question. If forced to answer, he simply replies with a type of non-answer, that 'he wisdom of the-

---

[18] Interestingly this seems to conflict with his view in *On Human Dignity*. There he argues that hard and laborious human work is also meaningful precisely because it corresponds to the hard and laborious work of Christ in redemption.

ology ends with the liberty of the children of God.' (*TP*, p.16.) Here there is no utilitarian reason, no 'purposive rationale' that answers why God created. The world is not necessary to God. God is free, (but not capricious). The ground of creation is God's good will or pleasure. (*TP*, p.17.) This line of reasoning leads Moltmann to a climactic conclusion. 'Hence the creation is God's play, a play of his groundless and inscrutable wisdom. It is the realm in which God displays his glory.' (*TP*, p.17.)

Whatever can Moltmann mean in claiming that creation is God's play? Here he is speaking symbolically. He quotes Hugo Rahner suggesting that 'when we are saying that the creative God plays, we are expressing with this image the metaphysical insight that, although the creation of the world and of man constitutes meaningful divine action, this action is in no way a necessary one.' (*TP*, p.17.) 'Meaningful but not necessary' then describes God's actions. This is likewise the best description of human play, and it finally provides the distinction between play and 'productive and gainful labor.' (*TP*, p.17.) Play not labor, meaningful activity but not productive toilsome work which involves compensation, characterizes God's creating. God's creation is God's play.

Moltmann does offer a theological qualification. He refers to the Hebrew word to create, *bahrah,* and points out that in the Old Testament it is only used to describe God's activity and never the 'works of men.' Therefore,

> when we say that the creative God is playing, we are talking about a playing that differs from that of man. The creative God plays with his own possibilities and creates out of nothing that which pleases him. When man is playing he is himself at stake in the game and he is also being played with. (*TP*, pp.17-18.)

We should notice here a creative, imaginative, playful turn of meaning. The word *bahrah* is most often translated as create. Usually this creating is construed in terms of God's work, not play. Indeed as we shall see, Moltmann himself follows this normal reading in the essay on work in *On Human Dignity.* What has happened then? Has Moltmann contradicted himself? Possibly, but not necessarily. It may be better to view this move as a 'play on words'. This would mean that he is offering a qualification, not only to the nature of the concept play, but also to the nature of the concept that we call work. God's creative 'play' can still be called his work. However, this work must not be understood in categories of necessity or utility, that is, as labor. Rather, God's work is a free playful expression of joy.

Do these characteristics of freedom, joy and play also apply to human work, as opposed to human labor (which by definition cannot be play for labor is not free but utilitarian and gainful)? Should they apply? Yes, seems to be the answer. Human activity, work, should correspond to God's (even though *bahrah* cannot apply directly to humans). Here however, instead of being explicitly construed as work, human correspondence to *bahrah* is construed as play. Moltmann, in the paragraph discussing *bahrah*, and after qualifying man's play as necessarily different from God's states:

> Still there are points of contact. Like the creation, man's games are an expression
> of freedom and not of caprice, for playing relates to the joy of the creator with his
> creation and the pleasure of the player with his game. Like creation, games com-
> bine sincerity and mirth, suspense and relaxation. (*TP*, p.18.)

Given Moltmann's play on the word *bahrah* in this essay, one could as easily substitute the word 'work' for play and game in this quote and find no substantial contradiction. Work and play, if work is properly understood, are the
same thing on this view. Work and play are meaningful, expressive, serious
activities. Neither however, includes the extreme seriousness that comes with
burden and utility. Only toilsome work, that is labor, involves this utility and
would therefore be excluded from the work / play concept.

Moltmann then moves from the general question of why did God create, to
the more specifically utilitarian question; for what purpose did God create the
world? He finds this an even more threatening and horrifying question than the
first, for God did not have to create something to realize himself. God did not
create for a purpose, but rather he created for sheer joy. In this answer the very
question itself is abolished. The purpose of my existence is a non-question. The
answer, for sheer joy, 'does not indicate ethical goals and ideal purposes but
justifies created existence as such.' (*TP*, p.19.) We should not confuse the enjoyment of God and existence with goals or purposes. The questions themselves, for what purpose am I here and am I useful, are inappropriate.

As the discussion progresses, Moltmann elaborates on this concept that God
created for joy and not for goals or purposes. Self-representation, liberty and
freedom, the 'demonstrative value of being', relate to God's joy. Man's 'free
self-representation has to be the human echo to the pleasure of God in his creation. The glorification of God lies in the demonstrative joy of existence.' (*TP*,
p.21.) It follows that no person needs to justify his or her existence in doing.
Utility, or goals simply do not apply.

> Our existence is justified and made beautiful before we are able to do or fail to do
> anything. If we are working at something, we have started out from leisure...
> When labor is successful, joy has already been there at its beginning. Leisure
> earned by working and self-created joys do not satisfy. (*TP*, p.21.)

Further,

> The human element in labor and the production of food, in social patterns and cul-
> tural expressions, always involves self-representation. All things men use always
> contain in their respective processes an expression of the *demonstrative value of
> being*. Whenever man produces something, he demonstrates himself as well, even
> if only by a small individualistic departure from the work rules. He presents and
> represents himself, and in a manner of speaking, answers a call with his presence.

This self representation is not identical with self-realisation by labor, for the creative play of expression does not depend on successes and accomplishments, although it does not preclude these. (*TP*, p.22.)

Moltmann ultimately argues that free activity is called play. Our activity is able to be play because we correspond to God. This play is not oriented toward any goal or utility precisely because joy, not utility, is the characteristic of creation. Existence in joy, not purposeful activity, is the answer to the question; why / for what purpose / did God create? Play not work (at least not labor) is foundational.

Play as world symbol goes beyond the categories of doing, having, and achieving and leads us into the categories of being, of authentic human existence and demonstrative rejoicing in it. It emphasizes the creative against the productive and the aesthetic against the ethical. Earthbound labor finds its relief in rejoicing, dancing singing and playing. This also does labor a lot of good. (*TP*, pp.23-24.)

Even concerning the eschaton, Moltmann argues that our imagery is from the realm of play and not labor. 'Christian eschatology has never painted the joy of existing in the new, redeemed, and liberated creation in colors of this life damaged by... labor... Christian eschatology has painted the end of history in the colors of aesthetic categories.' (*TP*, p.34.) Further, 'the images for the coming world do not come from the world of... work and achievement'. (*TP*, p.35.)

Given comparisons like these between work and play we are led to inquire whether this section is primarily a discussion of play or whether it is actually a negative appraisal of work. For our purposes what we are beginning to detect throughout this section on the 'The Theological Play of the Good Will of God', is not simply the development of a theology of play. More significantly we also see emerging at the same time the basics (negatively construed) of a theology of work.

One more important discussion in *Theology of Play*, which relates to our current purposes, is found in the section 'The Human Play of Liberated Mankind.' In this section the question with which we are ultimately concerned is: can labor become creative play?

Earlier, Moltmann had reaffirmed that the final purpose of history is no purpose at all, but is rather the liberation of life. (*TP*, p.36.) In his comments on the liberation of man, Moltmann argues that 'if a man is what he makes of himself, then his *being human* depends on what he *does*.' (*TP*, p.46.) Further, 'so if man is what he makes of himself, he is precisely not free when it comes to his own actions but dependent on them and subject to them.' (*TP*, p.46.) There is no way to get from doing to being. The quest for self-realisation then, is opposed to liberty, because it depends upon the categories of utility, goals, necessity and compulsion. Man does not have to make himself. (*TP*, p.47.)

When we come to labor (which in Marxist terms is supposed to create history and lead to humanization and self-realization) the question is whether it can become creative play? (*TP*, pp.53ff.) The answer is not surprising. It is no. Remember, Moltmann is talking here about labor; that is, instrumental and toilsome work. He is not talking about creative work which in corresponding to God's *bahrah* has come to be understood as play.

Moltmann begins his exploration into the question considering the Marxist vision that labor will cease and will be replaced with self-induced activity when exploitation is overcome. He cites the Czech Marxist Vitezlav Gardavsky who believed that love will transform labor into creativity and that creativity will be the means of human self-realisation. He then cites Marx's belief in his later writing that labor cannot become a form of play, but that it can lead to leisure where there are better opportunities for self-realisation. Moltmann then briefly considers the neo-marxist Herbert Marcuse who sees the possibility of finding freedom in labor rather than beyond it. Ultimately, Moltmann finds each of these proposals unsatisfactory. They do not break the compulsion of work. They do not lead to freedom which is where one finds happiness.

Work as a Right

An important part of interpreting Moltmann's specific reflections on work is to determine contextually his overall reason for discussing it. Is his concern to explore work itself, or is it primarily to make a related ethical point? If it is the latter, then care must be taken to interpret his text accordingly.

Moltmann's specific discussion of work is found in his essay 'The Right to Meaningful Work.' This is located in the volume *On Human Dignity* which is a collection of essays, not about work, but rather about the issues of human dignity and human rights.[19] Here, a reflection on work's nature and meaning is offered, but is designed to be understood as a continuation (the implications and applications) of the discussion on human rights. Therefore, to understand what Moltmann will suggest concerning work we must first grasp his broader understanding of human rights.

Following in the tradition of the United Nations *Universal Declaration of Human Rights,* Moltmann argues that human rights refers to the right to life in general. (*HD*, p.4.) This right to life however, is not one single right, but rather an umbrella under which a number of rights must be considered together. 'All human rights be they social, economic, religious, or political are interrelated. They must be taken as a whole.' (*HD*, p.8.) The right to life in general then is

---

[19] Douglas Meeks in his introduction to the volume suggests that: 'By proposing a Christian perspective on human dignity Moltmann intends in these essays a contribution to the wider debate on human rights... Human rights spring from human dignity and not vice versa. Human dignity however, requires human rights for its embodiment, protection and full flowering. Human rights are the concrete, indefeasible claim of human dignity.' (*HD*, pp.x-xi.)

logically prior to any specific claims to other rights.

> The right to life and to the means which make continued living possible stands in the forefront. The St. Polten Report, therefore, just like the Roman Synod of Bishops, *[Message Concerning Human Rights and Reconciliation]* places the right to life, to nourishment, and to work at the beginning of the catalog of human rights. (*HD*, p.6.)

Interestingly, here we find the first indication that work is a human right. The right to life has the priority, but since work contributes to life, it too becomes a right.

In theologically grounding this concept of human rights, Moltmann employs a contextual / political methodology. The starting point is to be 'out from one's own life experience.' (*HD*, p.14.) The inhumanity of a dictatorship, economic exploitation, racism, or the destruction of nature should be our starting points rather than abstract speculations.

> We have learned from liberation theology to begin where we ourselves really exist in our own people. Experience in the praxis of liberation from inhumanity is for Christians and churches the concrete starting point for the commitment to human rights. (*HD*, p.14.)

For Moltmann, the concrete concerns with reference to human rights leads him directly into a reflection on the doctrine of the image of God in human beings.[20] This doctrine becomes the theological point of orientation for understanding human rights. The image of God in persons, which interpreted means God's claim upon human beings, is the basis for all human rights.

Moltmann then goes on to list and describe four 'fundamental' human rights which, on his view, follow directly from the dignity of being created to be the image of God. (*HD*, pp.23-28.) These are the four rights which essentially belong to being truly human. Although he does not use the phrase himself in this essay, they seem to be four rights which are foundational to the 'right to life' referred to in the first essay. The first fundamental right involves the freedom to be responsible before God in all areas of life; that is, the freedom of conscience. The second involves the right of humanity to live in community. The third involves the right of human beings to rule over the earth and be in community with the non-human creation. The fourth involves a right to our future; that is, to self-determination and to taking responsibility for our future and the future of those still to come.

Interestingly, although he does not say so until half way through his discussion, the third right includes the right to work, for the human activities of ruling and preserving creation are work. Why and how work has come to be consid-

---

[20] See the second essay in the volume: 'Christian Faith and Human Rights'. pp.19-35.

ered a 'fundamental right,' as well as the implications of making it a right, are
important for they indicate (at least for this essay) what Moltmann understands
work's nature to be.

In considering work to be a fundamental right, Moltmann appeals to Genesis
1:28ff. Here 'the creation of human beings as the image of God is followed by
the blessing of God and the human calling to be fruitful and rule over the non-
human creation.' (*HD*, pp.26-27.) This blessing and calling to work stems from
being created to be the image of God. The image of God (God's claim upon us)
is the basis for human dignity. Human dignity requires the rights necessary for
its flourishing and this flourishing requires both the production and consump-
tion appropriate to it. Work therefore, is not only a necessity, but a right.

This right construed negatively would mean that work and its resultant fruits
cannot be denied someone because of their race, gender or the like. People cannot be denied the opportunity to work or to work's fruits. Moltmann however,
does not appear to stop with this negative orientation. He seems to assume the
positive corollary that work (or employment) for all, and nourishment, and
housing and material possessions must be guaranteed.

> If the right to the earth is given to human beings, it follows that each and every
> human being has the basic economic right to a just share in life, nourishment,
> work, shelter, and personal possessions. The concentration of the basic necessities
> of life and the means of production in the hands of a few should be seen as a dis-
> tortion and perversion of the image of God in human beings. It is unworthy of
> human beings and contradicts God's claim upon them. (*HD*, p.27.)

It does not seem that Moltmann understands the right to work generally to
be a right to freedom which allows opportunities or choices for work. Rather,
employment or the economic fruits of employment appear to be the right.

The result of making employment itself, rather than simply the opportunity
to work, a fundamental right has consequence. Although it preserves human
dignity as the starting point rather than the result of work, it also has ramifica-
tions for work's relationship to politics and economics. It actually requires one
to assume as given some type of welfare state. Total or near total employment
is the foundation, and economic and political functioning must accommodate
itself to this reality. Indeed this would have been the underlying social assumption behind the thinking of the *Universal Declaration of Human Rights,* and of
social assumptions in Europe and particularly in Germany during the post-war
period. It is certainly the thinking behind Moltmann's two essays.

When we come to the essay, 'The Right to Meaningful Work' Moltmann
continues his explorations on human rights. Here, however, it is not simply
work, but 'meaningful' work which is construed as a basic human right. It is
the subjective dimension of work, its human meaning, which is to be guaranteed as a right. While Moltmann's subsequent analysis of work may have implications beyond this limited concern, his primary emphasis is on work's sub-

jective aspect, both its potentialities and its limitations for human life. His guiding questions early in the chapter show us these concerns.

> Does it make sense, however, to seek the meaning of life in work? Can work have such power? Does such an expectation not lead to excessive demands on work and to torment for human beings?... How does the right to work relate to the *meaning of life,* and how is the meaning of life connected with the right to work? (*HD*, p.38.)

Further, from the structure of his own arguments on the nature of work, one can see where these questions lead Moltmann.

> Here we will look at the concept of meaning broadly and develop it in three dimensions: (1) What is the significance of work for the working person? (2) What is the significance of work for the human community? (3) What is the significance of work for life in general, for the meaning of the whole? (*HD*, p.38.)

Thus we see from Moltmann's contextual or ethical concerns how work is ultimately going to be construed. Not only does work's nature demand that meaningful work be a fundamental human right. It further demands that it be primarily depicted in subjective terms in relationship to human meaning.

Here then the questions become: How does Moltmann proceed theologically to construe work? Which doctrines does he look to, or not look to, for his construal of work? Which model for construing work does he adopt? Which models does he reject?

I begin by mentioning the three theological or philosophical models for understanding work which Moltmann finds to be inadequate. The first model which Moltmann considers is Luther's understanding of work as vocation. Generally, he is sympathetic to Luther's view. He recognizes how work as vocation infuses meaning into people's common life and work. He sees how the doctrine of vocation, the divine call which fills the whole world with the charismata of the new creation, could be understood as the beginning of the eschatological reformation of the world. (*HD*, p.45.) Yet ultimately, he finds the model inadequate both theologically and socially.[21] Theologically it is too close to natural law. Socially, it is too static and conservative.

Next, Moltmann considers the motif of work as enterprise. In his analysis here he follows Max Weber's thesis and identifies this as the understanding of work associated with Calvinist Christians and the groups on the so-called left wing of the Reformation. (*HD*, p.48.) Moltmann is quite critical of this model of work which he understands to be proposing the view that success alone justifies work. (*HD*, p.48.) Theologically he seems to distrust this economics–

---

[21] He does not completely reject the possibility of using this model. He suggests that today the vocational ethos is still possible, but only in a very limited way. (p.47.)

centered view of work as undermining human dignity. Socially he finds the
'spirit of capitalism' which it produces to be a cause of human self-destruction
and environmental disaster.

Moltmann finally considers the motif of work as achievement. This view he
associates with the philosophies of Hegel and Marx. The idea here is that all
work should be truly humanized if it is to have meaning for people; that is, all
work should be creative activity leading to self-realisation. Ultimately, Moltmann finds this view to be theologically inadequate for it expects work to provide too much meaning for human life. It tends to suggest that people can 'realise' or save themselves through their work.

Moltmann does not address these three models simply to reject them.
Rather, he uses them to highlight important social and theological considerations related to the function and meaning of work. The question which must
now be considered is, what doctrine or doctrines does he appeal to for his understanding of work? We will then be able to consider what type of model he
offers as an alternative.

According to Moltmann 'a person's conception of work always stands in
close relationship to his or her understanding of the gods or of the meaning of
his or her life.' (*HD,* p.40.) Thus, he begins his theologizing on work by focusing on the doctrine of God, and specifically on the idea that God is a worker.
His main premise concerning human work is that it should 'correspond' to
God's work. The argument follows that from creation it is known that God is a
worker. Human work however, can never be exactly the same as God's (for
God's work is distinguished from ours exegetically by the verb *barah*[22]). Nonetheless human work can and should 'correspond' to the creative activity of
God. Moltmann cites the command to work and to keep the sabbath found in
Exodus 20:9-11 as the Biblical support for this idea. (*HD,* p.40.) He then turns
to the doctrine of the initial creation to suggest that human work was part of
God's good created purpose for humanity. The point is that when human work
truly corresponds to God's, that is when it is actively creative but also seasoned
with Sabbath, it becomes truly meaningful. (*HD,* p.41.)

From these doctrines of initial creation and Sabbath, Moltmann then moves
elsewhere, to the 'work of redemption', to suggest that the human work should
correspond to God's. This doctrine expresses Moltmann's main theological
point in the essay. The idea is that God is not simply the effortless creator (initial creation) but that he also is engaged in hard and painful work. Such work is
the 'work of redemption.' Moltmann appeals to Isa. 43:24ff, and 53 to suggest
that the redemption brought by the 'servant of God' is wearisome work. (*HD,*
p.42.) The implication is that this servant is a worker. Jesus is a worker then,
not because he was a carpenter, but because he was this servant. Moltmann then
suggests that Phil. 2, in calling for the imitation of Christ's servanthood, should

---

[22] Also transliterated as *bahrah*.

be the theological basis for work.

> The point here is God's action in his suffering, in his renunciation, in his volun-
> tary servanthood and self-surrender. God creates salvation by suffering the tor-
> ment of prisoners. He frees them by his renunciation. He wins them by his ser-
> vanthood.

> In the designation of this redemption as the 'pain and work of God,' the word
> *work* gains a new meaning. It is filled to the highest degree with theological con-
> tent. *Work* becomes the embodiment of the doctrine of salvation. (*HD*, p.42.)

Further, Moltmann states that 'the transference of the human concept of work
to God and especially to his redeeming activity, then the redirection of the concept to human beings who are supposed to correspond to God, has had an
enormous effect' on what we understand work's nature and meaning to be.
(*HD*, p.43.)

From this consideration of God's toilsome work, Moltmann turns to Paul
and suggests that he understood his apostolic activity as work. It was not that
Paul understood his general work for survival (tentmaking) as anything more
than a necessity. Rather, in considering his ministry as work and placing it in
the service of Christ's lordship and thus in the service of the Kingdom of God,
Paul was extending and ultimately transforming the very meaning of work. All
work would then be placed on the level of Phil. 2. (*HD*, p.44.)

Moltmann suggests here that work then ultimately finds its messianic and
eschatological meaning.

> What happens in work is nothing less than co-renunciation with Christ and co-
> regency with him. In this way work 'for the sake of the Lord' receives a meaning
> that reaches beyond every success of work. (*HD*, p.44.)

In summary then, we can see that the key concept for Moltmann in relation
to human work is that it should correspond to God's work. Although correspondence appears to presuppose some kind of doctrine of the image of God,
Moltmann rather develops the idea by appealing to the concept of the work of
redemption, the theology of the cross. God is a worker, but this is not seen primarily in the fact that God created the universe. More prominently it is seen in
redemption. As we identify with Christ our work corresponds to his work. In
our work then we both suffer as a servant, and anticipate his lordship and our
rule with him. This dual identification of servanthood and lordship, (suffering
and success) built on the doctrine of redemption, is the ultimate theological
basis which Moltmann gives to work.

So what model does Moltmann offer for understanding work? What does he
ultimately understand the nature of work to be based on this theology of redemption? Moltmann wants to be careful to avoid making a claim to a 'comprehensive, generally binding understanding of work.' (*HD*, p.53.) Nonetheless,

he does see 'common threads concerning the meaning and humanity of work.' (*HD*, p.53.) Combining the understanding of 'work as correspondence' with the doctrine of the cross leads to Moltmann's ultimate construal of 'Work as Participation in God's History.' (*HD*, p.53.)

To demonstrate what this means Moltmann returns to the three dimensions of work offered at the beginning of the essay: (1) What is the significance of work for the working person? (2) What is the significance of work for the human community? (3) What is the significance of work for the meaning of life?

WHAT IS THE SIGNIFICANCE OF WORK FOR THE WORKING PERSON?

Moltmann's main purpose here is to suggest that it is consistent with work's nature that a person can affirm and develop him or herself through their work. He says that 'work is experienced as humane when it provides latitude for individual formation and thereby allows possibilities for self-expression.' (*HD*, p.54.) Here, a relational-existential dimension of work is affirmed as making work significant for the working person. This concept has its limits however.

> No one *has* to justify himself through work. No one *has* to demonstrate her right to existence through work! No one *has* to realize himself through work. Were that true, then the unemployed would have no rights and the handicapped no reality. (*HD*, p.54.)

This makes a good point, and it is apparent that Moltmann is drawing here on his earlier view that dignity leads to rights and not rights to dignity. However, there is also another concern influencing such a statement. This is Moltmann's general suspicion of the instrumental, or, necessity / economic utility of work in relation to human meaning.

From early in the essay Moltmann has made it clear that 'humane work cannot consist only in acting for purpose and usefulness.' (*HD*, p.41.) Later, his primary critique of work as enterprise rests in denying that success alone justifies work. In the section on the significance of work for the working person, Moltmann argues that if one experiences either an inward (existential) or outward (economic or political force?) compulsion to work, it has become dehumanized. (*HD*, p.54.)

Of course Moltmann is not totally against work's utilitarian aspect. He assumes that some utility is necessary as we see by his use of the words 'only' and 'alone' as qualifiers. He even suggests that one concept of work (the relational) cannot be set against another (the instrumental). 'On the contrary they can complement each other and provide mutual protection against one-sidedness.' (*HD*, p.56.) Nonetheless, statements like the following suggest Moltmann's bias and his suspicion of letting the instrumental or economic utility of work impinge too closely on work's ultimate human nature and meaning.

> But work is too narrowly defined if one speaks only of vocation, hired labor, en-

terprising and thus productive work, and the like... Work is wrongly defined if one means only productive work and forgets reproductive work... For a long time, work was understood only as a means to an end... [This] robs work of its human significance. (*HD*, p.55.)[23]

In this section on the meaning of work for the working person, Moltmann wants work's essence to include more than its instrumental economic function. Similarly to what we saw in his essay 'The First Liberated Men in Creation' he wants to affirm a non-utilitarian vision of work which becomes meaningful to the person precisely because it is not concerned, (or is not primarily concerned) with the necessity to work. In terms of my hypothesis, Moltmann is concerned that work's relational-existential dimension be given priority over its instrumental-sustenance aspect.

WHAT IS THE SIGNIFICANCE OF WORK FOR THE HUMAN COMMUNITY?

In this section Moltmann's main purpose is to suggest that it is work's nature to aid in human socialization. (*HD*, p.55.) This is, Moltmann argues, the human significance of work. In fact, he suggests that this becomes the comprehensive sense of work. 'We recommend, therefore, that work be understood in a comprehensive sense as active participation in the social process.' (*HD*, p.56.) In terms of my hypothesis, this means that the relational-social / structural side of work is not only affirmed, but that it is also taken as work's highest functional value. Again, this suggests that the relational aspect of work has the priority over the instrumental.

WHAT IS THE SIGNIFICANCE OF WORK FOR THE MEANING OF LIFE?

In this final section Moltmann summarizes and comments on his theological understanding of the nature of work. As he sees it, what I have classified as the relational-existential and relational-social aspects of work, which have been shown to be its highest human functions, must also have a transcendent meaning related to all of life.

It is not inconsequential whether or not the work of people and the working process of society have meaning for the whole. Statements on the theology of work in antiquity, in the biblical traditions, and in modern Protestantism have shown that. (*HD*, p.56.)

From this statement, Moltmann then briefly summarizes the basic theological concepts surrounding work.

In his or her work a person corresponds to the creating God. In his or her work a

---

[23] Here, productive work is work undertaken for economic production / utility. Reproductive work is work which is intended as the self-expression of the worker.

person participates in God's self-emptying for the purpose of liberating humanity. In his or her work, even if not in it alone, a person realizes his or her call to freedom. In his or her work and through it, a person is on the promised road to the kingdom of freedom and human worth. (*HD*, p.56.)

How do these ideas give a 'meaning for the whole'? They do so because they offer something like what I am calling an ontology of work. They suggest that Moltmann himself, knowing or unknowingly, is probing for some sort of ontological understanding of work by which he can both describe work itself, and provide the coordinates for its transcendent meaning. It seems clear that Moltmann is probing toward a theological / ontological basis for work's relational aspects. Where does he ultimately find this basis and how do these theological points fit together to form something like an ontology of work?

Instructively, once he has offered several summary answers Moltmann begins considering work's meaning eschatologically. Herein lie the resources in Moltmann's thought for understanding work ontologically.

If one seeks a concept that includes the significance of work for the person and for society, then the expression 'work in the kingdom of God' is near at hand... it is also able to show the eschatological meaning of all work and of society itself in its historical dealings with the natural world. (*HD*, p.56.)

Moltmann goes on to paint an eschatological-teleological picture of creation which involves work.

The world is not finished. Through their work people take part in the destruction or the preservation of the world. They serve not only with the creating God; they also work together with the redeeming God...

In the promise of the kingdom of God which renews heaven and earth, there comes against the growing destructive potential of human societies an urgent call for resistance against death, passion for life, and community within history. It seems sensible to me to consider this perspective in dealing with the questions of vocation, work, wages and the like. For in the end this is 'the one thing that is necessary': 'Seek first the kingdom of God, and all these things will be added unto you.' (*HD*, pp.56-57.)

The various theological points made concerning work come together and this provides its transcendent meaning in God's coming kingdom. Work is not simply about human development, social or existential. It involves more than this. Ultimately, work is about God and God's eschatological renewal of heaven and earth. If work were only about existential or social development, the work as achievement model would suffice. Since however, there is a transcendent aspect of work, the relational dimension is caught up in the eschatological. Work is more than its function, relational or instrumental. Work is ontological. Work is participation in God's history.

Yet there is still one other important aspect of Moltmann's discussion on the nature of work which deserves special attention. We have already seen how Moltmann has a tendency to be suspicious of the instrumental-economic/utility aspect of work. We also have seen his concern that work be free, unforced, non-compulsory, and 'reproductive' so as to allow room for human self-representation. To understand why such concepts of work stand at the heart of his overall understanding of work, it is helpful to recall Moltmann's discussion of work in relation to play. Then, in this latter essay the key concepts to consider which relate to play are rest, joy and Sabbath.

Within his argument that human work should correspond to God's actions in creation, Moltmann develops the idea that in theology meaningful human work, like God's, must be construed so as to include rest or the Sabbath. In its essence work is not simply a productive activity. Moltmann's view here is similar to Barth's understanding of the Sabbath and the active life.[24] Moltmann argues:

> Work is thus meaningful not because it alone provides the meaning of life, but precisely because it is limited by the goal of rest and joy in existence. The Sabbath does not simply interrupt work. Rather, work is understood and defined through the Sabbath... they also overflow into each other and affect each other. (*HD*, p.41.)

This results in a picture of work seasoned with the Sabbath; that is, a dynamic combination of the producing and presenting aspects of work. By the producing aspect of work, Moltmann is referring to that aspect which consists of acting for purpose and usefulness. By the presenting aspect he means that through our work we present ourselves before God, in the joy of our existence, as we are and as we understand ourselves. (*HD*, p.41.) This does not mean that we make or realise ourselves through our work, (this would be justification by works) but we do express ourselves in and through it.

Moltmann sees 'producing' as humanly meaningful only when it is caught up into work's corresponding presenting aspect. In production we present ourselves and our understanding of ourselves. Ultimately then, beyond its usefulness, humane work must also 'encompass freedom for self-presentation and thus playfulness.' (*HD*, p.41.) Freedom and play become essential characteristics of true work. These must ultimately qualify or transform our understanding of production in work (subordinating the productive to the presenting aspect hierarchically). Of course, work has a serious side. Through it we plan, and in some ways, produce history. However, 'in the seriousness of work also belongs, in a human sense, the relaxed joy of existence: "Let it be!"' (*HD*, p.41.)

So what have these discussions of Moltmann's understandings of work and

---

[24] Barth, *Church Dogmatics*, III 4., (1961).

play ultimately revealed? What picture of work finally emerges and how should this be evaluated?

A Critique of Moltmann's Understanding of Work

General Contributions

The strength of Moltmann's approach to and understanding of work is his practical focus on the concrete experience of work. I mean that Moltmann gives the problems which many workers currently face center stage: this involves, finding joyful meaning in their work, knowing that their work contributes positively to broader social development, and retaining dignity while working in less than perfect jobs. Here, Moltmann's political / contextual methodology is an asset for it fosters a more detailed exploration into these themes than might be possible when using other methodologies.[25]

Moltmann's originality, however, does not lie in his identifying these concerns. Rather, it lies in how he embeds these ethical concerns into a broader theology. Although he begins with narrower ethical issues, he then broadens the discussion so that work may be further explored in the light of both Christology and eschatology. What this produces then is not simply a work ethics, but rather a particular understanding of work which is implied by a wider systematic theology. What Moltmann offers specifically are new possibilities for understanding work based on eschatological Christology.

Beyond this, Moltmann also offers a theological grounding for and legitimation of the idea that some of our work is toilsome. Of course we have seen that he is critical of 'labor' which is toilsome due to an overemphasis on success; that is, an overemphasis on purpose or utility. Nor does he want to justify oppressive forced labor. However, by joining human work to Christ-the-suffering-servant's 'work of redemption,' Moltmann has allowed that some work, (or even all work to some degree) will involve difficulty and suffering. Often, contemporary theological explorations of work suggest that any justification of suffering in work amounts to an ideological abuse of work (an attempt to keep workers in oppressive situations).[26] The strength of Moltmann's point however,

---

[25] Moltmann does not find a 'concordance method' for arriving at an understanding of work to be adequate, (an example being Alan Richardson's *The Biblical Doctrine of Work.*) Nor is he satisfied with the theology of work offered by M-D Chenu. (*HD*, p.43. note 8.)

[26] West, (1986), 'Cruciform Labour', pp.12-13. Here he argues against Moltmann's suggestion that all human work is a participation in the lordship of Christ. He suggests the possibility that Moltmann's justification of painful suffering work is open to ideological abuse.

is that it is realistic from a theological point of view and not simply for prag-
matic reasons. It avoids unduly optimistic expectations about what can be experienced in work. Moltmann's theological point here corresponds to common
experience that not much work, if any, in this initial creation can be completely
and totally released from every possible difficulty.

These strengths notwithstanding, I now begin my critique by offering some
cautions about Moltmann's project stemming from the approach he has taken to
reflecting on work. Ultimately, it is his methodology that restricts the contribution of his project.

Cautions and Limitations

At this point, when addressing Moltmann's method of inquiry into the nature of
work I do not want to be unduly critical. Rather I want simply to point out that
Moltmann's project as it stands has several internal weaknesses. These stem
primarily from the fact that the project is not as such a broad theology of work.
This is not to criticize Moltmann for not producing what I wish he might have.
Rather, it is simply to recognize that his political / contextual approach to work
has weaknesses in addition to the strengths just outlined.

The project's main weaknesses stem from its not being sufficiently focused
on the phenomenon of work itself. Since this project is not a theology of work,
it cannot be expected to function as one. One cannot therefore expect to find in
such a secondary reflection on work the same nuanced discussions and wide
ranging detail that one would in a proper theology of work. Thus, my caution
involves not demanding Moltmann's reflection to answer questions which are
beyond its scope.

This caution, however, in addition to safeguarding the project, also suggests
that its usefulness in concrete social, political and spiritual contexts might be
limited. There is simply not enough breadth to his discussion as it stands to
make it widely and directly applicable. For example, most would agree that it
would be desirable for a person's work to be meaningful and involve many of
his or her creative faculties. However, the question arises concerning how concretely such work can be guaranteed as a right, rather than simply as a desire, in
a context where opportunity and resources are limited; that is, in a context
which takes seriously economic realities. There may be ways to move toward
opening up opportunities for more meaningful work. However, these have not
been suggested by Moltmann, nor is it certain that questions like these have
been anticipated in his discussions. The point here is simply that a limited discussion also means a limited usefulness.

Work: Labor or Play?

Having suggested these general cautions, I now move on to a more specific
critique of Moltmann's theological reflections on work. The underlying criti-

cism is that Moltmann has muddled, and therefore inconsistently presented and interrelated the concepts of work, labor, and play.

At times in Moltmann's discussions the concepts behind the words 'work' and 'labor' are identical and interchangeable. In the essay on play for example, there are several places where there seems to be no differentiation between the ideas involved within each concept.[27] Also, there are instances where, within the same argument, the words are simply and uncritically intermingled.[28] Further, in the essay on work, although the word 'work' rather than 'labor' appears, Moltmann clearly presents a combined idea of laborious and toilsome work when relating human work to the work of Christ.

This lack of differentiation in itself however, is not a problem. The inconsistency arises in that at other times one finds a sharp distinction drawn between the two concepts of work and labor. This most often appears in the essay on play where labor is constantly being contrasted with play. In this essay, forced, productive and necessary labor, is differentiated from those work projects which are free and creative (bahrah) and thus play. The key concept within this differentiation is the idea of 'necessary'. Work that corresponds to God's will will be playful; that is, it will be free but meaningful. This means that it must not be done out of any necessity. Labor on the other hand by definition involves necessity. Thus, true work (which is play) and labor are distinguished from each other and are even antithetical. This differentiation in kind is also seen within the essay on meaningful work. Here, Moltmann distinguishes between the 'effortless' work (barah) of God in creation, and the painful, toilsome, and laborious work of Christ in redemption.

This inconsistency of sometimes drawing a distinction between work and labor and sometimes arbitrarily not, may not be seen in itself as too serious a problem. It could be argued that although this is a weakness, it is not one which undermines the general thrust of his argument. Further, one might want to argue that this distinction between work and labor introduced with the concept of necessity shows promise. However, a further complication adds weight to this criticism.

---

[27] See *TP*, p.17., where the argumentation would just as easily allow the phrase 'productive and gainful labor' to be read as productive and gainful 'work.' See also p.24. Here, the phrases 'Earthbound labor finds relief...', and 'This also does labor a lot of good.' should probably be better read as 'work' for he has already argued that creative work 'bahrah' can be play, and in a future section he is going to argue that labor cannot become play. See this argument also with reference to the use of 'labor' and 'creativity' on page 56.

[28] See *TP*, pp.21, 22, 35. Page 22 is particularly revealing for Moltmann uses the word 'labor' here in the context of a discussion on self-representation. This same discussion on self-representation reappears in the essay 'The Right to Meaningful Work.' In this instance however, he uses the word 'work' rather than 'labor' thus indicating their interchangability.

As we have seen, Moltmann argues that true work basically is, or should be, play. In his essay on play he interprets *barah* from the Genesis creation account to mean play. Then, in the essay on meaningful work he discusses this same passage, only this time *barah* means work. Likewise, in this later essay he interprets work through the Sabbath rather than depicting the Sabbath in contrast to work. This offers the qualification that all work, including labor, should be seasoned with the Sabbath and thus be more relaxed and playful.

Now, true work is and should be play. Further however, and following on this view, is the idea that work / play should not be, or should not become, necessitated or utilitarian labor. These points form the thesis of *Theology of Play*. Yet, in 'The Right to Meaningful Work' Moltmann argues that the theology of the cross justifies laborious and toilsome work (labor). Of course in this essay, (with the appeal to Isa. 43 and 53) this work of Christ is viewed as laborious and toilsome but without involving necessity or utility. Here, 'work... receives a meaning that reaches beyond every success of the work.' (*HD*, p.44.) However, ultimately it would be an inconsistency if Moltmann were to argue that the cross is somehow simply a creative or playful innovation of God. Rather, Moltmann elsewhere understands the cross to be an (almost necessary) outworking of God's loving and therefore suffering nature. The cross, although the free act of God, is not for Moltmann either an auxiliary or playfully arbitrary act affecting only humanity. According to Moltmann's theology, the cross is central to and necessarily bound up with God's character.[29] What I am suggesting is that the distinction between necessary labor and free work loses its force once Christ's work on the cross is appealed to for work's / labor's justification. The work and labor distinction begins to blur when the cross is described as both. The distinction between the words, based on the characteristic of necessity, simply does not hold.

This point is further complicated by the fact that Moltmann explicitly argues that, contrary to work, labor cannot be construed as or become play. Yet, as we have been demonstrating, in 'The Right to Meaningful Work', work is positively construed as laborious precisely because of the cross. If then the distinction between work and labor has essentially blurred, and, if work is play, then labor and play also begin to converge. But this is precisely what Moltmann does not want to have happen. The point is that if, as we have already established, the sharp distinction between laborious work (labor) and playful work (work) begins to collapse (as the pillar of 'necessity' crumbles in relation to the work of Christ), then the antithesis between labor and play also collapses. Why then should it be that labor cannot be construed as play if work, which is laborious, can?

At this point the very basic distinctions between the concepts of work, labor and play begin to disappear. How can it be that work equals play equals labor,

---

[29] See especially: Moltmann, *The Crucified God* (1974), and *Theology of Hope* (1967).

if each word is to continue to mean anything distinctively?

The fundamental problem with this whole set of concepts is that Moltmann has not sufficiently defined his terms and therefore he has not been able to remain consistent within specified fields of meaning. He has been, at best confusing, and at worst contradictory. There may be some substance or promise to his nuanced renderings of work, labor and play. Indeed he hints at the fact that work's designation before the fall, and thus its future transformation, is positive and creative work as compared to that which is cursed as labor after the fall. (*HD*, p.40.) Yet Moltmann does not develop this point, nor does he integrate it into his discussion. Had he carefully defined his terms and their fields of meaning he might have been able to theologically suggest some important characteristics of work based on these concepts of work, labor and play. He has not done this however. Therefore, he has simply left the reader wondering what he means exactly, and whether his overall thesis might not be flawed. I am inclined to suggest that there is a deep inconsistency in Moltmann's understanding and use of the words/concepts work / labor / play. However, what his entire discussion does suggest positively is that, corresponding to human experience, work is not nor can it be a simple concept. It is a multifaceted complex phenomenon both conceptually and in practice.

Moltmann's Reflections on Work and My Hypothesis

Having suggested that work is not a simple but rather a multifaceted concept, I now want to consider how Moltmann's understanding of work compares with the threefold hypothesis that work should be construed as instrumental, relational and ontological. Of course Moltmann neither specifically outlines work in these terms, nor does he conceptually interrelate his perceptions along these lines. Nonetheless, as has been shown, his reflections do quite naturally lend themselves to such classification and analysis. My approach here will be to use the hypothesis as a tool for a more detailed critique of Moltmann's construal of work. The strength of using this hypothesis for these critical purposes is that it readily highlights either the fluidity and complementary inner-workings of a construal of work, or it reveals within it areas of tension and weakness.

Using my hypothesis I will show that although Moltmann has made contributions toward a broader understanding of work, ultimately his construal falls short in each specific aspect of work which in turn is necessary for this broader vision. I will thus conclude that his overall theological understanding of work is less than adequate.

WORK'S INSTRUMENTAL ASPECT

I begin this analysis by considering Moltmann's construal of work instrumentally with reference to questions of sustenance. As was shown, Moltmann recognizes work's fundamental connection to questions of sustenance or 'life-support.' (*HD*, p.53.) As such, utility will be at least minimally a part of work's makeup, even though to Moltmann humane work cannot 'consist only in acting for purpose and usefulness.' (*HD*, p.41.) Further, I have highlighted how Moltmann does not wish to have one concept of work (the relational) set against another (sustenance). Rather, he desires that these concepts complement and protect each other. (*HD*, p.56.) These points show that Moltmann assumes and allows for some type of utility (instrumentality) to be a part of work's functional nature, even if it is ultimately hierarchically subordinated to work's relational aspects.

However, these qualifications granted, through his critique of utility Moltmann does show himself ultimately to be, at best, little concerned with questions of sustenance, and at worst, dismissive of it. I have shown that Moltmann is finally critical of any concept of work which places too much emphasis on necessity, utility or purposefulness. His rejection of the model of work as enterprise, his suspicion of usefulness in his discussion of Sabbath, joy and playfulness in work, and his argument that earning a living has little to do with questions of work's meaningfulness, all serve to counter any high valuation of work's utility.[30] Further, as I have also demonstrated, the thesis of *Theology of Play* is intended to critique the 'spoilsport' who places an over emphasis on necessity, utility and purposefulness in human action, including work. It is the discussion in *Theology of Play* that I now want to address more critically and herein to consider how those ideas minimize the importance of work for the sake of sustenance.

The essay 'The First Liberated Men in Creation' was written in the context of, and notwithstanding its more abstract generalizations, as a critique to redress some perceived excesses within certain activist Marxist students movements of the 1960's.

> A second major contention raised by Moltmann, particularly in the context of the radical student disruptions of the last dozen years, is a criticism of what he perceives to be a certain legalistic fervor and lifestyle of socialism's 'new man.' This legalism is derived from the Aristotelian doctrine of virtue– 'practice makes a master'– taken over later by Marx in his premise that humans create themselves in their labor, in working productively. Thereby if the conditions of production could be restructured so that they are no longer alienating, we then could move from a preoccupation with 'having' to 'being,' and from the drab 'realm of necessity' to the splendid 'realm of freedom.'[31]

Given these concerns, Moltmann purposefully placed a strong emphasis on aesthetics over ethics and then on 'being' over 'having' or 'doing'. As we have shown, Moltmann believes that utility and purpose (ethics) hinders the freedom and beauty (aesthetics) which leads to happiness. Within that discussion, he

---

[30] See respectively: *HD*, pp. 48-50, 40-41, and 53-55.
[31] Chapman, (1981), p.443. See also: Bauckham, (1987), p.49.

very directly argued what he perceived to be the danger of 'necessity'. Necessity hinders the demonstrative value of being and free human self-representation. It hinders the joy of existence and implies that we need to 'justify' our existence.

The question, however, is why must utility or necessity necessarily prevent or preclude free, creative, self-representative action? Of course it might often be the case that it does. I concede that utility could, and often does, destroy freedom and joy. However, it does not necessarily follow that a utilitarian motive, economic necessity or some other intrinsic or extrinsic motivation for work totally excludes the possibility that one could still also find joy and self-expression in his or her work. Indeed, concrete common experience shows that very little work is completely freed from economic or utilitarian necessity. Do we really believe, however, that people never could or never do experience a sense of freedom and joy in that work? If we do, we are clearly incorrect for my experience shows at least one example to the contrary. In writing the thesis on which this book is based, I found ample opportunity for self-expression and self-representation. The freedom and thus joy which I experienced, however, did not in any way diminish the fact that I also wrote the thesis for several utilitarian purposes. First, it served as a means to the end of receiving a Ph.D. Second, another purpose for writing it was to learn what is needed to be able to do something else, namely, to teach theology and ethics. Third, throughout the writing process I had hoped that the thesis would eventually be published. While this in itself will not provide much if any financial resources, it may do so indirectly, for having a published thesis may provide me with better employment. The point here is simply that the thesis and this book represent work which is both playful and utilitarian.

If Moltmann wants to demonize utility and necessity, he needs a more persuasive argument and defense for the premise than that by definition necessity destroys freedom and thus joy. Against the backdrop of the legalistic socialist 'new man' his argumentation may need little authentication. When more broadly considered however, it becomes suspect.

This leads then into Moltmann's view of freedom which gives the hierarchical priority to 'being' over 'having' or 'doing.' Moltmann is clear in his belief that, contrary to both capitalism and Marx, 'there is no way to get from doing to being.' (*TP*, p.46.) One commentator aptly summarizes Moltmann's view:

> it is Christian faith that must reverse the relation between doing and being. As human beings we receive our worth and our identities from God, and not from what we produce; only then are we in turn freed to act and to create... The future in its newness brings a taste of absolute freedom, which is qualitatively different

from necessity and yet can be experienced in the midst of our work.[32]

It is very interesting and also very uncharacteristic of Moltmann to introduce such an abstract ontological distinction as he has with this 'being' verses 'doing' metaphysic.[33] It is nonetheless perfectly in line with his broader understanding that worth and dignity follow from created existence rather than human achievement. For Moltmann this is foundational. However, at least two other factors in this essay also build into his argument. First, contra Marxist anthropology, is his attack against any attempt to conceive of persons as creatures of their own works or as products of their own achievement. (*TP*, pp.48,51.) Second, appealing to Luther, Moltmann insists that justification by faith rather than works demands this metaphysical distinction with the priority given to being over doing. Moltmann interprets Luther's 'man is justified by faith' to mean that 'no form of human action leads us from an inhuman to a human reality of man'. (*TP*, p.46.) On this particular interpretation of Luther, justification means becoming human, thus being and doing do become antithetical, and the hierarchical priority of 'being' naturally follows.

My criticism however, is that Moltmann offers false options. One does not have to believe that a person is wholly or solely responsible to 'create' him or herself through one's works to believe that a person contributes to his or her human formation positively or negatively through those works. The options in this context need not be justification by faith or by works, Luther or Marx. Nor does one have to hierarchically posit being over doing, or doing over being.

On this latter point, we do not need such an abstract hierarchical dualism to preserve human dignity. Generally in life we do not have the situation where a person can 'be' without doing something (even if this means simply contributing via existence to a relationship in which the person is involved). Nor can a person 'do' without already being something (an existing person). The distinction itself is mostly artificial. It is better as a general principle to argue for a complementary 'being in doing' and 'doing in being' metaphysic / anthropology.[34] Of course in cases of severe disability, persistent vegetative state, old age, or even young age we will want to qualify this general principle with an additional argument (presumably from the doctrine of the *imago Dei*) that existence is still valid even if doing in some instances is not possible. However, such an addition does not necessitate the metaphysical dualism which Molt-

---

[32] Chapman, (1981), p.444.

[33] Of course, 'being' here should probably be understood dynamically as 'becoming' rather than statically as a fixed existence. This is due to Moltmann's overall 'not-yet' metaphysics which he builds in critical dialogue with Bloch.

[34] I want here neither a hierarchy of being over doing (as Moltmann has offered), nor of doing over being. The latter might possibly (by implication) open the door for euthanasia.

mann has introduced. If Moltmann really does want to preserve the being over doing distinction he will need to suggest more compelling arguments as to why it is necessary. It may be a way to combat the excesses of activist Marxism, and even to preserve the dignity of the handicapped and unemployed, but as a broader anthropological insight it is too reductionistic.

One may argue however, that we still need to deal with the force of his argument about justification by faith rather than works. However, as suggested, Moltmann has presented us with false options. We need not be limited to the options of justification by faith or by works with reference to our question. The problem I suggest here (and will return to later when dealing with the instrumental-spiritual argument) is that Moltmann has unnecessarily and imprecisely combined two related but differentiated theological concepts; those of justification and sanctification. Of course, Christian theology denies that a person can save him or herself through works of any kind, including work. That is why, against Marx's reductionistic anthropology, Moltmann is right to argue that a person does not need to create him or herself through work. A person does not receive his or her fundamental being or acceptance with God or others through work or works. A person simply cannot justify him or herself.

However, we need to introduce here the doctrine of sanctification, not merely consider the question of justification. If sanctification rather than justification is in view, then theologically it is less problematic to argue that what a person does (including work), in some qualified way, contributes either positively or negatively to what he or she is or becomes. Moltmann does introduce a separate category which he calls sanctification in the section on free works (which follow from justification). (*TP*, pp.48-49.) He does not in this essay however, entertain the idea that these free works have a formative or transformative role positively or negatively on the becoming individual or group.[35] Only in a more isolated earlier instance does he suggest that more may be at issue: that when a man is playing (working included) he is also 'at stake as he is himself being played with' or affected. (*TP*, pp.17-18.)

By failing to offer a more nuanced discussion distinguishing between justification and sanctification Moltmann has built his case around false options. If justification only is in view, then his could be the only legitimate options. However, if sanctification is being considered, and if one allows that justification and sanctification are in any way distinguishable in the salvation process, and if sanctification involves any formative or transformative element, then more possibilities open themselves up. A person does not have to save him or herself through work, nor does being have to be abstracted out and hierarchically established over doing. Rather, with sanctification in view, a person's

---

[35] He does appear more open to this possibility in his essay on 'The Right to Meaningful Work.' I will return to this later both in this section and then when discussing the relational-existential aspect of work.

choices and actions can have real effect on who he or she is and becomes.

Related to my hypothesis, the importance of setting aside Moltmann's critique of utility stems primarily from questions of moral purpose on the one hand, and questions of economics on the other. Both of these are important to any theological construal of work. Any theology of work must address the moral questions which involve determining for what purpose we work. I work for myself, I work for fun, I work to get wealthy, I work to serve others, I work simply to survive - all involve evaluative judgements and thus questions of moral purpose. If utility goes, ethics go. But if ethics go, can we then say anything meaningful about work which goes beyond the mere description of what actually happens? How can we make any prescription with reference to work? Yet, as we have seen, Moltmann himself is paramountly concerned with the ethics of work particularly (making prescriptions) as they relate to meaning and rights. The point is that while Moltmann's critique of utility may contribute something to the quest for joy and thus meaning in work by calling into question an overdone, neurotic, obsessive quest for success, its very arguments ultimately undermine the ethical value that it offers; that is, Moltmann's argument proves to be self-defeating.

Furthermore, I have suggested that debunking Moltmann's critique of utility is important to my hypothesis because of economic questions. I mean here that Moltmann's construal of work, with its primary focus on rights and meaning, and its specific critique of utility, erroneously subordinates economic issues to relational issues in the sphere of work. I suggest that any theology of work, or theological construal of work, needs to be able to equally take account of economics as a discipline (this however, does not mean capitulate to the discipline). I am not implying that Moltmann's reflections completely ignore economics. Nor do I mean that he is completely misguided in questioning an exclusive focus on necessity and utility in work. His intention to have work's nature and meaning include elements going beyond its economic life-support value is indeed consistent with the concern for a multifaceted construal of work which is presented in my hypothesis. I am suggesting that Moltmann's critique of utility and necessity ultimately undermines the ability of his construct to adequately value the experiences faced by most people of the importance, through work, of gaining sustenance with limited resources.

I now want to consider Moltmann's view of work's instrumentality as it touches upon human spiritual development. Protestants have traditionally emphasized the idea that through a person's obedience to God and service to others in their daily work, he or she grows spiritually in relationship with God. In his discussions Moltmann does not address these ideas as stated. He simply does not use this language in talking about work's relationship to spiritual growth. Nor does he specifically deny these concepts. His appeal is that our human work should correspond to God's. Why should it? Presumably there is some view behind these assertions that obedience, or at least the imitation of God, is a good. Although it is possible that this would be a strictly deontological appeal to our duty as created beings, it is doubtful whether Moltmann views this desired correspondence in work to be a good strictly apart from any benefit that we ourselves might receive. After all, his whole point is that when our work corresponds to God's it infuses into our work new meaning. Is this meaning, this humanization of work, not another way to talk about spiritual growth?

Further, Moltmann believes that in our work we should come to the point where we experience the joy of existence and the joy of our self-presentation. Life is a material embodied life and this necessarily involves meaningful activity and work. Is our coming to this understanding and experience not another way to talk about spiritual growth? Does this not also mean that work will necessarily also be a part of one's spiritual development?

The problem however, especially in *Theology of Play,* is that Moltmann is reluctant to allow for any view that even approaches Marx's assertion that we form ourselves through our work. He is theologically convinced, as we have seen, that any such construal would violate the principle of justification by faith. Again, the problem is that he has not allowed here for any distinction between the doctrines of justification and sanctification. Of course he argues that justification leads to free works and free relationships (and it is here that he chooses to introduce the idea of sanctification). Nonetheless, by not entertaining here the idea that sanctification as part of the broader category of salvation has formative or transformative power, he is necessarily constrained by his argument that we cannot be formed through our work lest we violate the theological truth of justification by faith.

On this view then, we ultimately become spiritually stranded in that we isolate work from our spiritual growth. It is for this reason that I find weakness in Moltmann's instrumental construal of work with relation to spiritual growth. It does not ultimately account for what traditional biblical, Protestant, and even more recently Catholic construals have. It does not affirm that how we work and what we produce affects both positively as well as negatively who we are and what we become. It does not affirm the role of work in sanctification and thus spirituality.

The picture is only somewhat improved in the essay 'The Right to Meaningful Work.' Here, there is more room given for 'individual formation,' a concept which closely parallels spiritual growth or sanctification. However, in this context, the concept seems to be understood in a very limited way in relation only to our self-expression in our work and not as a means through which God and the person can develop our human being. Thus, even in this context the criticism stands that Moltmann does not ultimately allow adequate room in his construal of work for spiritual development.

WORK'S RELATIONAL ASPECT

Although Moltmann does not structure his reflections using the terminology I use, his construal of work is nevertheless largely concerned with what I have called the relational aspect of work; both in its social-structural and existential dimensions.

We have seen that for Moltmann, the social-structural is the highest functional value of work. Indeed, throughout both articles we find a strong emphasis on concerns such as social justice (particularly human rights and the right to meaningful work) and the protection of the environment. The difficulty is not with Moltmann's lack of concern for specific social-structural issues, but rather is with what he understands the substance of these concerns to involve. It is not our purpose here to provide an exhaustive critique of, for example, Moltmann's understanding of human rights or environmental protection. Broadly however, his weaknesses in the instrumental area, (particularly with respect to utility, sustenance and economics,) carry over into and adversely affect his vision of what is socially good with relation to work. One example here is his concern to make employment a basic human right for every able person. If one focuses rather exclusively on the relational dimension of work, minimizing for the most part the instrumental dimension related to sustenance, then it is understandable how one could arrive at such a conclusion. This however, is precisely what cannot be done, for when it is the content of the ethical standard becomes imbalanced and skewed. The opportunity of employment for everyone may be a good social goal to move toward. However, if this goal is not then taken in relation to other social goals and social realities (for example, economic realities) then the goal itself becomes so abstract that it becomes useless for practical ethical purposes.

Another way to formulate this problem is that Moltmann has not been sufficiently comprehensive in his social-relational analysis. He has simply not taken into account the complex matrix of social structural levels and issues which he must. It is not wrong for him to be concerned with only a few ethical issues, for example, international social justice, the right to work, or environmental protection. It does create problems however, when moral accounts and moral prescriptions fail to factor in and inter-relate all of the relevant and related data. If we want to understand work on a social structural level, we will need to be sufficiently comprehensive in our social analysis so as to avoid unbalanced reductionistic moralizing or abstract utopian idealization with reference to only one or two concerns. Moltmann here has left himself open to this charge.

Of course, Moltmann is not solely concerned with social-structural aspects of the relational dimension of work (even though he has built his arguments around the right to work). Rather, he has raised this and other social ethical issues in connection with and growing out of the existential dimension dealing specifically with human meaning. Meaningful work, the existential dimension, is as much of a concern to him as the right to work.

Moltmann's main concern in this area is that work neither be understood as providing too much nor too little meaning for life. Work cannot be the sole locus in life in which meaning is established, nor can it be divorced from questions of its human existential meaning. Moltmann has thus attempted a view of work which can provide qualified meaning for the working person, the community, and life in general.

Although Moltmann is careful to offer several qualifications, he does affirm that work can play a significant role in the life of the working person. He sees work as instilling in a person feelings of independence and ability, and thus self-consciousness. (*HD*, p.54.) He suggests that work is humane when it offers latitude for individual formation. (*HD*, p.54.) He reasons that work is signifi- cant for the community when it is perceived as an active participation in the broader social process. He then argues that work is significant for the meaning of life in general because it relates to the Kingdom of God (a point which will be discussed shortly).

The criticism is not that Moltmann uses these terms, for in themselves they could be helpful and appropriate concepts with respect to work. Rather, the critique is with the way that Moltmann has restricted and qualified their mean- ing so as to exclude the idea that work in any way involves self-realization. 'The expression *self-realization* is too strong because it threatens the young, the old, the handicapped, and the unemployed with nonexistence.' (*HD*, p.54.) As seen, Moltmann's argument against Marx is that work is not to be a form of self-realization, but rather only a form of self-expression, self-representation, and self-presentation. These are important concepts indeed and I want to affirm that an ethical goal of work should be that it allows room for people to express and reveal themselves through their active and productive lives. The problem however, is the assumption that work is or should only be an expression, repre- sentation or presentation of the already existing self. It surely is this, in either a humanizing or dehumanizing way. However, it is also more than this.

Work also has an effect, either positively or negatively, on the becoming self and its identity. In and through the process of working people do change. They become something that they were not before their working began. This change can either go in the direction of growth or destruction. The point is that people do not simply present who they are, but also in some way become something, and thus in one sense realize themselves in and through their work. Moltmann is correct in criticizing Marx by arguing that work is not the only way for the self to change / become. Indeed, Marx was too reductionistic on this point in that he allowed no room for God, personal relationships or simply non-working existence. However, Moltmann has gone too far in his reaction against Marx and has excluded from work a very real and important characteristic. Work is one way, and for most people a very central way, by which the self becomes realized, and this can be either positively or negatively.

Again part of Moltmann's resistance to this idea seems to be his problem theologically that any affirmation of self-realization (or humanization) in work would necessarily be an affirmation of justification by works. Work needs to be free and needs to flow from the changed or justified self for there is no way to get from doing to being. If work contributes to this change, a move from doing to being, then it becomes a means of self-justification. Moltmann prefers Luther to Marx.

The problem however, is that Moltmann has tacitly equated self-realization with justification. Although it may be appropriate to conceptualize justification as in some way a type of, or contributor to self-realization, the reverse does not necessarily follow. It need not be true that self-realization is a type of justification or eternal salvation. Of course many, especially those who do not hold to a Christian view of things, may view self-realization (even through work) to be their secularized version of salvation. On a Christian view, this would be a type of salvation by works. However, it is also possible from within Christian theology to affirm even a non-believer's positive growth, development, or change through their work and to view this as something other than and short of justification or salvation. The doctrine of common grace would seem to apply here. People can still learn and grow in areas of their lives even if we want to affirm that they ultimately still need to experience God's justification and salvation for their whole life.

My problem with Moltmann is that he has been compelled by his own theology to exclude an important and central characteristic of work. Again, Marx has gone too far with his secularized version of salvation. However, this does not mean that Christians need to, or even can, exclude self-realization from the working process.

What are we to conclude then concerning Moltmann's understanding of the relational aspect of work? Positively he has highlighted both the social-structural as well as existential dimension of work. Further, he has also provided a very important check and corrective to Marx's anthropology. Negatively however, his construal is ultimately unsatisfactory. Although it offers some helpful points of insight, it is too lacking in scope to be of real use. On the social-structural side it is too incomplete to be of much help. On the existential side Moltmann has unnecessarily divorced from work an important existential characteristic, that of self-realization.

Further, the theological difficulties raise questions about its doctrinal coherence. I am not suggesting here that these theological weaknesses necessarily undermine all that has been said. Rather, I simply mean that with such difficulties, Moltmann's view of work's relational aspects falls short of the standard highlighted by my hypothesis.

WORK'S ONTOLOGICAL ASPECT

As stated, Moltmann does not call for or address an ontological understanding of work precisely as I have here defined it. Nor does his construal approach an ontological understanding of work to the degree that it highlights both work's instrumentality and relationality. Nonetheless, I have suggested that his theological summary with respect to work, in attempting to provide a theological basis for the significance of work with respect to the meaning of life as a whole, can be understood as a tacit probing for an ontological understanding of work.

As outlined, Moltmann is concerned to present a theological understanding of work which has a meaning, not just for the worker or the society, but also for the whole of life. Ultimately, Moltmann wants to ground work, through and because of its significance for the person and society, in the Kingdom of God, that is, through Christ in eschatology. Work is a way for people to take part in either the destruction or preservation of the unfinished world. It is a way to serve the creating God and work together with the redeeming God. Without detailed explanation, Moltmann suggests that work in the Kingdom of God in some way closely relates to God's renewing of heaven and earth. There is then a transcendent meaning and value to work itself.

We might wish that Moltmann had more fully developed these ideas and explained his meaning more precisely. Unfortunately, he has not. Nonetheless, what he has provided indicates that he recognizes a transcendent aspect of work, theologically conceived, which involves more than its penultimate personal and societal value. What Moltmann seems to be probing for is a view of work as a form of correspondence to God and as bound up with the new heavens and new earth which approaches transcendental or eternal significance.

For my purpose, as it relates to my hypothesis, it is not only significant that he is probing in this direction. It is also important to consider the theological grounding meant to give work this significance for the whole. Of course there are elements, for example, of protology and eschatology throughout the discussion. Generally however, we have seen that the doctrine of God the Father, and then more significantly Christology have been the points from which Moltmann has built his construal. Although it could be done, I shall not challenge any specific formulations with reference to these doctrines.[36] Rather, I want simply to highlight that Christology, or even the doctrine of God more broadly, is one doctrinal starting point for establishing something like an ontology of work. With reference to my hypothesis however, the question is whether this is the best doctrinal basis or whether by itself it is a sufficient one.

Obviously any Christian theology, including a theology of work, which is probing ontological questions will need to be (like Moltmann's) in some form built upon the life, cross, and resurrection of Christ. Any construal which is completely unrelated or contrary to these realities cannot be specifically Christian. However, there are other ways particularly with reference to a Christian theology of work, to accomplish this Christological goal which Moltmann has highlighted. One need not necessarily call for the imitation of Christ the working carpenter, nor, as Moltmann has done, develop a model of work based on Christ's painful and difficult work of redemption. This is not to completely invalidate these approaches. Rather I believe that ultimately there is a better and more convincing way to establish an ontological understanding of work.

My strategy is to develop the two interconnected and multifaceted doctrines

---

[36] For this type of criticism see the brief critique offered by West, (1986), 'Cruciform Labour'.

of theological anthropology and a theology of nature, and to do so teleologically (building upon protological, eschatological and Christological foundations). These, I shall show, are better starting points for the task of establishing an ontology of work.

This does not mean that the type of ontological grounding which Moltmann indirectly offers is useless. Moltmann has done theology a great service by pointing toward and offering an understanding of work which highlights its meaning for the whole of life and not only for the person and society. However, ultimately Moltmann's attempt is insufficiently developed, and thus inadequate for providing an ontology of work.

We have now come full circle to the original conclusion concerning Moltmann's construal of work. It has been shown that although Moltmann has contributed ideas to all three of work's aspects (the instrumental, relational and ontological) ultimately his construal falls short in each area. Further, I have highlighted how weaknesses in one area carry over into and adversely affect the other. The overall conclusion then is that Moltmann's theological understanding of work is less than adequate.

The Way Forward

Where does this lead then with respect to both Moltmann's theology, and a way forward concerning the hypothesis of this book? With respect to the hypothesis, having demonstrated in this first half of the book that this threefold construal of work is both appropriate and necessary, the task is now to develop a more adequate ontology of work building from theological anthropology and a theology of nature. In this process I will likewise explore how the ontological aspect of work both establishes and then further gives the parameters to both its instrumental and relational aspects. From this I will demonstrate how each of these three aspects in turn affects the others, and then the whole of work. With this, I will finally have presented a more comprehensive theological picture of the nature of work than has hitherto been provided.

Concerning Moltmann, I propose to develop many of my ideas in critical dialogue with his broader theology. I am not suggesting that the formulations which I finally present are Moltmann's. I will reconstruct and summarize his views only in as much as I intend to critically dialogue with them for my own purposes. The method then is to critically plunder Moltmann's theology for my own theological construals, and then to apply these constructs specifically to work.

Hence, I am not proposing to construct a theology of work directly from Moltmann's broader systematics, even though I am convinced that a better one would be possible than he himself has offered. Rather my project is to develop my own understanding of an ontology of work using Moltmann and his broader systematics as a dialogue partner.

PART 2

The Ontology of Work:
A Proposal

Chapter 4

Teleological Foundations for the Ontology of Work

So far, this book has argued for the need to develop a more explicit and theologically shaped ontology of work. In so arguing I have shown that both Catholic and Protestant theology have been moving toward this kind of construct, but that neither has yet to achieve a satisfactory formulation of it. What remains to be done in this book is to develop a more adequate ontology of work, and then to demonstrate what this will do for understanding work's nature and meaning. The next three chapters develop the theology through which this ontology of work is shaped by establishing in turn - a teleological orientation, and then an analysis of and contribution to Christian theological anthropology. However, though making wider contributions to this doctrine, the analysis of theological anthropology is necessarily narrowed toward the overall goal of finally establishing with it a more adequate ontology of work.

Thus, although I do not outline herein a fully detailed teleological Christian anthropology, I do nonetheless recognize that there are a wide range of interrelated issues that any anthropology must consider if it is to be appropriate in the current world situation. Paramount among these is the concern for an ecologically appropriate doctrine of humanity. This concern is all the more pressing given that my overall intention, based upon work's ontological aspect, is to suggest a quite high evaluation of the importance of human work. Now it might initially seem that there is an irreconcilable conflict of interests between these concerns. Can human work realistically be highly regarded considering the ecological crisis that has to a large extent been caused by our work? I believe that work can be highly regarded. However, this is a seriously important and complicated question that cannot be resolved by simplistically arguing for a revised kinder and gentler form of work (as important as this change in work style might be). Rather, what is more fundamentally needed, and what I shall propose, is a theological anthropology (and a resultant ontology of work) that is developed with a constant reference to a broader theology of nature.[1]

---

[1] For an overview that categorizes and lists several theologies of nature see: Northcott, (1996), pp.124-163. See also: Hendry, (1980). For a recent and helpful theology of nature see: Page, (1996).

The anthropology and ontology of work in this book will be primarily developed in critical dialogue with the theology / theology of nature proposed by Jürgen Moltmann.

Of course, the very distinction between anthropology and nature is somewhat artificial and therefore problematic. On the most basic level of material existence it is ultimately not possible to speak of humanity without also making a comment about nature; since a person is a material / natural being and therefore a part of what we call nature. Even theologically, both humanity and nature come under the same category of created being. By virtue of this they stand together and alongside each other in relationship to God as part of one and the same created, contingent, and material reality. Indeed, ecological theology is rightly concerned to show that many of our environmental problems appear to have developed from a context where we have drawn too sharp a distinction between humanity and nature.

These challenges notwithstanding, I believe that it is legitimate and even necessary to allow cautiously this somewhat artificial and problematic distinction to stand. Firstly, there is the practical reality that humanity does often understand itself to be (and thus acts as if it were) in opposition to nature. This is at the root of the ecological crisis. Secondly, for all of our similarities and common properties, humans in important ways transcend the natural world of which we are a part, and indeed are distinguishable from the rest of creation. Theologically this difference is defendable by pointing to some formulation of the concept of the image of God in humanity. Certainly we must be careful to recognize that even this doctrine does not draw so sharp a boundary as to cut humanity off from our natural existence or from non-human entities. Nonetheless, this doctrine does introduce an important, though not absolute distinction between the two. This then suggests is that it is appropriate to consider theological anthropology in itself, as long as it can be located within the context of a theology of nature and as long as it is constantly remembered that both anthropology and a theology of nature are essentially and irreducibly linked to and a part of one another.

Too often in recent ecological studies humanity is collapsed into nature in such a way that we lose our place within nature and thus our unique identity and transcendent particularity (something needed for these studies to be undertaken in the first place). On the other hand, there has been a tendency in the history of Christian anthropological studies to so differentiate humanity from nature that nature loses its unique place and therefore identity in relationship both to ourselves and to God. I believe that in my anthropological study these problems can be minimized by giving particularized space both to humanity and to nature. Furthermore, I suggest that the way to achieve this is by conceiving of both humanity and nature according to their respective and related ends, that is, with a dynamic and theologically grounded teleology.

Prior then to the detailed discussion of anthropology / nature that will follow, it is vital first to explore the concept of teleology and therein to show how it will be used within the remainder of the project. For this book the question of 'teleology' is not that which has dominated ethical theory for much of the 20th century; the debate between teleological and deontological ethics. That is, I am not directly concerned with the debate about consequentialism as opposed to rules based ethics (although this discussion has implications for that debate). Rather, my interest is broader and is with teleology as suggesting what are the purposes or ends of something. Here, I want to consider whether it is possible to determine the moral 'ought' by extrapolating from a thing's purposes and ends; and if this is possible, how it can be done. Therefore, with reference to humanity specifically, the teleological questions involve how we understand our *telos*, our purposes and ends, and what bearing these have on our morality. With reference to nature (non-human creation), the teleological questions involve how to understand its *telos*, or purposes and ends, and what bearing these have on both its particular identity as nature (in itself and before God), and then on our human moral relationship to it.

In both science and in ethics the dominant way that this approach to the concept of teleology has been expressed is by referring to the 'natural' or supposed inherent purposes and ends of a thing. Generally, this understanding follows from Aristotle's conception of teleology; though in Christian ethics this approach was first adopted, modified, and then placed within a theological context by Thomas Aquinas. Here the modification revolves around the idea that the 'inherent' purposes or ends of a thing are established, not primarily by logic or observation, but rather by God's initial design in creation for a given thing. Teleology on this account addresses what is natural to a thing, but not 'natural' in the modern sense of being independent of or autonomous from God. Rather, here something is natural in as much as it coheres with God's initial design for a thing, that is, in as much as nature is understood from within a Christian worldview to be creation rather than simply to be neutral nature.[2]

The proposal on teleology that follows is sympathetic to this trajectory begun by Aquinas, though it will show itself to be quite different in theological detail. These differences notwithstanding, what I propose below is that a revisioned teleological framework is both possible and necessary for theological ethics in general, and in particular for the project of establishing an ontology of work.

To accomplish this however, the concept of teleology first needs to be revitalized. Given contemporary skepticism surrounding this possibility, what must first be shown is that it is possible to reason from the descriptive *is* to the prescriptive *ought*. This means that it is essential to establish at the outset the possibility of talking about a thing as having purposes or ends and that it is appropriate to reason from this to determine a moral ought.

To accomplish this task I will enter into dialogue with two contemporary thinkers: Alasdair MacIntyre, (a moral philosopher) and Oliver O'Donovan (a

---

[2] Although stated somewhat differently, this is the basic argument presented by Jean Porter in her discussion of Aquinas' general theory of goodness. See: Porter, (1994), pp.34-68.

moral theologian). I begin with MacIntyre.

Alasdair MacIntyre: Reviving Teleology

Let us first look briefly at the possibility of a philosophical grounding for teleology. Alasdair MacIntyre in his seminal study *After Virtue* (1985) offers an important contribution to ethics (philosophical and theological) with his proposal for the reintroduction and revitalization of the concept of teleology; that is, that one can and must derive the ethical *ought* from the descriptive *is*.

The thesis of *After Virtue* is that moral philosophy since the Enlightenment has lost its bearings and has finally become stranded in a *cul-de-sac* of emotivism with no clear way out. The problem which MacIntyre outlines is that moderns have experienced a loss of language with which to talk about morality. Although key moral words and phrases that indicate concepts of the good and right and wrong have survived, they have been divorced from their historically derived philosophical and theological contexts to such an extent that what they signify becomes unverifiable and thus mostly meaningless. What MacIntyre argues for is the rebuilding and restoration of these lost and missing contexts. For this task he ultimately calls for a return to either Aristotle or 'something very like it.'(p.117.)[3] Although this return to Aristotle by MacIntyre is complex and involves multiple interrelated Aristotelian concepts, one central element in this scheme needing restoration is the concept of teleology.

With Chapter 5, 'Why the Enlightenment Project of Justifying Morality Had to Fail', MacIntyre specifically begins his revitalization of the concept of teleology. Throughout the chapter MacIntyre argues that the problem for modern moral philosophy has been the loss of an Aristotelian teleological framework and / or a theistic version of it as was common from the European Middle Ages to the modern period. He argues that with classical and theistic ethics there was a three-fold scheme operating. These included; 'untutored human-nature-as-it-happened-to-be', 'human-nature-as-it-could-be-if-it-realized-its-*telos*' and practical reason, which is 'the precepts of rational ethics as the means for transition' from the former to the latter state. (p.53.) MacIntyre argues that all three of these concepts need to be present and operating if the moral project as a whole, and thus the moral language which grows out of it, is going to function and be intelligible.

The error as MacIntyre understands it, is that this three-fold scheme was

---

[3] This quote is made in the context of a discussion on whether Aristotle or Nietzsche provides the way forward for moral philosophy. I am interpreting this discussion to be paradigmatic for MacIntyre's whole thesis. For MacIntyre, Nietzsche is the inevitable outcome of Enlightenment morality. Aristotle, or something very like it if it could be sustained would make Nietzshe's entire project pointless and provide a general way forward for moral philosophy.

abandoned. Lost primarily was the idea that reason could genuinely be used to comprehend man's true end. (pp.53-54.) In science (following Pascal) and philosophy (following Descartes) anti-Aristotelian directions set the boundaries for reason. The result of this is that reason is perceived as not able to discern any essential natures or teleological features in the objective universe. This finally leads to the rejection of any 'teleological view of human nature, and any view of man as having an essence which defines his true end.' (p.54.) These developments in science and philosophy, (even in theology with Protestantism and Jansenest Catholicism) eliminate any notion of man-as-it-could-be-if-it-realized-its-*telos*.

> Since the whole point of ethics - both as a theoretical and practical discipline - is to enable man to pass from his present state to his true end, the elimination of any notion of essential human nature and with it the abandonment of any notion of a *telos* leaves behind a moral scheme composed of two remaining elements whose relationship becomes quite unclear. (pp.54-55.)

Stated succinctly, a content for morality has survived but it has been cut off from its teleological context. A certain view of untutored-human-nature-as-it-is has survived, but, since moral pronouncements were originally meant to correct, improve and educate human nature 'they are clearly not going to be such as could be deduced from true statements about human nature or justified in some other way by appealing to its characteristics.' (p.55.) MacIntyre concludes:

> Hence the eighteenth-century moral philosophers engaged in what was an inevitably unsuccessful project; for they did indeed attempt to find a rational basis for their moral beliefs in a particular understanding of human nature, while inheriting a set of moral injunctions on the one hand and a conception of human nature on the other which had been expressly designed to be discrepant with each other. (p.55.)

What MacIntyre argues for by way of correction is a re-establishment of the lost three-fold understanding of ethics. He suggests that it is possible to perceive the human *telos,* and that the knowledge for doing this is derived from essential human nature by reason. Ultimately MacIntyre argues that if we reintroduce this three-fold concept we will be able to develop moral statements from factual premises so that morality will then be based on fact rather than emotional wishes. Basically, there will be a way to get from the *is* to the *ought.*

Essential to this project, according to MacIntyre, is to reintroduce the concept of function to an understanding of a thing's essential nature. (pp.57-58.) He illustrates this by quoting A.N. Prior that logically one can accurately conclude from the fact that someone is a sea-captain that he therefore ought to do what ever it is that a sea-captain ought to do. He further illustrates that if something is a watch, it ought, if it is a good watch, to keep time accurately. The key here is to think of something's essential nature as including its function. If this is allowed, then what a thing *is* implies inherently how it *ought* to be or behave. The *is* to *ought* step is rehabilitated. This move, MacIntrye argues, will only be a problem if one insists on excluding functional (and I shall add to this argument relational) concepts from the understanding of the essence of a thing.

Concerning humanity specifically, MacIntyre argues that in the classical Aristotelian tradition, Greek or Medieval, humanity was understood as having an essential nature and an essential purpose or function. (p.58.) It is only when this functional understanding of the person is rejected that it becomes difficult to get from the descriptive *is* to the prescriptive *ought.*

Where however, does this functional description come from according to MacIntyre? It is rooted in the various forms of the social life. (Hence my comment that functional concepts are ultimately relational concepts.) Functionality is derived from the various roles a person might have; be these family member, citizen, soldier, philosopher, servant of God or the like. (pp.58-59.)[4] MacIntyre argues that: 'It is only when a man is thought of as an individual prior to and apart from all roles that a "man" ceases to be a functional concept.' (p.59.) Another way which one might say this is that it is only when the essence and identity of the person (self) is conceived of non-relationally that functionality ceases to be appropriate for understanding something of the essential nature of the person.[5]

MacIntyre's argument then, is that teleology based on reason is a necessary category and needs to be restored in ethics if we are to make moral statements and judgements which are meaningful (factual) and which go beyond emotivism. Indeed on his view, intelligent moral discourse demands that we make such a move.

This brings us back to the point where we began. According to MacIntyre, if moral philosophy and moral theology want to get out of the *cul-de-sac* of emotivism, they will need to restore the lost three-fold understanding of ethics, or something very similar to it. They will need do this by reintroducing and reviving the lost concept of a functional (rational) teleology. They will need to return to Aristotle or 'something very like it' – at least with respect to these particular points.

---

[4] It is interesting to note that at this point MacIntyre comes very close to Luther's understanding of stations or calling in relationship to moral obligation.

[5] For a relational anthropology see: Gunton, 'Trinity, Ontology and Anthropology: Towards a Renewal of the Doctrine of the Imago Dei.' in *Persons, Divine and Human: King's College Essays in Theological Anthropology,* (1991), pp.47-61. And. Zizioulas, (1993).

Oliver O'Donovan: Theological Teleology

When carefully examined, Christian moral theologian Oliver O'Donovan in *Resurrection and the Moral Order* (1986) provides theology and theological ethics, not with a return to Aristotle as such, but rather with something (at least to a significant degree) like it. As a point of departure, O'Donovan like MacIntyre believes that for ethics it is possible and necessary to affirm the move from the *is* to the *ought*. (p.17.) For both, a teleological framework is an essential part of an ethical system. In this respect O'Donovan's framework can be seen as a complement to MacIntyre's Aristotelian teleology.[6]

To begin I offer two summary observations about the teleological framework which O'Donovan has developed. First, he does not take Aristotelian philosophy as the conceptual starting point for his understanding of teleology. This does not mean that he fails to incorporate Aristotelian perspectives, for as we will see he does. Rather, the necessary observation is that he begins with biblical and theological concepts. For O'Donovan it is essential, at least for an Evangelical / Christian ethics, (including teleology) that we begin with theology. He begins his book:

> The foundations of Christian ethics must be evangelical foundations; or, to put it more simply, Christian ethics must arise from the gospel of Jesus Christ. Otherwise, it could not be Christian ethics. (p.11.)

For O'Donovan however, even this is not yet precise enough. He goes on to say that this means that Christian ethics starts with and depends upon the resurrection of Jesus Christ from the dead. (p.13.) It is then from this starting point of the resurrection that O'Donovan develops the two doctrines essential for his theological teleology; creation and eschatology. Orientationally for O'Donovan, creation and eschatology in light of the resurrection (rather than Aristotelian philosophy) forms the basis for teleology.

The second summary observation is that O'Donovan presents teleology fundamentally as a relational concept (one which necessarily involves a multiplicity of relationships.) Teleology involves an ordering to, for, and alongside the other, and the like. It does not, as some critics of teleology suggest, imply a rigid understanding of being which negatively restricts either science or human freedom. (pp.45ff.) Rather, the multiple relational orderings imply some sense of openness, fluidity and dynamism within 'being'. I am not suggesting by this that O'Donovan understands created existence as open in the sense of being

---

[6] O'Donovan does argue however that MacIntyre does not follow Aristotle's natural teleology as closely as he should. (p. 221.) Thus, it seems correct to suggest that in some respects O'Donovan is more in line with Aristotle than with MacIntyre. However, I am only suggesting that O'Donovan complements Aristotle. The fact that O'Donovan differs in places with MacIntyre's own Aristotelian scheme is here irrelevant.

random and therefore dependent upon subjective human interpretations to provide its order. He argues pointedly against this. I am suggesting however, that in casting teleology in relational terms, he has allowed room for openness in ethical reasoning, or, for Christian ethics to be open to that which might be a 'new' conclusion. More on this later.

O'Donovan first begins to develop his concept of teleology in Chapter 2 when discussing the created order. He begins by arguing that the resurrection is the vindication of creation and that creation therefore is to be taken seriously in ethics. Creation however, implies more than the raw material of which existence is composed. Creation implies also the order and coherence in which it is composed. (p.31.) This order is both vertical and horizontal. Vertical order means that creation is ordered to God. It is contingent upon God. Horizontal order refers to creation's ordering among and between its parts. From these two directions O'Donovan forms the concept of order as both end and kind. (p.32.)

An order of kind refers to a generic ordering. This means that things are related to each other reciprocally. A thing can be recognized to have a commonality with another thing and thus have its identity defined relationally with reference to the other. (This would also mean that it can also have its particularity similarly defined within this reciprocal relationship.) An order of kind means that things are ordered 'alongside' of each other. A is in some respect 'like' B, and B 'like' A. (p.32.) This idea of kind and generic ordering is intended to repudiate the idea that we live in absolute disorder where a plurality of entities are so unrelated that the concepts of 'a world' and 'relationship' become meaningless. Ultimately, generic ordering, or relationships of kind, make sense of the idea that we live in a common universe.

With an order of end O'Donovan develops the idea of teleology. Teleology suggests that things are related to other things directionally. In classical Platonic terms this is depicted as an ordering-to-serve. Thus, A is ordered-to-serve B, and B is A's end. (p.32.) In biblical terms O'Donovan illustrates this idea by showing that in Col. 1:15-20 the concept 'for him' (Christ) is an indication of teleological order in creation. Creation is ordered to, and for, Christ. (pp.32-33.) Teleological ordering then, in both Platonic and Biblical senses involves the idea of ordering-to or ordering-for.

When considering the relationship between an order of kind and an order of ends, O'Donovan argues that the only pure teleological relation, unqualified by any generic ordering alongside, is the relation between the creature and its Creator. However, he goes on to suggest that within the created order as a whole there is a complex network of teleological and generic relations. (p.33.) Some creatures which have a generic ordering-alongside, (both man and vegetables are generically ordered-alongside as both are creatures), can also have teleological ordering-to each another. Vegetables are ordered-to men, for example, as food. (He elsewhere also suggests that they may be ordered-to other entities like animals distinct from their ordering to humanity. p.35.) Some generic ordering however, can have no teleological ordering-to. For example, one race cannot make another slaves for the ordered-alongside negates the ordering-to in this instance. O'Donovan's point here with these illustrations and orderings is that we must be careful to remember both generic and teleological relations and the complex way that they interrelate in reality.

Following this discussion O'Donovan turns his attention specifically to a fuller depiction of teleology. So far he has only been referring to teleology in the Platonic sense, as an ordering-to-serve. He now introduces the Aristotelian sense, that is, the idea of an ordering-to-flourish. A is ordered-to-flourish as A. (p. 34.) Vegetable creation is ordered-to grow luxuriantly, animal creation to move with strength and vigour, and rational creation to think. On this view we can imagine a purely natural ordering, or natural teleology within the created world.

In this Aristotelian and natural sense one does not raise the larger relationally defining cosmological questions. Platonic teleology does, for example, when it speaks of an ordering-to-serve divine truth. In Aristotelian teleology however, one asks questions more intrinsic to the nature of a thing itself.

Scholastic Christianity, O'Donovan argues, even though it followed Aristotle in its teleology, nonetheless found it necessary to also include the Platonic concepts of teleology so as to safeguard a unified and whole concept of reality. It did this by posing both natural and supernatural teleological questions. (pp.34-35.) What is the natural end of a thing, and what is the supernatural end of a thing? The Scholastics wanted to show by this that things existed within themselves but also in some type of broader defining relationship, both to others and to God.

As O'Donovan develops his own arguments he wants to preserve and interrelate both of these senses of teleology. So, the content of the natural teleology of an individual thing will in part be understood and determined by how it relates to the wider order of which it is a part. This nuancing means that teleology becomes open, not only to relationships with other natural things, but also to a relationship with the supernatural; and it is the supernatural which determines what the flourishing of the natural order is to be. (p.35.)

O'Donovan illustrates this idea when considering the teleology of mankind. A supernatural teleological ordering suggests that mankind's end is to serve God. A natural teleological ordering suggests that mankind's end is to flourish as mankind by functioning as nature's ruler. Of course, it must be remembered that mankind is generically ordered alongside the rest of nature, and that nature also, as creaturely, has its own generic and teleological orderings. The entities of nature have their own orderings to each other, but they also have their orderings to flourish as individual entities. Thus, mankind's rule over nature will be a rule which liberates other beings to be: to be in themselves, to be for others, and to be for God. (p.38.)

Although he wants to preserve both senses of teleology, both the natural and supernatural, in this chapter on created order O'Donovan is ultimately concerned to show the legitimacy of natural (generic) teleology, and its connection to morality. He argues that there is a natural teleology which implies with it a corresponding natural morality. This morality likewise is generic in nature. That is, it is a morality which is not dependent upon varying situations. Nor is it a morality restricted to Christians. Rather, it is a universal morality. It is a morality which must necessarily transcend time-place particularizations and always be the case. (p.39.)

The existence of a generic universal morality (really a natural theology), he argues, is not a theological problem as some have contended. It does not limit God's freedom by imposing upon God an extrinsic moral standard. Nor does it make creation and thus morality a type of emanation of God.

> There is no reason why this proper theological concern should not be fully accommodated within a teleological and generic understanding of created order. In speaking of kinds as independent of time-place particularity there is certainly no need to attribute to them an eternal transcendence such as belongs to God himself. Kinds are not independent of the temporo-spatial universe. No claim is made for their existence 'before creation'. They are simply, by virtue of their role as ordering principles within the temporo-spatial universe independent of any *particular* time-place determination. (p.39.)

Following on this, and on his response to further objections to a natural teleology, O'Donovan concludes his chapter on the natural order by reaffirming that teleology is ultimately about relationships. It involves links which make it possible to get a picture of the universe as a whole. For him, a natural teleology, (not ignoring supernatural dimensions), is needed so that one does not end up with a fragmented knowledge, which is ultimately no knowledge at all. He says: 'Knowledge of the world without ends can never become a unified knowledge.' (p.50.)

Further, he argues that any abstraction denying teleology creates a dangerous misunderstanding of the place of humanity in the universe. It implies that humanity encounters an inert creation, that is, a creation without movement and without a point to its movement. At this point the mind will create its own teleological order and impose it upon created order. One negative result of this perversion of the given order involves what we are experiencing currently, that is, a lack of respect for, and protection of, the environment. A teleology which recognizes the given and established order will be necessary if we are to avoid such problems. (pp.49-52.)

Next I turn to consider the implications of eschatology for O'Donovan's teleology. As previously stated, O'Donovan does not derive the content and shape of his teleology solely from Platonic and Aristotelian ideas. Nor does he form his content for teleology only from the natural, that is, from within the doctrine of creation and created order. Rather, the ultimate shape to O'Donovan's teleology comes in Chapter 3 where he discusses eschatology and history.

The resurrection vindicates created order. In this respect it looks backward to creation. However, the resurrection also looks forward eschatologically in that it at the same time fulfills that which it has vindicated. Indeed, this fulfillment was always implied in creation even though it could not be realized in the fallen state of man and the universe. (p.54.)

The theological content of teleology then comes from two places or two directions; redemption and transformation. The former looks backward, the latter forward. Redemption recovers mankind, but it also recovers the natural order which, in addition to having its own relation to God, is also mankind's context as humanity is the ruler of the ordered creation that God has made. (pp. 54-55.) Redemption however, goes beyond mere restoration. It implies the eschatological transformation of the world. (This will be a crucial issue in my ultimate evaluation of work.) It implies the destiny and direction to which the Garden of Eden was always headed.

> The eschatological transformation of the world is neither the mere repetition of the created world nor its negation. It is its fulfilment, its *telos* or end. It is the historical *telos* of the origin, that which creation is intended *for,* and that which it points and strives *towards.* (p.55.)

The resurrection brings together both redemption and transformation. It unites both creation order and eschatology. Herein lies the content and shape of teleology. The origin and the end are inseparably united. (p.57.)

A Christian teleology which involves transformation is not content to be historical (or historicized) teleology. This would mean that the end would be construed simply as development within time. (pp.58ff.) Rather, the eschatological *telos* is the *telos* of history (rather than the *telos* which is history), and is at the same time the *telos* of the created order. Therefore, a Christian view of history, and thus a Christian teleology, must include the idea of a beyond time eschatology. The destined end is not imminently present within the historical process. (p.64.)

This means that a natural teleology (Aristotelian and Platonic) although valid, necessary, and providing a generic morality, is not sufficient by itself. A Christian teleology according to O'Donovan's overall construct will incorporate these, but also go beyond them since a Christian teleology will be transformed by the eschatological element which looks forward to a new creation.

This brings us back to where we started in considering O'Donovan. Does he offer something like an Aristotelian recovery of teleology for morality? The answer broadly is yes. In incorporating Aristotelian teleology he has, to a significant degree, met MacIntyre's criteria. However, O'Donovan has finally produced a version of teleology for ethics that is more theological rather than philosophical, and for which the resurrection / transformation is necessarily the starting point. It does not reject philosophical contributions, but essentially it is a Christian rather than an Aristotelian teleology.

Constructing a Teleological Framework for this Project

What then is one to make of the two views of teleology presented? What formulation of teleology is needed and appropriate for exploring Christian anthropology and establishing an ontology of work? First there is MacIntyre's proposal. MacIntyre's thesis is that the current moral landscape which is dominated by emotivism is a wasteland. This is a compelling argument. Emotivism with its non-verifiable and non-factually based approach to morality makes morality itself and the language of morality meaningless, or, in the worst case simply a guise for those with power to manipulate the weak. Emotivism is not therefore morally viable even if one is convinced that it is the only available ground on which to stand. Similarly compelling is MacIntrye's argument that the way out of this dead end street will involve re-traversing the road of modernity that we have been on, by among other things, revitalizing a teleological framework. That is, it is reasonable to argue that for a system of morality to be both coherent and useful it is essential that it is able in some way to perceive the *ought* from some conception of the *is*.

In addition to these general directions however, there is one specific area of MacIntyre's proposal that deserves attention and that I want to incorporate critically into the teleological framework for this book. This is the idea that it is appropriate and even essential to consider concepts of function in determining a thing's essential nature, and thus its *telos*.

Concerning humanity specifically, some may object to this inclusion of function as part of a person's essence arguing that purposeful function is destructive in that it diminishes both a person's essence and value by making these dependant upon what he or she does. Rather it is argued that simple existence determines a person's essence rather than any function or activity that he or she might incidentally undertake. This, as shown, was Moltmann's concern where he argued against self creation / justification through work. Likewise, from the Foundationalism initiated by Descartes to contemporary Existentialism (both modern projects interestingly) this is the contention. This of course is a valid concern, especially in a day when the value and dignity of the sick, old, handicapped, pre-born and even unemployed is under attack from those reducing all human value and moral reasoning to some form of utility.

These concerns in themselves however, do not finally undermine the suggestion that function is central to a thing's, or in this case, a person's essential nature. On the contrary, only when function is extremely narrowly defined or when one attempts to quantify the value of someone, in, for example, economic terms, might such criticisms be valid and necessary. As flagged earlier however, the very notion of function leads into the broader realm of relationship. This is with respect to persons as well as things. Function in itself does not necessarily suggest the concept of utility as the *apriori* foundational category, or starting point. Rather, function when disentangled from the ideology of modernity is primarily a relational concept operating with and within relational categories. The notion of function in fact binds together the things/persons that utility pulls apart. Function likewise guarantees that connectedness and interdependence are integral to a thing/person's essence in a way that Foundationalism and Existentialism cannot, beginning as they do with individual existence. As the key category of function, relationship rather than either utility or solitary existence safeguards a person's value and corresponding dignity by showing them to be a valuable part of an integrated whole; rather than in an individualist way making their essence prior to and thus detached from and incidental to that whole.

Both horizontally with reference to the inter-relationships of created beings, and vertically with reference to a relationship to God, function always directs a thing or self toward the other. It always, and at the same time, incorporates (provides a means for inclusion) and yet differentiates (allows for distinct particularities) in this directing relationship. Even those listed above (the sick, old, handicapped, pre-born and unemployed) are enmeshed in a matrix of directing and functional relationships, which shapes who they are (their essence) positively in a way that utility and mere existence cannot. Each relationship necessarily carries with it its own type of functional directedness; that is, each relationship functions for different purposes and in different ways with respect to another being; be that a person, animal or other being. For example, the handicapped person has dignity and is of value precisely because he or she brings something valuable, their particularity, into a relationship with the other who is different. It is this distinctiveness, relationally bound together that gives richness to the whole. This matrix of relationships then, functioning as it does so widely, implies that all involved, by virtue of their connectedness, have relational space and thus a place in creation. This suggests that function in fact highlights a person/thing's value. Far from devaluing a person or thing by undermining their dignity, function as a category of relationship guarantees their dignity and value. Importantly this applies to function/relationship within non-human and not simply human creation.

Therefore, it appears that MacIntyre's proposal that function is needed to determine a thing's essential nature (and thus *telos*) need not ultimately be a problem. This is especially true if one believes (as shortly to be argued) that the essence of the self (and thing) is properly perceived relationally.

One further point: the relational understanding of function as I am arguing here is not something alien to MacIntyre's proposal. Rather it is supported by MacIntyre's argument that one's function is in many different ways rooted in the social life. One's roles, for example, are integral to one's identity and thus one's essential nature and *telos*. The Reformation doctrine of vocation though in different formulations grasped this well.

However, at this point I also want to continue carefully to expand MacIntyre's framework by emphasizing the vertical dimension to this concept of relationship. I want also to identify a thing's function and thus its essence with more than simply its social roles. Theologically, it is important to consider a thing's function in light of its relationship to the ultimate, that is, to God.

Everything that exists, as a created thing, has some relationship to its Creator. As such, it will have some function specific to this relationship. Following on this, an entity's essential nature and thus *telos* will take into account and ultimately be dependant upon this relationship. Even one's understanding of social roles will be significantly shaped and defined by this relationship. This does not deny the importance of social roles for determining one's functions and thus one's essential nature and *telos*. It does however, mean that even these social roles have a transcendent point of reference, which if not determining, at least sets some boundaries on the social roles themselves.

Here then, I want to affirm that in this book teleology that incorporates function will incorporate vertical as well as horizontal relationships. What then in summary can be finally be said about the relationship between function and teleology?

The essential nature of anything is inextricably linked with the concepts of function. In as much as concepts of function involve both a rooting in the social life and a standing before God, they necessarily are relational concepts. As relational concepts they hold things together and safeguard things against being conceived of in an excessively individualistic or atomized manner; which is sometimes associated with the teleological idea of a thing flourishing as itself. Thus, the concepts of function central to teleology, rather than being destructive and alienating, are liberating. They allow things to be what they are both with, and distinct from, others. Teleology which incorporates concepts of function adds a richness to our understanding of the essential nature of a thing rather than robbing it of its dignity and worth.

Thus far however, discussion has been focused primarily on outlining and developing the stronger aspects of MacIntyre's teleological framework. Yet, these reflections, in as much as they have supplemented and modified MacIntyre's view, have begun also a broader critique of his framework. Now, building upon what has been argued, and in moving on specifically into a discussion of O'Donovan's teleology, it is important to point out what are the significant weaknesses philosophically and theologically in MacIntyre's proposal, and why ultimately his teleology is less than adequate.

In philosophical terms Aquinas and other Christians have recognized that Aristotelian natural teleology (meaning here a thing's ordering to flourish as itself) brings to light an important ethical dimension within creation generally. However, by itself it is insufficient philosophically. At least for Christian ethics O'Donovan is correct when he argues that philosophically something like a Platonic understanding of teleology must also be incorporated. Both the natural dimension of a thing's ordering to another thing, and the supernatural dimension of a thing's ordering to the Divine must be represented. Admittedly, with his concepts of social roles and function MacIntyre, whether knowingly or unknowingly, does include the natural aspect of Platonic teleology in his scheme. For, social roles and function necessarily involved this relational kind of order-

ing. However, this concession granted, on the other side MacIntyre has not sufficiently integrated the supernatural aspect of Platonic teleology into his understanding. That is, he has not taken sufficient account of a thing's ordering to the
Divine.[7] At least, he has not made this part of Platonic teleology central to or
essential for his framework. Why has he failed to do so? Why has he only incorporated part of Platonic teleology? Whatever the reasons, for a Christian
teleology such a philosophical omission is catastrophic and makes the proposal
inadequate.

In a similar theological vein, Aristotle's natural teleology as incorporated by
MacIntyre amounts to a teleology solely embedded in and thus limited to 'creation'. This is not to deny the importance and value of teleological relationships
derived logically from within 'creation'. However, for Christian theology a
teleology must primarily be grounded within the reality of Christ; that is, it
must be built upon the eschatological hope that stems from Christ's death and
resurrection. This much was O'Donovan's argument.

Going further, a Christian teleology stemming as it does from Christ will be
a hope for, rather than the loss of creation. However, this hope only is a hope
for creation if it comes from outwith creation and the inherent possibilities
therein. Creation itself needs a saving relationship, or ordering to God. Thus, a
teleology for Christian theology will necessarily go beyond both Aristotle and
Plato. Although it will include elements of natural teleology (and an ordering to
the Divine whatever that may be), this teleology will ultimately need to be
gathered up specifically into Christ in such a way that creation itself is fundamentally transformed. That is, creation itself will have a *telos* outwith its own
potentialities. Thus, rather than being the foundational source for teleological
reasoning and from which ethical conclusions are derived, nature (itself open
and in process) will become simply a qualified or derivative source for such
reasoning. Teleology here will still be natural (dealing with created reality) but
it will be so in the sense that it is grounded in both God's initial creation and
new creation. For a Christian teleology the locale of natural teleology will be
creation rather than self sufficient or self contained 'nature'.

With these critiques then, it is obvious that MacIntyre's teleology as presented in *After Virtue,* although helpful in pointing moral thought in the right
direction, is ultimately unsatisfactory; at least for a Christian understanding of
teleology. As these critiques indicate, for a Christian teleology it is necessary to
find a way after MacIntyre.

As O'Donovan's ideas have already begun to prove helpful in the critique of

---

[7] This is so in the argument being examined here from *After Virtue.* However, as MacIntyre's thought has subsequently developed he has begun to work with the concept of an
ordering to the Divine. This is particularly seen in this later book *Whose Justice? Which
Rationality?* (1988) where he has identified himself with a Theistic / Thomist version of
Aristotelianism.

MacIntyre, it now becomes appropriate to evaluate his teleological framework. With one substantial qualification, a teleology for this book can be built from O'Donovan. Here, rather than simply repeating approvingly the already out-lined contours of his argument with which I agree, I will focus on modifying and further developing O'Donovan's argument where it is flawed.

Throughout *Resurrection and Moral Order* O'Donovan is concerned to combat anti-foundationalism. (pp.7-8.) He wants to combat a view of reality that sees order, and thus moral constructs, as human inventions imposed upon the natural un-ordered stuff of existence. Rather, he argues that the concept of creation itself requires a given created order, and thus moral order. Beyond creation however, order is an ontological given that the resurrection substanti-ates and vindicates. For O'Donovan, 'The order of things that God has made is *there*. It is objective, and mankind has a place within it.' (p.17.)

Thus far O'Donovan's argument, with its appeal to objectivity might seem convincing. Yes, if God has created then there must be a given order. The diffi-culty however, is that in combating the excesses of anti-foundationalism (a necessary and useful critique of postmodernity) O'Donovan has simply by-passed the legitimate observations and challenges of his opponents against strong foundationalist objectivism. It is here that O'Donovan's argument begins to unravel.

The inadequacy of his position shows up in how he depicts the ontologically given order of things in creation. O'Donovan sees the created moral order itself as fully established, that is as in every way complete and thus unalterably closed. Herein lies the moral order's objectivity. According to O'Donovan, the primal (ontological) order has always been there, but it simply could not be realized or experienced because of human sin. (p.54.) This however, would suggest that creation or created order itself contains within it its own solutions to its problems; they have always been there they are just suppressed. Salvation then is inherent in creation although it is obscured by human sin. This vision of an already completed and self saving creation however is fundamentally at odds with O'Donovan's own broader eschatology. Regrettably, though attempting to rescue morality from subjectivism, with his commitment to objectivism (a strong foundationalism) O'Donovan inadvertently undermines his own project. Though possibly winning on one front, his project loses by failing to see and work through the implications and logic of the resurrection's transforming or salvific significance for the created 'given' order itself (an idea that will be-come clearer later when looking at Moltmann).

In failing to grasp that the resurrection's transformation of creation requires that in important ways creation and created moral order remains open even now to the genuinely new, O'Donovan develops an ethics that is finally at odds with his eschatology. On the surface he may have safeguarded the value and ethical significance of the givenness of the initial creation, but with his foundationalist commitment to objectivity he has ultimately excluded and thus undermined the ethical order implied by the new creation. Lost here is the possibility that order, or the moral order, (along with humanity) is actually open to its own salvation. Contrary to his intentions, creation then is lost, not reaffirmed with O'Donovan's construct. Furthermore, creation on this account is understood as closed or static rather than open to process and development from both outwith and within itself; the later as an anticipation of its salvation. Importantly, this is not simply a philosophical problem associated with contemporary shifting metaphysical conceptions from static to process ontology. No, more importantly for O'Donovan his contention that the moral order is fully given in the initial creation (but obscured by human sin) is a theological problem. Such a view makes both salvation and genuine moral development in this life an impossibility. It is thus self-defeating.

Likewise, parallel to this theological inadequacy stands a negative spiritual effect particularly with reference to a theology/spirituality of work. His conception of the givenness of creation order does not ultimately allow human activity to be spiritually meaningful. If creation order is completed and thus closed with pre-fall creation, then human life and co-operation with God becomes at best backward looking and negatively restorative rather than creatively an anticipation and participation in God's new creation. At best human stewardship means simply clearing away sin so as to recognize what God has already established. However, here the theological value and meaning of Adam's initial work, the naming of the animals is lost. Adam is not first recognizing the parameters of creation (the given order), but then also as a reflection of the image of God constructively forming further that order. Rather, on O'Donovan's view, Adam would at best be going through the motions for instructive or rhetorical value. Adam's freedom is simply the freedom to recognize what is already there. This is an important freedom but hardly an adequate reflection of the image of God. Spiritually, O'Donovan's conception of the moral order as fully established with the initial creation does not leave open the possibility that God could use, or indeed often seems to use humanity to further form the order which he has given. Spiritually, this would mean that earthly work is of little heavenly value.

Care must be taken here however, for this does not mean that O'Donovan wants to exclude freedom or creativity (the new) from Christian ethics (or work). On the contrary, he refreshingly desires to embrace both grace and freedom in the Christian life and ethics. To O'Donovan, Christian freedom involves a genuinely human freedom in Christ through the Spirit to respond creatively as God's moral agent. (p.23.) This indeed is something new to humanity with the coming of Christ. It is a participation in Christ's authority within the created order, meaning that humans are now free to do what we were not able to before. We are, according to O'Donovan now able to grasp the objectively given moral order and subjectively discern how and where it applies within creation. In Christ through the Holy Spirit we are able to make moral responses creatively.

He *[the Christian person]* has the authority to designate the character of the reality which he encounters, not merely to adhere to certain designations that have already been made for him. As a moral agent he is involved in deciding what a situation is and demands in the light of the moral order. As a moral agent in history he has to interpret *new* situations, plumbing their meanings and declaring them by his decision. This kind of authority is not a challenge to the authority to God; it is a restoration of Adam's lordship in the natural order, the lordship by which he calls things by their names (Gn. 2:19.). (p.24.)

On this view however, the givenness and finality of the initial created order has not changed. Adam calls things by their names he does not give them there names. The order is closed. It is simply that now, in Christ, humanity can assume its supposed proper place of dominion that God had assigned to Adam, whatever than might mean. The creativity which we are called to is not really a further shaping of the given order. Rather, it is a creative discernment of the 'mind of Christ' (1 Cor. 2:16.). (p.25.) It is discerning something which has already been established. It is a recognition of and respect for the given natural order and thus God's place as the giver of order.

The view of freedom and moral order here has merit. It does allow for newness, creativity and love in discerning situations while at the same time arguing for an objective God given basis for morality. The question however, is whether it allows for as much human freedom and participation in the created and moral order as is theologically (particularly eschatologically) warranted and ultimately needed for a genuinely Christian existence. Herein lies the problem. The theology I am developing suggests that this conception of freedom is insufficient.

Reasoning from this theology, could we not still affirm some givenness within the initially created moral order and the moral boundaries that this implies, while at the same time also affirm that humanity not only recognizes but also in significant ways (as creatures imaging God not as God) contributes to and participates in the further forming or shaping of that order? Is it not possible to see creation as complete in the sense that God has established order, setting the generic parameters for morality, but that within these parameters God has designed and built in space for genuinely creative innovation that does essentially further form that very order itself? Is it not theologically possible to suggest that God has created the world in such a dynamic way that both God and his creation are genuinely open to new and human contributions? This is, I believe, what the resurrection suggests; a gathering up of *that which is* but likewise a divine transformation of that which is with the eradication of evil. There is thus the newness of recreation. This does not mean however, that humanity saves itself and creation in some kind of cooperation with God. Rather it means that in the resurrection, God gathers up and ultimately transforms specifically that which he has made, and, that which humanity has done with the creation he appointed humanity to steward.

It is possible to illustrate these theological points with the category of family. Theologians have generally affirmed that the concept of family is itself a part of the created moral order. (Family is a creation ordinance, mandate...) The Genesis narrative likewise seems to affirm this. However, the given order here simply sets the parameters for, rather than determines, all of the particulars with reference to both family structures and the ethics tied up with and related to them. The specifics of family order and structure are simply not prescribed (in and by initial creation) beyond an affirmation of the existence and roles of a husband and wife, and children. There is a silence here that allows for openness concerning the particulars beyond this. Must family be ordered as an extended clan, or a tribe, or as a modern nuclear family? Each of these models of family and others can be developed so that they remain within the general parameters given in the initial creation.

When humanity, or a particular culture, organizes itself along specific lines it has the God given freedom, within the parameters (initial creation directed toward the new creation), to form its own reality in important ways, and thus, to form its own order. And, in so doing, the teleologically derived morality or moral rules necessitated by these humanly created structures will likewise be developed. Their specifics, their objective order, will depend upon which structure is humanly chosen. This view of freedom is similar to but more than that suggested by O'Donovan. Here is neither foundationalism nor subjectivism. It is not simply that we now in Christ recognize new situations and play on the surface of things with their order. Rather the resurrection suggests that through human choice and organization (work) we create these new situations and along with this we necessarily give further shape to the ontologically given order itself. We do not change the parameters as such, but nor do we simply apply a set of given rules creatively. Rather, we also give further form to the rules themselves. Reality is not set-in-stone as foundationalism suggests. It is plastic. Though it is not infinitely malleable as subjectivism suggests. By developing new structures for reality, the inherent teleological rules that emerge from these are likewise genuinely new, for they are particular to these new realities. The *is* of the relational structures which we create will produce their own particular and new *oughts*. Here the moral order is still a given, but there is an openness within it to real and new particularity and thus innovation, even to human innovation.

This does not mean that everything humanly imaginable is now permissible. Indeed, further related *oughts,* derived either teleologically from other relationships or from specific divine injunctions will likewise need to be incorporated into the evaluative process. Scriptural commands and prohibitions for example, will still be important parameters, or provide the space in which to exercise our freedom. They will not however, simply be used as commanded moral rules or proof texts to substantiate traditional agendas.

The point here is that the created order and moral order need not be as complete and closed as O'Donovan argues. One can still fight against postmodernity, stand on absolute moral givens and discern the 'mind of Christ' without concluding that the mind of Christ is necessarily made up on every particularity and eventuality which might be encountered or created by humans. God judges creation but is likewise open to it as the incarnation suggests.

Finally then, to summarize this particular discussion as well as the broader discussion in this chapter, I suggest that an adequate teleological framework (and ethics) will recognize and accept the given in the created order, but it also, in open anticipation of the new creation that has already but not yet come, will allow for a further shaping of that created, and thus given, order. Theologically, this means that an adequate teleological framework will approach nature (a theology of nature) and humanity (anthropology) from a dynamic interplay of both protological and eschatological perspectives. Importantly then, this further shaping of created order (which is occasioned by our work) will not be an undermining of the initially given and created order. However, given the logic of eschatological transformation, this further shaping, though including elements of the old, will while preserving these, genuinely introduce that which is new and creative to that order. This newness will be neither a repetition of that order nor an abandonment of it. It will be its transformation.

Therefore, ethically an adequate teleological framework does establish formally that the created (initial and new) *is* implies the moral *ought*. However, materially the prescriptions derived from the *is* are open to and in significant ways are bound up with humanity as we shape that reality. It is not the case that this framework undermines the objectivity of God's creation and thus God's sovereignty. Nor is it the case that this teleological framework binds theology hopelessly into subjectivist moral reasoning. Rather this teleological framework is primarily theological in that it points to the design and desire, and thus to the will of the Creator for human participation in the moral order. Herein is a robust and theologically derived teleological framework that will be fleshed out in the next chapter as I build constructively toward an ontology of work. Both MacIntyre and O'Donovan have been helpful dialogue partners but neither, left undeveloped, has been able to provide a conception of teleology adequate for Christian ethics and an ontology of work.

CHAPTER 5

Theological Anthropology: An Historical and Contemporary Appraisal

The Doctrinal Foundations

The previous chapter argued that a teleological framework was necessary for the development of an adequate Christian theological anthropology; one cognizant of a theology of nature, and from which an ontology of work can be built. Having established the shape and direction of this framework, it is now necessary to determine which doctrines specifically should be looked at in developing this anthropology. Likewise, it is important to identify what the broader issues are that need to be addressed so that an adequate formulation for today can be developed. A brief critical evaluation of the history of Christian anthropology with an examination of current trends in the field will highlight what these doctrines and issues are.

Every doctrine in some way relates to and affects one's theological anthropology. The creation, the doctrines of sin, salvation, Christology and so on each suggest something important about who we are, why we are, how we came to be where we are, what are our limitations as well as our potential, what we are to become and the like. This notwithstanding, three areas of doctrine especially stand out as foundational to theological anthropology. The first involves doctrine associated with the initial creation (protology). Here the anthropological questions include the origins of humanity, humanity's created nature / essence and God given purposes, the image of God in humanity, humanity's 'original' state, and then the fall and the results that follow from it. Following from the question of the fall, a second area of doctrine has proven to be central in the Church's quest for understanding what it is to be human. This is soteriology, with its related counterpart, eschatology. Soteriology looks to the questions of human salvation, (whatever this is understood to be) and restoration. Eschatology proves to be important in as much as questions of salvation include aspects of humanity's future final state and destiny (*telos*). The third area of doctrine that has proven to be essential to a Christian anthropology is Christology, and extending from this the doctrine of the Trinity. With Christology the issue since the New Testament has been how Jesus has become the true man, or new Adam in God's image, and how a subsequent understanding of what it means to be human must start with Him.[1] Concerning the Trinity, it has been suggested that personhood in the Trinity and the intra-trinitarian relations provide the basis for understanding what humanness or human essence is. As I will examine, there has recently been a trend to look to a social understanding of the Trinity as model for understanding the human and personhood.[2]

In developed formulations of Christian anthropology each of these three areas of doctrine has found some place. However answered, questions of origin (creation) and then the end (salvation) have been unavoidable. Further, as a consequence of this, essential too have been questions of how persons relate to, and are understood in light of, Christ and the triune God. However, the ways that these three areas of doctrine have been interrelated, and the emphases placed upon each have varied depending upon the particular tradition and the formulation's unique context; that is, its social - cultural, philosophical, apologetic and theological settings.

The Image of God

Integral to most traditional Christian anthropologies has been a discussion and some formulation of the doctrine of the image of God in humanity. This does not mean that all constructions of Christian anthropology are formulated exhaustively around the image concept. However, most have given the image symbol prominence in their overall constructions. Given this centrality of the *imago Dei* concept in the history of theological anthropology, much of the following discussion will necessarily consider its meaning and the views of humanness that stem from it.

What the image (and likeness) means or might imply has been and continues to be the subject of much speculation and debate. Millard Erickson in *Christian Theology* (1983-5) suggests three fundamentally different ways to approach and understand the image concept. The three views he suggests are the substantive, the functional, and the relational. (pp.489-510.) This threefold nomenclature though obviously artificial is nevertheless helpful, for each of these concepts approached as a category provides a way to emphasize the particularities found in often-diverse approaches to the doctrine. I will use these broad categories and this basic nomenclature in what follows. However, I will use the categories more loosely and less exclusively than Erickson has for I do not mean to imply by their use that the various views are always or necessarily mutually exclusive of each other. Indeed, they are not. For as will be seen, as well as sometimes

---

[1] Cairns, (1973), pp.40-60.
[2] This idea that the image of God in humanity might be understood with reference to the Trinity is not new to contemporary 'social' trinitarians. It was explored previously by Augustine albeit using what has been termed the psychological model of the Trinity rather than the social model. See: Cairns, (1973), pp.99-107.

being formulated into a distinct view, aspects of the functional view have also been incorporated into some substantive and some relational views. However, having acknowledged this ambiguity and artificiality, I have nevertheless presented these three categories separately in what follows, for, by doing so I am better able to demonstrate three fundamental differences in approach to Christian anthropology.

The Substantive View

The substantive category incorporates many formulations of the *Imago Dei* and personhood arguing that there are essential characteristics, qualities, or faculties within a person which either in themselves correspond to God, or, which constitute that person as in the image of God. These capacities or endowments are the keys for understanding what it means to say that the person is a person and in God's image. These qualities for example may be understood to be the capacities of reason, will, or, more narrowly they may be construed as 'spiritual' capacities such as consciousness or an awareness of God.

Basically, substantive views are labeled such because they adopt and are dependant upon a substance approach to metaphysics, or being. This means, they result from substantive ontologies. Thus, 'being', and therefore a human being, is defined as – and is essentially understood to be – a combination of various substances / qualities. The person is a person because he or she *has* a body, soul, emotions, will, intellect and so on. This approach also means that substantive views tend to emphasize the image of God in terms of and with reference to the individual. It follows from this that substantive anthropologies have tended to focus upon questions of constitution; questions concerning the constituent parts of the individual person.

Substantive anthropologies, in so emphasizing the individual and his or her constitution, have usually been formed with reference to two types of interrelated questions. Colin Gunton labels these questions usually asked in Christian anthropology (he means here substantive views) as ontological and comparative.[3] According to Gunton the ontological question concerns the kind of entity that the human is. It is a question of what, rather than who, is the person. Throughout the history of the western Church in particular, this ontological/substantive 'what' question has taken center stage and has most often been answered along the lines of a rather radical Platonic, and later Cartesian version of dualism that has started with and stressed the distinction between the body and spirit-soul. Matter and spirit are here perceived as separate mostly distinct

---

[3] Gunton, 'Trinity, Ontology and Anthropology' in *Persons, Divine and Human* (1991), pp.47-49.

substances that together constitute a single person.[4] They are the things that a person possesses that makes them a person. Often in the Eastern Church, and also in some recent Western theology, the ontological type of question has been cast quite differently by starting with and emphasizing the composite unity of the person. Only after this unity establishes the boundaries of personhood is attention given to a distinction between substances, the spiritual and bodily aspects of the person.[5] Importantly however, answering the ontological type questions in this way, at least within recent Western theology, usually indicates a desire to move away from substantive views.

The other question according to Gunton that is quite common (and likewise embedded in the substantive view) is the 'comparative'. It addresses the way or ways that the human being is understood to be different from other non-human beings. This first involves a comparison and contrast between God and humans. Then, it proceeds to a comparison and contrast between humans and non-human entities. Humans are what God and other non-humans are not. For example, we are human because we are lower than God but higher than the animals. Using this comparative approach, it became common for the Church to argue that a person is in the image of God by virtue of fact that he or she, like God and unlike the animals, possesses reason/rationality or has a free will. By virtue of possessing these things, we are human. Gunton's point is that what results from asking these types of ontological and comparative questions is a more individualistic understanding of the human being, and an atomized understanding of human 'being' where the essence of personhood lies in individual substances, qualities or characteristics rather than elsewhere. Historically these qualities have mainly been some conception of the will and the intellect.

This substantive view of the image of God in humans, including both questions of kind and contrast, has been the dominant approach in Western Chris-

---

[4] Examples of this dualistic view in the history of the Western theological tradition will be suggested shortly. However, for a discussion which offers an up to date philosophical grounding for this type of dualism see: Swinburne, (1986), and, (1987), pp.33-55.
Here however, it should be noted that Swinburne argues for a version of dualism which, although emphasizing two distinct components, nonetheless allows that these are combined in an intimate unity in the human on earth. (1987), p.33.

[5] Concerning the Eastern view of a composite unity see: Ware, (1987), pp.197-206.
A contemporary Western example of this composite unity view is encountered later in the anthropology of Jürgen Moltmann.

Further, it should be noted that there is a strand of Christian theology which wants to move even further away from dualistic concepts. See for example: Thatcher, (1987), pp.180-196. Although Thatcher is not a monist in the same way that a reductionistic materialist would be, he does tend (more than the Eastern Church and Moltmann) toward the monistic end of the continuum. He favors a 'broad materialist position' ontologically, but does nonetheless allow for distinctions conceptually. (pp.182-183.)

tian anthropology.[6] Irenaeus was the first of the Church Fathers / theologians to pay particular attention to the *imago Dei* concept and he inextricably framed his discussions of the person within the conceptuality of a substantive metaphysic. In the very way that he formulated his argument against gnosticism, that a person's body and soul (as two distinct substances) are destined for salvation, he introduced into the subsequent tradition a substantive way of describing the person and image of God.[7] Irenaeus' basic approach was adopted and then systematically developed by Medieval Scholasticism. This tradition firmly embedded the substantive view of the image into the Western tradition. On Aquinas' view for example, the image became directly equated with a person's qualities or characteristics. Specifically these were his or her intellectual capacities or rationality.[8]

Further, even though they were reacting to Scholasticism, Luther and Calvin also framed their discussions of the image of God according to the grammar and structure of substance. In opposition to Roman Catholic soteriology they reformulated their views of the image. However, they continued to understand the questions mainly in terms of the individual and his or her constitution. That is, they still thought of the image of God as 'in' an individual person and with reference to his or her constituent parts.

In *Imaging God* (1986) Douglas Hall offers a challenge to this view that Luther and Calvin continued to represent a substantive anthropology. He argues that with the Reformers of the sixteenth century there was a break from the classical substantialist view. (p.98.) He suggests that stemming from their focus upon the biblical testimony, Luther and Calvin introduce into the Western tradition the beginnings of a relational ontology. Importantly however, he acknowledges that their views were still somewhat entangled in substantialist thinking, and he finally concludes that these Reformers mostly provided the initial resources and set the stage for a new direction toward a relational ontology. (pp.106-107.)

This view that the Reformers, at least for the Western tradition, began what would become a relational rather than a substance ontology and view of the person is also suggested by C. Stephen Evans.[9] He argues that 'a strong case can be made that relational anthropology is really the fulfillment of a trend be-

---

[6] For a good survey on the views of the image of God in persons, particularly as it developed in and throughout Western Christianity, see: Cairns, *The Image of God in Man.* (1974).

[7] Irenaeus did not develop his view of the image of God in persons into a mature doctrine. Rather he simply offered reflections, mostly secondary, which were only later taken up and more fully developed. See: Cairns, (1974), pp.79-88.

[8] Cairns, (1974), p.120.

[9] C. Stephen Evans, 'Healing Old Wounds and Recovering Old Insights: A Christian View of The Person for Today', in Noll, and Wells, (1988), pp.68-86.

gun by the protestant Reformers, who rejected the scholastic equation of the *imago* with rationality and instead views the *imago* as the original righteousness people possessed by virtue of their relation to God.'[10] This notwithstanding, he finally concludes that Reformation theology 'did not go all the way toward a relational anthropology but preserved, whether consistently or inconsistently, the substantial category of the soul, and even the view that sinners possess a "relic" of the image of God.'[11]

There is an ambiguity here and questions persist as to whether as transitional figures the Reformers should be considered as representing the substantive or relational view. While not disagreeing with the analysis of Hall or Evans it does seem more appropriate to conclude that since they continued to work within a substantive grammar it is better to consider them as part of the substantive tradition. This acknowledges however that they may be said to offer the beginnings of and some resources for a new direction.

In summary, Irenaeus, Aquinas, (and also others like Clement of Alexandria, Athenasius, and Augustine,) – those who by and large established the tradition, – as well as the great Reformers Luther and Calvin, each fundamentally viewed the image of God in human beings substantively with respect to specific characteristics or qualities. This does not mean that other functional and relational elements were not present within the developing Christian tradition. These other elements however, were not the primary categories used to describe the concept of the image of God in the person.

The Functional View

Another approach to Christian anthropology can be described as a functional view. This is one that is sometimes classified as a distinct view but it can also be included as a part of either the substantive view or the relational view. The functional category like the substantive actually incorporates many sometimes diverse formulations. The common characteristics of functional views however, are that they argue that the image of God and the person in that image are best understood through the conceptual grid of God's call upon humanity to specific activity. Particularly, this means that persons and the image are best perceived in terms of what humans do, or are supposed to do, according the call of God. Human function rather than something we are, have, or experience relationally is what sets us apart as human. Essentially, the content of this call is seen to be to dominion or the stewardship of creation (human work), and often following from this it is the call to develop culture.

Admittedly the functional view, with its emphasis upon the primacy of performance / action may initially seem strange or even repulsive to contemporary

---

[10] Ibid., p.73.
[11] Ibid., pp.73-74.

Western culture which, through the pervasive influence of existentialist and personalist philosophy among other things, has become accustomed to hierarchically value existence over function. Also, given its emphasis upon dominion and cultural development, especially at this time when these very concepts are reckoned to be the culprits in the ecological crisis, some may immediately consider the functional view suspect. It might be seen as a theological perversion, reflecting not biblical teaching but rather the modernist triumphalistic spirit which has optimistically attempted to dominate nature in an oppressive way. It might be argued that a Hegelian or Marxist notion of progress has co-opted this theology. Or, the functional view might be argued to be simply a contemporary reaction against the speculation of substantive views and the trendiness of relational views.

Although one might be able to argue each of these points to a degree with reference to specific formulations of the functional view, for the view as a whole these criticisms do not hold. G. C. Berkouwer in his classic book *Man: The Image of God* (1962) highlights two important observations about the functional view. The first is that it is a longstanding position found within the tradition of interpreting the image. He suggests as an example that it surfaces in the Socinian Racovian Catechism (1605). (p.70. note. 11.)[12] Admittedly, this theologically suspect document was composed at a time when the influence of Renaissance humanism (not yet the Enlightenment) would have been present. This notwithstanding, what it demonstrates is that at the very minimum, the basic idea of the functional view existed prior to the Enlightenment and modernity. Further, although it is possible, it is not obvious that its understanding of the image was more influenced by the emerging spirit of the age than by biblical insights and the exegesis to which it appeals. Indeed, this leads to Berkouwer's second observation that the functional view has been essentially derived from biblical exegesis, and particularly from an exegesis of the Genesis 1:26 account of the image. (pp.70-71.) My own reading of various other functional views concurs with Berkouwer on this point that the functional view is primarily an exegetically derived position. Of course it could be argued that the exegesis behind functional interpretations has been tainted, in the earlier catechism by certain humanist assumptions, or in the case of more recent formulations by modernist assumptions concerning the world. Doubtless it is true that all exegesis is to some degree affected by the particular context in which it is done. Nonetheless, if one examines the exegetical arguments used to support the view, especially as found in some contemporary and very thorough scholarship, it becomes apparent that there exists an ancient precedent for arguing that the idea of function and stewardship is meant to explain the content of the image concept as found in Genesis 1 and elsewhere in the Old Testament.[13]

---

[12] See also: Pannenberg, (1985), pp.74-75.

[13] Anderson, (1994), pp.11-18, 32-33, 119-131.

Having considered, admittedly briefly, some of the initial and possible reactions to functional views, I now return to consider another chief characteristic associated with these views. It is generally the case that when function becomes the orienting point from which to understand the person and image, the questions of individual versus social understanding of being, as well as of individual constitution, begin to recede into the background. These types of questions are not ignored, nor do they become irrelevant or unimportant. Rather, they simply cease to be 'the' central concern. They assume rather a subordinate place within the overall conception. For example, within functional views the call to stewardship / function as the defining principle of the image necessitates a corporate call, (it is intended for the whole of humanity in all places and at all times), yet it preserves individual particularity, (it concretely applies to each person uniquely). Neither communitarianism nor individualism is what is at stake. A functional understanding cuts across and can be equally at home in either. Thus, questions of individual constitution need not be ignored but they are left to one side. This question may still be important for anthropology but it is not discussed within the doctrine of the image of God. It can be explored elsewhere, possibly in other doctrines or in, science, psychology and so forth.

This discussion indicates that it is necessary to understand the functional view as dealing with different issues than the substantive (and likewise the relational which is most often developed as a counter to it). Specifically then, how does the functional view relate to the other two views being classified? In some instances it operates eclectically gathering up insights from the other views. Or it may appear as an emphasis within one or another of these views. Yet this does not mean that it is always, or ever, simply a combination view. In some places it proves to be a genuinely distinguishable view. Let me demonstrate.

The functional view is not primarily or necessarily concerned to establish one ontology, substantive or relational, above the other. Indeed it can appear on either side of the metaphysical fence. Sometimes the views that emphasize the importance of function for understanding the essence of persons operate within a metaphysical framework that incorporates (but is not necessarily limited to) substantive ontology. One example of this is seen in the view of the image presented by Cornelius Plantinga Jr.[14] Plantinga is careful not to argue for one metaphysic over another. Rather, he accepts that both substance and relation are appropriate and have a place within the same metaphysic. He reasons this by suggesting that in a non-reductionistic manner the image incorporates various ideas which include dominion (function), the capacity for fellowship and love (relationality), and reason / self-consciousness (substance).[15] He further states that 'the image will thus emerge as a rich, multifaceted reality, comprising acts, relations, capacities, virtues, dispositions, and even emotions... [and] I should

---

[14] Cornelius Plantinga Jr. 'Images of God', in Noll and Wells, (1988), pp.51-67.
[15] Ibid., p.52.

like to add that one can speak of each God-like act, relation, property, and so forth, as an image of God.'[16] The point here is simply that Plantinga has identified function / dominion as a major (but not the only) aspect for defining the image. He has likewise continued to use substantive concepts and grammar for understanding that image and the resultant person.

As suggested however, the functional view, or at least a view that emphasizes the centrality of function for an understanding of the person and the image, also appears on the other side of the metaphysical fence; that is, on the relational side. This is most clearly seen in Douglas Hall's presentation. In *Imaging God*, Hall explicitly argues for a relational over a substantive ontology. (pp.88-160.) However, he also argues that within this relational metaphysic the key for understanding the calling to be the image is the concept of dominion / stewardship. Hall argues that human dominion is the content that we give to the creaturely reflection of the glory of God, or, the image of God. (p.184.) Hall's position is a clear example of a functional understanding of the image and person while at the same time an affirmation of relational ontology.

Importantly however, I have also suggested that functional anthropologies can be understood as separate and distinguishable from substantive and relational views. I mean that it truly does present an alternative and essentially different approach to the question of the image and person.

Generally, in contemporary formulations, functional anthropologies surface in two places. Primarily it is developed in Biblical theology (and particularly in Old Testament theologies). Also, and often deriving from Old Testament theologies, it appears in some Reformed circles which place an emphasis upon what has been termed the 'cultural mandate.'[17]

Although there is not unanimity, there is a tendency in Old Testament theology when interpreting both Genesis 1 and Psalm 8 to describe the content of the image and likeness of God as human dominion or stewardship.[18] A classic representation of this view is offered by Hans Walter Wolff in *Anthropology of the Old Testament* (1974) in the chapter entitled 'God's Image – The Steward of the World.' Wolff's reasoning develops as follows. The special position of man in the world is described by the phrase *God's image*. This phrase points to a correspondence between man and God. This correspondence is more precisely

---

[16] Ibid., pp.52-53.

[17] For an example of this see: Marshall, (1984), pp.20-22. On page 20 (note 1) Marshall notes that his discussion of the cultural mandate, and here the functional image of God, relies heavily upon Al Wolters, 'The Foundational Command: Subdue the Earth', Toronto: Institute for Christian studies, 1973.

[18] In addition to the two theologies which I will now mention see also: von Rad (1972), p.60.

For a dissenting view however, one leading toward a relational view of the image see: Westermann, *Creation*, (1974), pp.55-60. Yet it should also be noted that Westermann does concede that there is a close linkage between the image and dominion. (pp.49-55.)

understood as conferring upon man an office which distinguishes him. (p.159.) Wolff then states that 'it is precisely in his function as ruler that he is God's image.' (p.160.) Further, 'the relationship of correspondence is to be seen in man's function as the ruler of the rest of creation.' (p.161.) He then suggests that this rule involves re-fashioning and making comparably useful alterations (human work). (p.163.) Finally, in quoting Ludwig Kohler he describes the task of ruling as the commission to establish civilization. (pp.163-164. note. 15.)

Admittedly, throughout his discussion Wolff shows very little of the exegesis upon which he has based his views. Nor does he show an awareness of the possible impact of his views upon the environment. Therefore, he is not able to anticipate challenges or defend his position against those who would consider it ecologically irresponsible.

However, another quite recent Old Testament theology supporting the functional view, which both offers exegetical detail and develops its position against the backdrop of the ecological crisis, is presented by Bernhard W. Anderson in *From Creation to New Creatio*. (1994). Concerning the image of God specifically Anderson says:

> But the main import of the statement about the *imago Dei* is not just to define human *nature* in relation to God but to accent the special *function* that God has assigned human beings in the creation. Human beings, male and female are designed to be God's representatives, for they are created and commissioned to represent or 'image' God's rule on earth. To be made in the image of God is to be endowed with a special task. (pp.14-15.)

Interestingly, according to this it appears that to Anderson the concept of the image of God has little to do with ontology as such. Although he has acknowledged that Genesis 1 presents man as a total bodily whole – a psychosomatic unity, (the question of individual constitution) his point is that function rather than nature is what is really at issue. (p.14.) This relativising of ontological questions is further seen in his subordinating both the concept of relationship and the concept of substance to the idea of function. Concerning relational questions he says:

> The worth of human beings lies in their relation to God. They are persons whom God addresses, visits, and is concerned about. But above all they are 'crowned' as kings and queens to perform a special task in the Creator's earthly estate. (p.15.)

Further, he also is clear that questions of substance are only of secondary importance. Concerning the phrase in Genesis 1 'Let us make humanity in our image, after our likeness' he says:

> One should not tone down the anthropomorphism of this statement by attempting to define the 'image of God' as something *in* the human body: 'spiritual nature,' 'soul,' 'rationality,' 'freedom,' 'self-transcendence,' and so on. The application of

the same language to Seth, a son in Adam's image (5:3; cf. v. 1), indicates that
human beings, in their total bodily (psychosomatic) existence, are made in the image of the parent, ... In Gen 1 however, the intention is not to define the essence of
humanity or the essence of God, but rather to indicate the task of human beings
and their relationship to God. As God's living image on earth, human beings –
'male and female' – are to act as God's representatives. (pp.32-33.)

Finally, after acknowledging ecological concerns, Anderson sums up and concludes his arguments on the topic. 'Thus the special status of humankind as the
image of God is a call to responsibility, not only in relation to other humans but
also in relation to nature.' (p.130.)

With Anderson, in contrast to some of the others who have adopted either
substantive or relational ontological categories, one finds a functional view of
the image of God that simply refuses to allow ontological questions the center
stage. Rather, the emphasis is upon human functioning.

What we have seen in this brief survey of the functional view is a position
that attempts to let the biblical material, especially although not exclusively the
Old Testament, define the meaning of the image of God. As such it attempts to
put aside much of the extreme and sometimes bizarre speculation that has sur-
rounded the doctrine. Given its clearly Biblical foundations, this functional
emphasis is a commendable and necessary ingredient for any developing theological anthropology. However, the image of God concept as well as theological anthropology in general, while building from specifics within biblical theology are really subjects for systematic theology. Scripture, here the Old Testament, sets the theologizing process in motion but it does not itself comprehensively explore all the potential of the concept. The main weakness of the functional view is its refusal to allow many questions asked by systematic theology
into the discussion. Ultimately the insights of the functional view will need to
be incorporated into this theological anthropology. However, teleological / eschatological insights will need to be emphasized further. Likewise, more attention will need to be given to what insights can be gained from both the New
Testament and Christology for the doctrine of the image of God. In summary,
although function should be central to any theological anthropology, it is not
the only thing that needs to be said.

The Relational View

The relational view of persons, personhood, and the image of God in humanity
is for Western theology a relatively recent development.[19] It has nonetheless, in
the West increasingly become a prominent view, particularly as it has come to

---

[19] For discussions of how relational understandings of the image and relational conceptions of ontology came into Western theology see: Hall, (1986), pp.98-108, Evans, in
Noll and Wells, (1988), pp.71-78, and Cairns, (1973), pp.152-186.

be a significant part of the renewed interest in and emphasis upon trinitarianism.[20] This is particularly evident in recent ecumenical discussions on the Trinity. The 1989 report by the British Council of Churches entitled *The Forgotten Trinity* shows an ecumenical body consciously building their statement about the person from within a trinitarian and relational framework. (pp.19-25.)

In Protestantism particularly, and notwithstanding the possibilities opened up here by Luther and Calvin, the genesis of what today is identified as the relational understanding of the Image of God and the person is found in the theologies of Brunner and Barth.[21] Yet formulations have moved on a great deal since these groundbreaking explorations. However, before considering one recently formulated specifically trinitarian relational conception, it will be helpful to sketch some general characteristics associated generally with relational constructs.

Broadly, relational views of the image and person are critical of a metaphysics of substance. Indeed often they are quite strongly anti-substantialists. However, this does not mean that, like many holding the functional view, they eschew metaphysical discussions in developing their formulations. On the contrary, establishing a relational rather than substantive ontological framework and a specifically relational ontology of personhood is the project. What rejecting an ontology of substance mostly means for relational formulations is that methodologically, they do not accept that questions surrounding the constituent parts of the individual person are proper to the definition of personhood. This is because personhood in relational views is not first and foremost dependent upon the person as an individual. At times questions of the constitution of persons may arise. Generally however, these views understand personhood to be a social category and when questions of individual constitution do arise, answers tend toward holistic and away from dualistic explanations.

The key characteristic of relational views is that ultimately relational ontology suggests a corporate understanding of being. Being is by definition being-with-others. According to its proponents, this ontology is superior to an ontology of substance for although an ontology of substance establishes individuality, it does so at the expense of the other by cutting the person off from the other. That is, it leads to individualism. A relational ontology is seen as superior precisely because it makes room within personhood for both particular individuality (otherness), but also for inclusion and connectedness.

Colin Gunton's Relational Anthropology

Having outlined these general characteristics it is now possible to consider an

---

[20] Thompson, (1997), pp.9-42.

[21] For a brief account of Barth and Brunner see: Erickson, (1983-5), pp.502-508. For a more in-depth discussion see: Cairns, (1973), pp.152-186.

example of a recent formulation of the relational view of the person and the image of God; one that is specifically associated with the contemporary revival of trinitarian thinking. The formulation examined here is that of Colin Gunton found in *The Promise of Trinitarian Theology* (1991).[22] Most of the analysis undertaken here comes from chapters five and six of this book, the first of which looks broadly at the concept of the person constituted in relation, and the latter more specifically toward a renewal of the doctrine of the *imago Dei*. Before turning to the arguments in these chapters however, a few contextual remarks are in order.

Gunton states in the preface that the book's unity is to be discerned from its being a quest for an ontology. This means that he wants to explore an understanding of the kind of being God is (Trinity), and through this to establish an understanding of what kind of beings we are and what kind of world we inhabit. (p.vii.) This ontological exploration understands itself to be specifically indebted to and a continuation of trinitarian concepts shaped by the Cappadocian Fathers. (p.viii.)

It is not surprising then that Gunton offers a chapter specifically critiquing Augustine's understanding of the Trinity. His main argument is that Augustine did not grasp the concept (and ontology) of 'person' that the Cappadocian doctrine of the Trinity suggested. Augustine could not see that for the Cappadocian Fathers the persons of the Trinity are what they are only in their relations with each other and not prior to them. That is, their relations qualify each person ontologically in terms of what/who they are. (p.41.) Rather, Augustine saw relation as a logical, not ontological, predicate. He therefore could not finally make claims about the particular persons of the Trinity. (pp.41-42.) The outcome of Augustine's neoplatonic philosophy was 'a view of an unknown substance *supporting* the three persons rather than *being constituted* by their relatedness.' (p.43.)

The implication of this, it seems for Gunton, was to bequeath to the West an inadequate and culturally dangerous doctrine of the Trinity which, in its inability to escape the grips of dualistic ontology based on Aristotelian logic, would pave the way for Western individualism.[23] Likewise, it further prepared the way for a later fateful definition of the person 'as' a relation, rather than a person 'in' relation. (p.40.) That is, Augustine's understanding of person as a relation contributes to the development of a view that dissolves the individuality of the person into the abstract concept of relation and thus dissolves the identity of the individual. Herein lies the paradox. On the one hand, the groundwork has been

---

[22] For a similar and related view developed specifically from an Orthodox perspective see: Zizioulas, (1991), pp.33-46. and, Zizioulas, (1993) *Being as Communion*. For an additional view similar to Gunton's which is developed in dialogue with the social sciences see: McFadyen, *The Call to Personhood* (1990).

[23] This idea is further explored by Gunton in *The One, The Three and the Many* (1993).

laid for individualism. On the other, it has been laid for the eradication of that same individual.

These preliminary observations and interpretations are necessary for they are the backdrop against which Gunton develops his own view of the person, and later, the *imago Dei.* I begin with his view of the person.

In his chapter entitled *The Concept of the Person: the One The Three and the Many* Gunton begins with the view that what we and what our institutions are is largely a matter of persons in relationship. (p.86.) The problem, he argues, is that in following Descartes' dualism which isolated and elevated the mind over the body / matter, modern Western culture has developed a dualistic and individualistic view of persons. The intellect is the only sure reality. The world outside of it, even the body, is suspect. The person is the mind. The person / intellect is seen as a distinct and abstract entity existing independent of and in isolation from its various relationships (which in reality have shaped its existence). On this understanding, even the possibility of relating to others becomes problematic, for they may in fact only be illusions. (p.87.)

In the West then, we have come to treat the person and the individual as the same thing. That is, we have come to define the person as an individual and the result is that we have lost both the person and the individual. (p.88.) This ironically has lead to modern collectivism as well as individualism. Both however, are mirror images of each other and both signal the loss of the person; the one into the many and the many into the one. (p.90.)

Gunton then turns to an alternative tradition in the West which presents a radically different view of the person than that presented by Cartesian thought. It is exemplified recently by the Scottish moral philosopher John Macmurray in his Gifford lectures, particularly in his 1954 lectures *Persons in Relation.*[24] Gunton gleans three main points from Macmurray. The first is that his ontology is different. 'Where Descartes began with the mind and its distinction from the body, Macmurray begins with the concept of action. As agents we are unities.' (p.90.)[25] Gunton does not take up and develop this ontology of action. Rather, he simply refers to this different ontology to show that an alternative to the Cartesian view of the person does exist in the West.

The second point that Gunton highlights from Macmurray is that 'the concept of the person is logically prior to the other notions that are associated with it. It is that upon which the rest of our knowledge and being depends.' (p.90.) This then leads directly to the third point. Gunton interprets Macmurray: '*As persons we are only what we are in relation to other persons*'. (p.90.) That is, the self is constituted by its dynamic relationships to other people. It has its

---

[24] See also his 1953 Gifford Lectures *The Self as Agent.* (1961). These two sets of lectures together constitute the Gifford Lectures given by Macmurray.
[25] This different ontology is developed by Macmurray in his 1953 Glasgow University Gifford Lectures, *The Self as Agent*, (1961.)

being in its interpersonal relationships. (pp.90-91.) Therefore we must 'centre our attention first not on the identity of the individual, but on the matrix within which individuality takes shape.' (p.91.). It is in community then that each individual remains distinct and the other really remains the other. On this view the individual is 'relativized without being legislated out of existence.' (p.91.)

After considering Macmurray's philosophy, Gunton moves on to discuss theology and anthropology, and then specifically, persons and relation. In doing this he sets out his own view of the person. His primary appeal is to the relational concept of the person that owes its development to the trinitarian theology of the Cappadocian Fathers, and particularly to Basil. He states, 'By giving priority to the concept of person in their doctrine of God, they transform at once the meaning of both concepts.' (p.96.) On this view, the *being* of God is understood as communion. Each person in the Trinity is perceived to be a person not with respect to itself, but only with respect to the other persons. Here Gunton appeals for support to Eastern Christian ontology as argued by John Zizioulas. He quotes Zizioulas, 'In God the particular is ontologically ultimate *because relationship is permanent and unbreakable...* In trying to identify the particular thing, we have to make it part of a relationship, and not isolate it as an *individual.*' (p.97.)[26] It is here that Gunton begins to distinguish his view from Macmurray's. Particularly, he takes a different slant on Macmurray's ontology of the active agent. Rather than a being in the process of action who, in encountering the other discovers the existence of another, Gunton opts ontologically for a person as a 'being-in-relation', which elsewhere Zizioulas calls an ontology of love.[27] With this Gunton concludes concerning the person:

> A person, we must learn and relearn, can be defined only in terms of his or her relations with other persons, and not in terms of a prior universal or non-personal concept like species-being, evolution or, for that matter, subsistent relation (and the list could be much extended from current political debate). (p.98.)

---

[26] One might want to argue that the ontology in the Eastern Church presented the image of God and human constitution (the person) substantively using the language of Platonic dualism. This would be true to a degree. However, as Bishop Ware has argued, if one probes deeper into the inner logic of the Eastern discussions one sees beyond the substantive / Platonic dualistic language an emerging more integrative holistic conception of the person. ('The Unity of the Human Person According to the Greek Fathers', pp.198-199). Also, Metropolitan John Zizioulas and Vladimir Lossky present discussions suggesting that ontologically a more relational view of the image and the person has been perceived in the Eastern tradition from the Patristic period. See: Zizioulas, *Being as Communion* (1993), pp.27-65, Lossky, (1974), pp.111-139. Thus, this ambiguity granted, I suggest that what was emerging in the East is an understanding of the image of God and the person that ontologically was more relational than substantive.

[27] Zizioulas, (1991), p.42.

Before moving on to Gunton's discussion of the *imago Dei* and the further aspects of anthropology developed in Chapter Six, it is helpful first to highlight some problematic questions that this chapter raises. Gunton's interpretation of Macmurray, and then his own concept of person understood as almost directly analogous to the concept of person in the Trinity, presents the view that the individual person's being is only defined and realized in and through its relations with other persons. However, why must a human person be understood *only* in and through his or her relations to other *persons,* (including of course, God)? Is this realistic? Should we as persons not also be understood in and through our relationships with other non-human 'beings' since our very existence is embedded within the context of, and depends upon, other non-personal realities? Must we define ourselves only through our interpersonal relationships simply because that is how we understand the concept of person to be operating in the Trinity? Following on from this, is it even legitimate to make such a direct analogy between God and humans, especially if one's theology already includes the idea of some distinction between God and creation?

If we are to extend this understanding of the person from the Trinity to humans, presumably with recourse to the image of God concept, and if we do so quite directly, does this not require us to consider the person (like God) as something essentially other than a 'material' being existing in a material context? Would such a direct correlation not lead directly back to a view that it is the immaterial soul that is the essence of the person and thus in the image of God?

Thus, is it even possible to postulate an understanding of personal human being by only considering his or her relationships with other people, and ignoring the complex matrix of his or her additional non-interpersonal relationship structures? Does not such an abstraction ultimately make any definition of persons growing out of the analogy of limited value, in as much as it is cut off from the real world of human experience? Should not the *human* person also be defined to some extent with reference to a host of additional material relationships within which he or she finds himself or herself? Should these determinate relations not also include relations with non-human creatures and other entities which are part of our creation environment? (A view that Gunton himself wants to affirm in chapter six.) Further, should the person not also be defined through its relationship to whole systems, structures, states of affairs, or the concrete product / results of human action, which of course, have been created by him or herself and / or other persons either previously or currently?

These are no small contentions for they have implications in many areas. Obviously, they affect what we can or cannot say about who and what we are as persons. Furthermore, as mentioned, they force us to consider whether or not the definition of person (person-in-relation to other persons) as found in the communion of the Trinity (i.e., the social Trinity) can really serve as a complete analogy for understanding what we as humans essentially are. Even with our similarities to God we are essentially different beings than God.

Interestingly, Gunton in chapter six presents a view of the person along somewhat different lines than in the earlier chapter. In chapter six his understanding of ontology has broadened to make space within personhood for human relations with non-human entities. He does this however for slightly different reasons (more ethical / ecological) than the ones I have outlined. Indeed, in this later discussion there is no indication that he has recognized many of the more conceptual philosophical problems posed by his earlier construct. Nor does he anticipate the possible implications or difficulties raised by how he has there defined personhood. How then does Gunton make this space within personhood for non-personal relations?

At the start of chapter six, *The Human Creation. Towards a Renewal of the Doctrine of the 'Imago Dei'*, Gunton argues that the traditional ontology of human being (usually built upon dualistic presuppositions) is expected to be derived by means of comparison (with God) and contrast (with the rest of creation). The result of this in the history of Christian anthropology has been the elevation of one characteristic, reason, above all others. Gunton finds this entire approach, and its results, unsatisfactory. He suggests that we need a different methodology, something other than 'speculative comparison and contrast', for developing our ontology. (p.105.) That is, he argues that we should root the contrast in ontology and not the ontology in contrast. (p.105.) The rest of the chapter is, in effect, his attempt to do this.

Again, Gunton offers a brief outline of what he sees the problem to be. He criticizes the tradition of anthropology in the West, including Irenaeus, Aquinas, John of Damascus and of course, Augustine. I have already mentioned his critique of Augustine and he offers nothing essentially new here. However, his statements concerning John of Damascus summarize his view well. John offered a definition of the image and person that relativised the dominant place given to reason by qualifying it additionally with the idea of free will. Gunton however states:

> While that definition has the merit of not limiting the image to reason, it is to be noted that all of the characteristics are static possessions of the human as individual, rather than (say) characteristics implying relation. (p.106.)

Here he is offering a quite standard critique of the tradition with its substantive ontology. His reason for being dissatisfied with the tradition is that it offers only a static (not dynamic or teleological) view of personhood.

Next, Gunton follows Coleridge in a discussion of the anthropologies resulting from three divergent cosmologies and in each considers where the space to be human is located. One view, the Phoenician cosmology, offers no space between God and the world and thus, no space to be human. The Hellenistic view, he suggests, offers space but locates it in the wrong place, between the mind and body. The result of this is too little space to truly be human. In the third cosmology, the Hebrew, there is space to be human. This is because of the freedom of the immutable God who created *ex nihilo;* that is, God created from nothing something that is truly other and thus particular. The problem here however, is that this alone makes too much space (the potential of individualism) and therefore, something else is needed to qualify it. Enter – the notion of the image of God.

As Gunton begins to discuss the idea of the image of God he acknowledges that the concept of the person is quite difficult to define. (p.112.) What he suggests, following an interpretation of Barth, is that 'person means primarily what it means when it is used of God.' (p.113, note 18.) This gives him warrant for beginning anthropology with the Trinity. It is here, in the conception of God as three persons in communion, that Gunton finds the space to be human which he has been seeking. This is a personal space for it is defined analogously by the three persons of the Trinity who exist for, and from, each other in their otherness. 'They thus confer particularity upon and receive it from one another.' (p.113.) Particularity then implies freedom and together these concepts, particularity and freedom, provide the needed space to be other, and thus they define being. Creation, God's creation of the other, 'becomes understood as the giving of being to the other, and that includes the giving of space to be: to be other and particular.' (p.113.)

From this Gunton concludes that the world's otherness from God is part of its space to be itself, to be finite and not divine. 'But as such it echoes the trinitarian being of God in being what it is by virtue of its internal taxis: it is, like God, a dynamic of beings in relation.' (p.114.) He is not saying that creation's particularity and contingency (which suggests a type of freedom) implies that all of creation is made in the image of God. That is, he is arguing against a view that simply being created implies that something is in the image of God. Rather, he argues that 'creation's non-personality means that it is unable to realize its destiny, the praise of its creator, apart from persons.' He cites here Romans 8:19 to demonstrate his idea and then suggests that this type of discussion / context is where one must seek the outlines of a theological anthropology. (p.114.)

Of course, we are in a day when the ecological crisis calls into question such an anthropocentric view of creation's subordinate dependence upon humanity. Therefore, it is highly controversial to suggest that creation in some way 'needs' humanity (persons in the image of God) for its fulfillment. However, biblically one must grant that in some respect creation cannot ultimately reach its destiny (*telos*) apart from humans (Romans 8:19). This is so even if the understanding that non-human creation cannot, or does not, praise its creator without humans seems incorrect. The Psalms often suggest the very opposite when, for example, Psalm 19 records 'the heavens declare the glory of God: the skies proclaim the work of his hands.'

Gunton's main point though should not be missed because of this secondary criticism. Here, even though controversial, his point is that the non-personal creation is bound up with and dependent teleologically upon the personal, (be that Jesus Christ and / or other humans incorporated in him). Nor is this concept simply a product of Western modernity's longing to control and dominate nature as some might be tempted to challenge. Rather, Gunton's point is primarily derived from pre-modern longstanding cosmologies. Firstly, it derives from the biblical narrative that sees all creation brought to fulfillment in the person of Jesus Christ through those incorporated into him. Secondly, such a view is similar to the anthropology of Eastern Orthodoxy which argues that humanity is creation's microcosm, mediator, and microtheos.[28]

Returning to Gunton's logic however, the questions are still how the created cosmos provides a context for anthropology, and, what are we to make specifically of the doctrine of the image of God? Gunton is clear that he rejects a view that 'the image is to be found in reason, or any merely internal characterization of the individual'. (p.115.) That is, he rejects substantive ontology. He points then to two contenders for a view of the image, both of which depend upon readings of the first two chapters of Genesis. The first locates the image in the human stewardship of the creation. (The functional view as I have called it.) The second, following Barth's relational construct in the *Church Dogmatics* III/2, locates the image somewhere in the plurality of the male and female created relationship. (p.115.) Concerning this second point, the location of the image in the male / female relation, Gunton finds some warrant in the idea, in that it recognizes the relational dimension of existence. However, he also suggests that it has two important weaknesses. First, he worries that the binitarian tendency of this view will promote an exclusion of the other rather than inclusive communion. Second, he is concerned that it underplays the way that Genesis brings non-human creation into the broader covenant. (pp.116.)

Concerning the first suggestion that the stewardship of creation is what is meant by the image of God, Gunton likewise grants that there is warrant in the idea, particularly in that it is closely dependant upon the Genesis text. Ultimately however, he finds the position too literalistic and too restrictive in light of the New Testament's re-orienting of the image of God doctrine to Christ. (p.115.) Ultimately, in relation to both of these suggestions, what is needed according to Gunton is more than an extended exegesis of Genesis 1:26 ff, if one is to reach a satisfactory use of the concept of the image of God. (p.116.)

Of course, Gunton is correct to suggest that the image of God concept needs to be developed more broadly than simply an exegesis of the Genesis account. He is right to highlight the fact that the New Testament itself re-orients the doctrine beyond its Genesis parameters to the person of Christ. However, it is questionable if or how the following supports his critique of Genesis' presentation of the image. 'Is the image of God as realised in Christ to be expressed in terms of his stewardship of the creation - indeed, part of the matter - or must other things be said?' (p.115.) His logic expects a negative answer: that it is other

---

[28] Ware, (1987), pp.200-204.

things should be said, particularly things like the primacy of relationality. Yet, it is perfectly possible to grant that things other than stewardship must be said, but, at the same time grant that it is fundamentally appropriate to describe the image of God in terms of Christ's stewardship of creation. Why would it not be correct to suggest that eschatologically and teleologically Christ (and those included in him) is the image of God specifically in that he is the redeemer, restorer, Lord, and fulfillment (*telos*) of all things / creation? Why can these ministries not be considered an eschatological dimension and vision of stewardship that fits well with both the mission of Christ, and the intent of the idea of dominion in Genesis? The Eastern Church seemed to approach just such a view in their understanding of humanity (in Christ) as microcosm.

To be fair to Gunton it must be admitted that he is not as dismissive of the stewardship idea as this particular comment on the topic might suggest. Interestingly in spite of his criticisms of the idea, in his own argument he does incorporate a form of the idea of stewardship into his concept of the image of God. In fact, he attempts to incorporate the positive insights from both of the identified contending views for the image; that of stewardship and that of male / female relationality. The former brings out important elements of humanity's relation to the creation. The latter brings out important elements of human relations with other humans. (p.116.)

Indeed, Gunton finds unacceptable any formulation that would force one to choose between two correct insights. He argues that both contending views are right in as much as they discern relatedness to be the clue for the solution of the anthropological question. He suggests that the weaknesses of both approaches can be obviated by finding a concept that bases them - and any other dimensions - in a theological ontology. (p.116.) Of course, that concept for Gunton, the conceptual link into a theological ontology as it were, will be the concept of 'person'. This logically follows given that Gunton is concerned with an ontology of human being and not just with human qualities and tasks.

> To be made in the image of God is to be endowed with a particular kind of personal reality. To be a person is to be made in the image of God: that is the heart of the matter. If God is a communion of persons inseparably related, then surely Barth is thus far correct in saying that it is in our relatedness to others that our being human consists. (p.116.)

Moreover, a more subtle aspect of Gunton's eclectic suggestion should not be missed at this juncture. It is precisely because insights from the stewardship concept, as well as Barth's insights, must be incorporated into one's conception of the image of God that one can find a further opening or expanding of the concept of relatedness beyond simply inter-personal relations as argued in the previous chapter. As Gunton suggests, stewardship itself is based in relatedness. Stewardship necessarily involves relations with non-human entities. Hence for humans, being-in-relatedness or personhood will necessarily include more than simply inter-personal relationships as was suggested earlier. It will include, by virtue of insights gained from the stewardship element, relatedness with non-personal creation. It will likewise open the way for teleological purposeful ordering to be a part of human being. Knowingly or unknowingly herein lies an important watershed in Gunton's argument.

Although a purely reductionistic functional ontology is ruled out, functional or stewardship elements become incorporated into a relational ontology; as does relatedness with other non-human entities. What Gunton's willingness to incorporate insight from both Barth's relational construct and stewardship concepts of the image does then, is to ultimately allow a view of being-in-relation without reducing our very being to relatedness. Here it is the teleological ordering implied by stewardship concepts of being-in-relation-to-non-human-reality that is the key to avoiding the loss of personhood into relationality.

Now in returning to the above quote and the relational aspect of the ontology, one might again want to question Gunton's wisdom of making a direct analogy between humankind and God as a communion of persons. However, when Gunton argues for a relational ontology he tries to preempt such criticisms by qualifying what he means by way of a double orientation. (p.116.) The first direction indicates that we are persons (thus in the image of God) in so far as we are in right relationship to God; because of sin this is necessarily realized in Christ through the Spirit. This means the 'image of God is then that being human which takes shape by virtue of the creating and redeeming agency of the triune God.' (p.117.) The second direction is the horizontal one and is an outworking of the first. It is that the human person is created to find his or her being in relation, first with other like persons, but second, as a function of the first, with the rest of creation. (p.117.) The ontology of the person is to be realized in human community first, but it must also be completed by our relationship with the non-personal world. (p.118.)

Gunton's argument emphasizes the concepts both of otherness and of relation. It implies a freedom in both the give and take of relationship. It specifically intends to 'rule out both the kind of egalitarianism which is the denial of particularity, and leads to collectivism, and forms of individualism which in effect deny humanity to those unable to 'stand on their own feet.'' (p.117.) It is further argued to provide the basis for an inclusion of what is usually called the spiritual and bodily aspects of existence, and therefore, it relativises all dualisms. Relations are of the whole person and not simply the mind or body alone. (pp.117-118.)

Given my earlier criticisms, I now become particularly interested in Gunton's assertion that 'we are not human apart from our relation with the non-personal world.' (p.118.) Here he indicates an awareness, previously undetected, of ecological questions, and the implications which his anthropology might have upon ecological issues. He argues that our human community with the world is not the same kind of community which we have with other persons; that is, it is not a community of equals. He does however, suggest that we do receive much of what we are from the world and that in the context of the world we also become persons. The world is in community with us in that both are promised a share in the final reconciliation of all things. (p.118.) However, even though the world is bound up with the human and depends upon humanity for its destiny, it is not arbitrarily at our disposal. On the contrary.

> Here, being in the image of God has something to do with the human responsibility to offer the creation, perfected, back to its creator as a perfect sacrifice of praise. It is here that are to be found the elements of truth in the claims that the image of God is to be found in the human stewardship of the creation. (p.118.)

Gunton, following John Zizioulas, specifically brings up here the idea that the very concept of person is eschatological. (p.118.) Being / personhood will only be realized when God is all in all. Yet, this is not to deny that we must also understand the person to be a protological concept. (p.119.) Origin is also an important concept in that it provides a dynamic orientation of human being to a proposed end. (This inclusion of protology within eschatology is essentially saying the same thing as my earlier conclusion that anthropology must be teleological.) This then leads Gunton to state that the image is not static but comes to be realized in various relationships in which human life is set. (p.119.) He further states that the New Testament in re-orienting the concept of the image to Jesus makes this point well.

> It is because Jesus is the 'the image of the invisible God' that God is 'through him to reconcile all things, whether on earth or in heaven...' (Col.1.15,20). The one through whom all was created is also the means of the re-establishment of the image in humanity. (p.119.)

Following this and in conclusion, Gunton again restates his view of the image.

> To be in the image of God is at once to be created as a particular kind of being - a person - and to be called to realise a certain destiny. The shape of that destiny is to be found in God-given forms of human community and of human responsibility to the universe. (p.119.)

Noticed here is that the content (shape) of the image is teleological and involves not simply interpersonal relationships, but also responsible activity; namely stewardship.

With this Gunton returns to one of the questions asked initially in the chapter, that is, how are we understand the idea of comparison with respect to the image? He concludes that human difference with the rest of creation is not an ontological distinction. Rather, it is an asymmetry of relation and is therefore only a relative difference. Our fate as humans is bound up closely with the fate of the rest of the universe and it involves our being stewards and not absolute

Lords of creation. The difference between God and those made in his image is not found in some structural difference. It is rather found in the distinction that God is the creator and we are his creation. (pp.119-120.) Gunton then concludes:

> The triune God has created humankind as finite persons-in-relation who are called to acknowledge his creation by becoming the persons they are and by enabling the rest of the creation to make its due response of praise. (p.120.)

What we find in chapter six then is clearly a modified and more nuanced view of the person than we were given in chapter five. I have throughout this discussion indicated what these differences are. I have also highlighted a few theological points as possible nuances that could be important for the attempted resolution of the earlier problems with Gunton that I raised. Ultimately, I shall not attempt to resolve for Gunton the tensions caused by the differences in his two accounts. Exactly how both views fit together, or even if they do, is a question posed to him. Also, I shall let my points of contention stand as questions indicating the kinds of issues that need to be addressed in a more comprehensive teleological anthropology. What I have done then is presented the views from these chapters, with their tensions and points of controversy, as a current approach to a relational view of the image and person. I now offer some concluding comments and assessments that will function as my own formulation.

Gunton's view of the person and the image, in as much as it is grounded in the doctrine of God, in as much as it recognizes some of the strengths and potentials of other approaches to anthropology, and in as much it minimizes some of the weaknesses of these other views, is overall promising. However, it is not without its conceptual difficulties, the most fundamental of which questions whether it is theologically possible to draw such a direct analogy between the sociality and ontology of being in the Trinity and the ontology of human persons. Even though the *imago Dei* doctrine does suggest that it is correct to posit some level of analogy between the two, the nagging question is whether Gunton has drawn the analogy too closely between two related and similar but also very distinct entities; namely God and humanity.

The Eastern tradition particularly reminds us that the reality of God is ultimately greater than our capacity to describe him. God will always transcend our formulations and descriptions of who he is. In this sense it is correct to say that finally God is a mystery. It follows then that any attempt to explain both the ontology of God and the ontology of the human in God's image, as promising as it may be, will be at best less than total, and, when pushed too far will show itself to be weak and fall short.

If humans are created to be in the image of God, and, if God is by nature trinity then it does follow that human essence / ontology will in some ways correspond to or reflect the divine essence. However, the step from the structure of the divine essence to the human is a large one. Ultimately the step involves a shift in kind and category from infinite to finite. Although theology calls us to posit an ontological correspondence between God and humans, it does so only in a somewhat guarded way. People are to be the image of God but in a human and not divine way. Thus, the correspondence between the ontology of God and the ontology of the person, although legitimate is not absolutely parallel. The persons of the trinity are unique persons, that is they have their being and identity, in their relationships to each other. Similar to God, humans have their being and identity in their relationships. However, our relations include our relationship with God, with others and with creation. We are finite and dependent upon these others, including things that are not God, in a way that God never is. Thus although the ontology of God is mirrored by humanity it is not identical to it.

All of this suggests that while Gunton's method of grounding an ontology of personhood in the ontology of God is promising and indeed right in many respects, it is nevertheless not a simple or straightforward process. For Gunton's own position to be more compelling he would need to address more closely these issues.

However, granting the seriousness of these weaknesses and potential difficulties inherent in Gunton's view, they do not necessarily undermine the fact that he has pointed out some very important truths. In general, his and other relational ontologies of personhood based upon trinitarian ontology does indeed seem the way forward.

What then are the overall conclusions concerning theological anthropology for this book? Granted it has not been my primary purpose to argue specifically for one approach to anthropology (substantive, functional or relational) over another. For the purposes of developing an ontology of work for a theology of work it has been necessary simply to use the debates in theological anthropology to set the parameters and directions for the discussion that is to follow. That is, by broadly sketching the approaches and both highlighting some of their strengths and offering some critical observations, it is now possible to see where one should and should not probe in seeking to establish from within a teleological Christian anthropology an ontology of work. In the process of establishing these parameters however, some general conclusions on the anthropological questions raised do emerge. Here, by way of summary and for the sake of a broader theological anthropology, these conclusions are offered.

It does seem that a version of a relational metaphysic and thus a relational conception of personhood is required when theological anthropology begins by probing the nature of the personal God we are created to image. Substantive and purely functional views are inadequate for they, while claiming to take the image of God as their starting point, do not give sufficient attention to who God is by nature. Thus, they are not able to make the step to who we must be by nature if we are to image that God.

Yet, although a relational ontology and conception of the image is required by the trinitarian nature of God, the understanding of relationship, when applied to human being, should not be restricted to inter-personal relationship. For humans, relationship and hence being and identity in relationship, must also include our relationships with the rest of non-human reality. This will include our relationship with the personal God but will likewise include our relationships with non-personal entities. Thus our being is bound up with all of creation.

Further, and building upon the previous chapter's discussions of teleology, to be adequate a relational view must also be conceived so as to encompass concepts of both human roles and functions (in this chapter implied by the concept of stewardship). However, these concepts are not to be seen as add-ons. Rather, roles and function are upon closer inspection intrinsic dimensions to relationship. Particularity implies uniqueness, and when speaking from the standpoint of teleology, uniqueness implies some kind of 'ordering to'. Ordering to in turn demands some kind of role and function. Thus, role and function are to relationship both implications and applications of the relational matrix. Essentially, there can be no relationship without concrete realization of these in various roles and functions.[29]

What then are the results of this kind of a relational conception of personhood? Generally, on the negative side it keeps us from the individualistic tendencies and unproductive speculations on the constituent parts of the person that are characteristic of the substantive view. Likewise, it helps us to avoid the unintentional reductionistic tendency of functional views of dissolving personhood and identity into a person's roles or functions.

On the positive side however, a relational view as here modified shows itself in practice to be sufficiently open for the many positive and necessary observations which its counterpart views, the substantive and functional, offer. It makes space within personhood for roles and function (stewardship) but does not limit personhood to these. It likewise picks up from substantive views the emphasis upon the particular identity of individual persons while not ending up in an untenable individualism as substantive views do. Likewise, this kind of relational view picks up from both other views that the image of God is the starting place for understanding personhood.

At this point however, having established these parameters for a teleological and relational ontology of personhood, and for the larger purpose of outlining from theological anthropology an ontology of work, it is now appropriate to undertake a more detailed analysis of and dialogue with Moltmann's theologi-

---

[29] This realisation is practical in that it helps us to keep our focus on real and concrete human life. It avoids the more speculative soul versus body, or image versus likeness dualisms that non-relational views make room for. There may be a place for these discussions (with or without conceiving of them dualistically) but a relational ontology incorporating teleological perspectives and thus roles and function keeps these from becoming the central point of the discussion as they have been for far too long in the history of theology.

cal anthropology. Moltmann too offers both a relational and trinitarian view of the image of God and persons in that image. I began the discussion with Gunton rather than Moltmann however, mainly because Gunton provides a more concise presentation of the overall model. Gunton introduces us more directly to the central debates and more polemically explores these than does Moltmann. However, Moltmann's presentation will both further theologically develop a version of this model, and, will apply it more widely than was possible in Gunton's more concise presentation. Finally though, the reason for turning to Moltmann is that when critically considered his anthropology offers additional insights which are needed for an adequate ontology of work.

CHAPTER 6

The Ontology of Work in Dialogue with Jürgen Moltmann's Theological Anthropology

Introduction

In this chapter, in order to demonstrate the ontological aspect of work, I am sketching the contours of, and dialoguing with, the Christian anthropology derived from the theology of Jürgen Moltmann. I have especially turned to Moltmann at this point for three reasons. First, with its eschatological orientation, Moltmann's theology in general is compatible with and complementary to my own conviction developed in the previous two chapters. This is the conviction that the very structure of a theological ethics must be teleological, and, that this teleology should be developed from theology, specifically eschatology, rather than simply from philosophy. A second reason for turning to Moltmann is, as I have already suggested, that his broader theology is a promising dialogue partner for the larger project of constructing a theology of work (especially here an ontology of work). Third, I have turned to Moltmann because his theological anthropology is developed within a broader theology that functions also as a theology of nature. The advantage here is that this will provide an anthropology that explicitly attempts to be ecologically friendly.

Now in sketching the contours of Moltmann's anthropology I am not suggesting that I will here provide a fully comprehensive reproduction of it. Rather I have selected the themes and issues that will ultimately serve the overall purpose of demonstrating from a theological anthropology an ontology of work.

Nonetheless, in addition to this stated purpose, the discussion that follows makes a broader contribution to the larger field of theological anthropology and not simply to a theology of work. How so? First, this study critically examines the overall shape and direction of Moltmann's anthropology. It does this by locating and evaluating the central anthropological insights from his theology, and by demonstrating where one would go if one were producing a more comprehensive formulation of it. Second, this study makes a wider contribution to theological anthropology in that it explores many of the related theological details that other more traditional formulations of theological anthropology either neglect or leave quite vague. As such, this study functions as a kind of anthropology testing ground for examining the impact and value of insights gained from doctrines not traditionally associated with theological anthropology.

Of course, in approaching anthropology within Moltmann it must recognized up front that he does not as such undertake to develop a fully comprehensive theological anthropology.[1] Rather what one finds scattered throughout his writings are the building blocks for a quite rich view of being human / human being. That is, throughout Moltmann's writings one finds to varying degrees reflections on humanity's nature, purpose and destiny. At times Moltmann does enter into extended arguments and develop themes traditionally considered within an anthropology. Often however, important anthropological insights arise from his theology either simply through an incidental comment, or as implications of the larger theological point that he is at that time making. For this project all three of these sources are essential although it is often the latter of the three that pulls the ideas together and produces the more interesting results.

Specifically, Moltmann's most developed anthropological discussions, representing his more mature theology, appear in: *God in Creation* (1985), *The Way of Jesus Christ* (1990), and *The Coming of God* (1996).[2] With one notable exception discussed next, in most of his other writings the anthropology presented is implied but not specifically developed. Conceptually however, the anthropology offered outwith these three books is either an anticipation in a less developed form, or a reflection of what is specifically discussed in more detail therein. Therefore, although the discussions in this chapter will range quite widely through Moltmann's theology, overall the explorations and structure focuses primarily on these three primary sources.

Having made this commitment however, as mentioned there is one other text that deserves some consideration initially. That is the earlier essay, *Man: Christian Anthropology in the Conflicts of the Present* (1974).[3] It may seem strange that I have not included this booklet specifically addressing anthropology in the list with the other three primary sources, but this has not been done for at least two reasons. Firstly, although it is an extended essay specifically on anthropology, it is an early work that does not represent Moltmann's most mature theological reflection. Secondly, it is not as the title might suggest a detailed discussion reflecting Moltmann's anthropology. Rather, it is by and large a critique of several dominant contemporary approaches to anthropology. This limitation notwithstanding, it is a helpful work to mention as it shows both where Moltmann's sympathies do and do not lie, and points to the directions that his own anthropological constructs will take.

Basically, in this booklet Moltmann argues that contemporary sociobiological, cultural, and religious (existential) approaches to anthropology, al-

---

[1] Moltmann, *God in Creation* (1985), p.xiv. Hereafter referred to as *GC*.

[2] *The Way of Jesus Christ* hereafter referred to as *WJC,* and, *The Coming of God* hereafter referred to as *CoG*.

[3] Hereafter referred to as *M*.

though offering several legitimate and necessary insights, fall short of a Christian anthropology. He is critical of the modern images of man which he argues, reductionistically attempt to locate human essence within humanity itself through either; economics / production (*M*, pp.47-59.), civic or racial identity (*M*, pp.59-67.), natural and judicial law (*M*, pp.67-78.), interpersonal relationality –at the expense of the material– (*M*, pp.78-86.), social role –the detached consumerist approach– (*M*, pp.86-96.), or the experience of 'naked decision' / will and choice (*M*, pp.96-104.). Rather, Moltmann wants to suggest that the Son of Man, and particularly the crucified Son of Man, is the essential beginning point and paradigm for Christian anthropology. He suggests that the suffering God and not the human as such is the key for developing a theological anthropology.

> The humanity of man comes to its reality in the human kingdom of the Son of Man. In the kingdom of the Son of Man man's likeness to God is fulfilled. (*M*, p.111.)

This suggestion however, is far from developed in this tract. Rather, this and related suggestions simply set the stage for the view of humanity that Moltmann will elsewhere later develop in more detail. Hence, what we find here is basically a marker indicating Moltmann's desired starting point for developing an anthropology.

With this in mind, and as a way into the more detailed examination of his anthropological ideas, it is interesting to consider where Moltmann's anthropology might be located within the survey of anthropology offered in the last chapter. Fundamentally, his concept of humankind (and of the *imago Dei*) is a version of the relational view, and specifically it is a trinitarian and a Christological construction.

Concerning the ontology with which Moltmann develops his anthropology, he is unequivocal in his call for theology to leave behind the traditional 'Aristotelian metaphysics of substance'. In connection with this, he further repudiates what he calls Cartesian 'subject' metaphysics. His search then, for a 'non-subjectivistic' and non-substantive metaphysics, leads him to conclude that: 'Both can only be done away with by means of a relational metaphysics, based on the mutual relativity of human beings and the world.' (*GC*, p.50.) Predictably this leads him later to the conclusion that it is the whole of human existence rather than a perceived characteristic (substance) that is God's image. (*GC*, pp.220-221.)

Moltmann is also equally forceful in his belief that being in God's image necessarily entails being in a trinitarian image. Thus, the image incorporates human interrelationship. 'Human beings are *imago trinitatis* and only correspond to the triune God when they are united with one another.' (*GC*, p.216.) This view of course, grows directly out of his understanding of who God is; a social Trinity. (*GC*, pp.234-244.) Moltmann argues that the human image of

God corresponds to God's 'inward nature.' (*GC*, p.241.) This inward nature is understood to be God's social trinitarian nature.[4]

Further, and in line with the focus on the Son of Man as the paradigm for the human, Moltmann's anthropology also encompasses a Christological interpretation of the *imago Dei;* or more specifically as he calls it, the *imago Christi.* The *imago Christi* is the *imago Dei* mediated through Christ. (*GC*, p.218.)

With reference to these points, Moltmann differs very little from the trinitarian and relational approach that I have already sketched. His anthropology becomes illuminating however, when considering the detailed outworking of these points, and the additional doctrinal points used to help him to fill out his broader picture of the human being.

Concerning the three primary sources, I begin examining this by looking at the earliest of the books, *God in Creation.* It is appropriate to begin here for at least three reasons. Firstly, it is the work most focused on creation, and in as much as our concern is with a teleological anthropology which builds upon issues of origins and intended purposes, it is a logical starting point. Secondly, it is where Moltmann himself begins to develop and fill in many of the details of his view of the human person that have so far in his writings been either underdeveloped or implicit. Thirdly, roughly half of the book is devoted to theological anthropology and it is the most fully developed anthropology produced by Moltmann.

Despite having said that it is a developed anthropology, it must be remembered that the ethical concerns behind the book, while embracing anthropology, are ultimately directed toward ecology and the preservation of creation. As such, what has been written about the human is presented in a polemical context that is intended to relativise the human and show the often neglected importance of non-human creation. This does not mean that Moltmann undertakes to depreciate the human. Rather, it indicates that the scope of the questions addressed concerning humanness will be directed and even limited by these broader ethical concerns. Care therefore must be taken to read Moltmann's anthropology in its ecological context, while at the same time allowing it also to be an anthropology in its own right and not simply a sub-point of ecological theology.

Human Purpose in the Initial Creation

Structurally, most of Moltmann's anthropological material in *God in Creation* appears in the second half of the book. In the first half, he is attempting to develop a 'theology of nature'. Yet it is important to notice that he actually begins to discuss anthropology in the section on the ecological crisis (the introductory

---

[4] Moltmann argues here for the social trinitarian model only after he has argued extensively against the 'psychological' model of Trinity.

section that functions as a bridge into the theology of nature). Specifically, he enters into a discussion of anthropology in this section when dealing with what he calls the 'crisis of dominion.'

This observation is important for it establishes the context in which Moltmann will develop his anthropology. Clearly 'crisis' is the key word describing this context. Yet for Moltmann the ecological crisis, narrowly defined as a crisis in 'nature,' cannot be the real problem. Rather, the crisis as he sees it is essentially 'a crisis of the whole life system of the modern industrial world'. This system in turn is a reflection of 'fundamental human convictions about the meaning and purpose of life.' (*GC*, p.23.) For Moltmann the heart of the crisis is located in human beliefs about life's meaning and purpose.[5] Perceptions of life's purpose, then, provide a logical entry point for examining what it means to be a human being. Therefore, human purpose becomes a foundational conceptual grid through which to interpret our humanness and personhood.

It is interesting that Moltmann chooses human purpose as entry point for anthropology. Doubtless this tack ultimately stems directly from his having identified this as the epicenter of the ecological crisis. Although, given Moltmann's arguments against purpose elsewhere, as in the *Theology of Play*, this would appear contradictory. Yet for my purpose it is helpful to begin here for it highlights what I labored to show in the last two chapters, namely that questions concerning the essence of human purpose (human teleology) are of foundational importance and should provide the directions and contours of a theological anthropology.

Now when discussing human purpose, I (in keeping with Moltmann) am not meaning a supposed 'intrinsic' purpose of a supposed 'autonomous' human. Rather, I, like Moltmann, begin with the belief that both human and non-human / natural reality together constitute one created and contingent reality. Following on this, I understand human purpose to mean God the creator's intended purpose for humans. (In this section of the chapter I am concerned with God's intended purpose in the initial creation, while in the next section I address God's intended purpose for humans in the new creation). Thus, when I refer to human purpose or when I present Moltmann's views in terms of human purpose I really mean human purpose as given to humans by God.

Having said this however, I suggest that the purpose or purposes given by God also necessarily involve the created provision of a sufficient design, (or

---

[5] It is not clear here whether the phrase 'human convictions about the meaning and purpose of life' is meant to refer only to the meaning and purpose of human life, or, whether it is a statement concerning human beliefs about the purpose of human as well as non-human life. Both options would seem to be plausible given Moltmann's overall concerns. At the very minimum however, we may conclude that Moltmann is concerned here to show that perceptions of human purpose are foundational to questions of anthropology.

potentiality in this design), and a general ability to act toward those purposes. Therefore, in a derivative and qualified sense, it is not improper to speak of human purpose as also in some way intrinsic to the human. Yet it is intrinsic only in the sense that it has been purposefully built into the creature by the creator as either a potentiality or actuality for the good of the whole creation.

What however is a theological understanding of human purpose? Theologically can humanity be said to have a purpose? What is God's intended meaning and purpose for life? How one answers these questions will have consequences for what one actually understands humanness to be, and on what one understands ethical human living to be. Further, and in addition to (and as an application of) these metaphysical and meta-ethical concerns, these questions are foundational for the quest of establishing an ontology of work from a human teleology / teleological anthropology. If theological anthropology is right to ask questions of human purpose, (and I have argued in the chapter on teleology that it must) and if intended human purpose is at all understood to incorporate human projects and the work involved in these projects, not simply as an instrument to achieve some additional purpose but also as an essential aspect of humanness itself, (a point in this chapter I will be demonstrating), then a view of work as ontological begins to emerge. At this point I am simply making this argument by way of illustration to suggest that a theology of human purpose is an essential category for both a theological anthropology in general, and, for the hypothesis that seeks to establish an ontology of work in particular.

In examining Moltmann's view of human purpose in the initial creation, and this concept's contribution to his overall theological anthropology, I will be considering three of Moltmann's discussions. The first considers whether theology should present an anthropocentric or a theocentric understanding of creation and the natural environment. This is really the wider question that asks 'for whom is initial creation intended?' As will be shown, the answer to this question functions as a type of pivot around which the idea of human purpose turns.

The second discussion centers around Moltmann's view of nature as humanity's 'home country'. For purposes of anthropology this is essentially a question of what constitutes humanity's working and yet also dependent relationships with nature. Again a particular vision of human purpose emerges as integral to the picture that Moltmann offers.

The final discussion that I will be considering in this section involves ideas connected with and stemming from Moltmann's understanding of the *imago Dei*. I have already indicated generally what his views on this doctrine are. Nevertheless, it is important to consider how for Moltmann the doctrine leads to certain roles and functions for humanity. It is with respect to these roles that I will further interpret what constitutes his view of human purpose.

Anthropocentric Versus Theocentric Conceptions of Nature

One of Moltmann's purposes in *God in Creation* is to argue against a strongly anthropocentric view of the world and the human domination and exploitation of the world that have stemmed from it. By this Moltmann means to deny the view either secular or theological (supposedly derived from the Genesis 2 creation account) that the world was created primarily for people, and for people to do with as they please.

> Interpreting the world as God's creation means precisely not viewing it as the world of human beings, and taking possession of it accordingly. If the world is God's creation, then it remains his property and cannot be claimed by men and women. It can only be accepted as a loan and administered as a trust. It has to be treated according to the standards of the divine righteousness, not according to the values that are bound up with human aggrandisement. (*GC*, pp.30-31.)

Moltmann argues that an erroneous view of the human as the 'crown of creation' has lead to an anthropocentric view which claims that heaven and earth were made for the sake of human beings. According to Moltmann this is not the biblical view, for as he argues, according to both the biblical Jewish and Christian traditions the crown of creation is not the human being but the sabbath. (*GC*, p.31.) He does not deny humanity's special place within the creation, but argues that 'God created the world for his glory, out of love'. (*GC*, p.31.) This then, is a '*theocentric* biblical world picture' rather than an anthropocentric one.[6] On this view the human being, with his special position in the cosmos, is simply given 'the chance to understand himself as a member of the community of creation' and he is not given the right to dominate it through the sciences. (*GC*, p.31.)

According to this view, the purpose of the whole of creation is God's glory. By implication and application therefore, human purpose is also to bring God glory. This position is a generally accepted Christian view and is therefore not particularly controversial. However, a larger question still remains as to what the specific meaning of this general claim might entail. Moltmann describes this concept metaphorically with the vision of humanity and nature together singing a 'hymn of praise of God's glory'. Further, his argument suggests that human purpose directed towards God's glory involves humanity's enjoyment (with the rest of creation) 'of God's sabbath pleasure over creation'. (*GC*, p.31.) The question still remains, what does this concretely mean in terms of human activity? Is the metaphor here meant to suggest an organized service of worship, or is it simply a general statement on the indispensability of worship and sabbath rest? If it is the former, then human purpose does indeed take shape around a somewhat hierarchical valuation of organized worship over the rest of

---

[6] Moltmann's theocentric position could be argued to fall under the heading of what in ecological ethics is called the 'weak anthropic principle'; which argues that while the human does not have the right to dominate nature (anthropocentrism or the strong anthropic principle) it does in some instances have a claim to priority over other species.

life's activities. If it is the latter, we are still left with a vague general description which, although providing a sense of meaning, still leaves us unsure of what the content of worship and enjoyment, or the sabbath rest, might be.

This picture of human purpose will be further developed as we proceed. At this point, the ambiguity not withstanding, what we see according to Moltmann is that in a theocentric rather than anthropocentric worldview, human purpose is turned away from the human as such and, is turned almost exclusively toward God. Herein lies the pivot previously mentioned. On this view the question of human purpose is redirected so that it has more to do with God and God's glory than with humanity and human reality. As important as this concept may be for the study of the doctrine of God, such a redirection of the question does not offer much beyond a general limitation for anthropology. Still needed is a vision of what is concretely involved in glorifying God both in the present world and in eternity. We need then to consider further what may be included in a theology of human purpose.

Nature as Humanity's 'Home Country'

In the second half of Moltmann's discussion of the ecological crisis he begins to sketch the outline of what he calls an ecological theology of nature. In the process he focuses his attention on a fundamental issue, the dichotomy and conflict between man and nature. The question that he is exploring is how to resolve this conflict which has in his view led to the ecological crisis. One concept, and probably the central concept, which Moltmann develops for this purpose is the idea of humanity's 'home country in nature'. I call this the central concept of the section for it functions as the pinnacle of his argument. Those discussions which precede it, (*Karl Marx and the Estrangement of Nature*, and *Ernst Bloch: 'Nature as Subject'*) build toward this concept, and those that follow (*Soul and Body*, and *The Naturalization of the Human Being*) provide further detail and explanation of it.

The term 'home country' is a concept which Moltmann borrows from Ernst Bloch.

> Bloch starts from a correspondence between the human being and nature: the counterpart of the creative person is productive matter, while the counterpart of the hoping person is the material sphere of the really-possible. Consequently Bloch assumes that there is a subject 'nature' which corresponds as a partner to the human subject. It is only when nature ceases to appear merely as 'nature for the human being' - that is to say, his object and raw material - but is recognized in its individual character as a 'subject' of its own that the history of nature can be perceived as something on its own, independent of human beings: and it is only then that nature's own independent future can be heeded. And only then, too, can a community between human beings and nature come into being in which both can find their 'home country'. (*GC,* p.42.)

Following on this Moltmann cites Bloch with respect to human technology / work. He introduces here the idea of 'alliance technology', or, as one might today call it – 'soft technology'. The idea is that the conflict relationship between man and nature (spirit and matter) can be resolved through their mutual mediation rather than through human exploitation. The human and nature both remain subjects, and both, rather than simply nature, become also and at the same time, objects. However, the point is that the objectivity is relativized and regulated by the primary condition of subjectivity. In summary,

> alliance technology... accepts the co-productivity of nature as subject. In this alliance, it is not only the person who desires to bring forth and manifest his true essential being. Nature too is to manifest herself in the alliance, in her own individual character. (*GC*, p.43.)

It is interesting here to notice that, according to Moltmann, Bloch sees the key point of contact and the resolution of the conflict between humanity and nature to be located correspondingly in what might be called work (of humanity) and productivity (of nature). It is in the actively productive (but also protective) 'manifestation of essential being' of both subjects that the dichotomy between man and nature dissipates.

Of course, up to this point Moltmann is simply interpretively, and selectively for his own purposes, outlining Bloch's ideas. Yet we can see where this is leading him. For, later in this same section on Bloch, Moltmann suggests that the problem with Marxism is that it 'only' conceives of man's practical (instrumental) relationship with nature. This practical relationship is man's work, and when so conceived the human is the only subject involved and he or she simply works on nature as a raw material (object) for his or her own purposes. (*GC*, p.45.)

When Moltmann turns to his own construal of the 'home country' he picks up and develops for his own purposes and within his own theological framework the ideas presented by Bloch. Reflecting the dual subjectivity already outlined, he points to two fundamental concerns. The first is work, and the second is 'the interest of habitation'. His point in the case of the first is that work – instrumentally described here as obtaining food and building up our own world – assumes that the person is the active agent and that nature is always passive. (*GC*, p.46.) This he accepts as a necessary and valid concern. Yet, humans also need to and do have an interest in habitation. Here humanity not only has to work on nature, it also has to live in it. Following on this Moltmann concludes that the 'interests of habitation are different from the interests of work.' *GC*, (p.46.)

For Moltmann the image of humanity living in a home country is a vision of a 'network of social relationships without stresses and strains.' On this view, when I am at home I experience equilibrium and relaxed social relationship without anxiety or struggle; that is, I experience tranquillised social relationships. (GC, p.46.) Hence, it follows that humanity will be at home in nature when it adapts to nature; when it has a relaxed relationship with it. Of course,

> Nature is not in itself a home for human beings. On the contrary, the human being's natural constitution shows that he is an unfinished being who is not adjusted to his environment at all. It is only when nature has been molded into an environment that it can become a home in which men and women can live and dwell. (GC, p.46.)

It follows then, that in order to achieve both this tranquility but also a molding of one's environment, the goal must be the 'symbiosis' between human beings and nature. (GC, p.47.) This means that both work and habitation interests are essential but must be 'balanced out'. (GC, p.47.) Only with both concerns, but both concerns in balance, will the dichotomy between humanity and nature be overcome.

To demonstrate this concept Moltmann then moves the discussion on to a consideration of the composite unity of the soul and body in the human being. He chooses this topic to show that the person in itself is really a prototype of the symbiotic relationship he is suggesting. (GC, pp.47-49.)

Finally, Moltmann turns the discussion to the concept of the naturalization of the human being. This is not to be conceived of as a romantic return to nature. Rather it means that men and women should come to interpret their own being from within the framework of nature rather than in opposition to it. (GC, pp.49-50.) This provides one example of how humanity, as the product of nature, also becomes its object rather than always its subject.

Both of these discussions are intended to follow on from the idea that a symbiosis or balance between work and habitation, humanity and nature, must be reached. The conflict between man and nature must be overcome. This call for balance, and the legitimization of the two concerns, work and habitation, are not in themselves problematic. However, here are a few critical comments about Moltmann's argumentation.

To begin I simply point out that his understanding of the nature of work here is solely instrumental. Sustenance and building up civilization / environment are the only ends in view. As such it is logical to conclude that in work the human is always the active agent and that nature is always passive (that the interests of work and habitation are different). Yet, if work is defined as more than instrumental; that is, if it is also ontological (allowing it to be an end rather than simply a means to an end) and as relational (allowing for personal / interpersonal exploration and demonstration leading to the related artistic / aesthetic and moral dimension) it is possible to see a more inter-dependent give-and-take relationship between the worker and his or her material / environment. Here it is possible to view both as subjects. As an expert wood craftsman works with rather than against the grain and unique (life) characteristics of a piece of wood to, in effect, release the historically produced qualities of the wood, and at the same time allows the processes of working with the wood to further form and affect him, so too can other workers (with this more holistic and less reduction-istically instrumental view of work) work together with rather than against the material elements of their trade. The point is simply that there is not and need not necessarily be a conflict between the interests of habitation (nature) and work. Indeed, it seems to be the whole point of Moltmann's discussion that symbiosis is desirable and possible. Why he needs initially to juxtapose the interest of work against the interest of habitation is unclear. To say that in common experience there is often a conflict of interest may be true. However, this is not the same as saying that the interests of the two are essentially differ-ent.

Another, and related critique concerns Moltmann's imagery in exploring the home country concept. He argues that 'home' is an environment characterized by equilibrium and relaxed social relationship and that it is a place without stress and strain (habitation is a different interest than work). The implication is that humanity's home in nature will also have these characteristics. However, there is a fallacy here. Home-life is not primarily characterized by a lack of stress and strain. Indeed, one may hope that this becomes part of the experience in home-life. However this state will usually be a by-product of much strenuous and continual work. Relationally, establishing harmony is a long and ongoing task, the fruits of which can be enjoyed but the work of which is never com-plete. Materially, having a home where relaxation is possible demands constant cleaning, maintenance, repair and the like. The home environment left to itself will deteriorate and become precisely not a place characterized by relaxation and harmony. Admittedly, these tasks can either work with the given reality of a home environment, in which case the work will be less confrontational, or it can work against it, in which case there will be conflict. The point here is sim-ply that the image of the home as harmonious only comes through much and sometimes difficult work. This then leads back to my critique of the idea that the interests of work and habitation are essentially different. They are precisely not different for if there is to be habitation there must also be work.

Moltmann acknowledged as much when he qualified his view arguing that humans, as unfinished beings, not only need to adapt to the natural environ-ment, but they also need to mold (work) nature into a liveable environment. (*GC*, p.46.) Here one begins to detect indications of what Moltmann perceives human purpose to include; the molding of an environment for habitation. Inter-estingly however, it is humanity that is said to be unfinished (whether this be because of a Fall and / or simply a condition of initial createdness) and no such pronouncement is made concerning nature. Here, non-human nature is not de-picted as either unfinished or in need of molding. Thus, since humanity is the incomplete of the two partners, we need to mold nature only for our, and not nature's, purposes. Does this mean however, as seems to be implied, that non-human nature is finished and that it does not need in itself to be 'molded'? Does this mean that if humanity were 'finished' we could simply adapt to nature as it currently is? Do we mean to imply that nature in itself could be a friendly environment and that it is simply our inability to live within it, due to our incompleteness, that forces us to mold it? Theologically, the answers to these questions must be no. It is not simply humanity that is unfinished, or not yet perfected.

Although 'nature' in the initial creation was completed and proclaimed good by God, it was not perfect and complete in the same way that it shall be in the new creation. Indeed, nature too has its own destiny in which it is brought to its fulfillment and completion. Nature too is theologically understood to be much more 'in the end' than it was in the beginning. Further, independently of how one views the literalness of the Fall, Genesis 3 does indicate that nature is bound up with humanity's condition and that it too, along with humanity, was 'cursed' and in need of redemption. Thus, as both directed toward its future as the new creation (as initially unfinished), and in need of redemption (as fallen and cursed), nature too must be viewed as open; that is, as open to and in need of some kind of 'molding'.

On this view, and in returning to the question of work it is not simply humanity that is unfinished and therefore needs to form its environment. Nature too is unfinished. As unfinished it is likewise open to be worked upon, not just for our human purposes, but for its own purposes and flourishing. Now care must be taken not to overstate this point. Nature is not there simply to be worked by humans. Nature is also a subject and not simply an object. Yet, because of nature's relationship to God, and God's appointment of humanity as its stewards, nature is theoretically open to our working on it both for our sakes and for its own sake. I would even argue that, in a qualified redemptive sense, nature likewise needs humanity. Nature needs at least a person, Jesus Christ, if it is to arrive at its *telos*; its redemption and recreation. Further, Romans 8:19-25 indicates that it even needs humanity (in Christ) for its redemption. Now of course this redemption of nature in Christ and through our adoption does not mean that our actual human working on nature is, or leads to, its salvation. I simply mean that it is not theologically wrong to posit that nature in some respect needs humanity for its ultimate flourishing. Concerning human working on nature, I simply want to suggest that theologically nature is a partner. It is productive (Bloch's term) but is also like us in that it is unfinished. Because it is unfinished, or open, like humanity nature must be both object as well as subject. It is not simply a subject, who happens also, for our sake only, to be an object.

This admittedly controversial conception of nature becomes less potentially problematic if we understand it according to our previously presented model of teleology. When applying an understanding of teleology (orderings along-side, orderings directionally to, and an ordering to flourish as itself) to this theological conception of nature we may say the following: In kind (generically) nature is ordered alongside humanity. According to its end (teleologically) nature is ordered both to God, and contingently through its relationship to God, nature has been ordered by God to humanity. (I would likewise caution that conversely humanity has been ordered by God to protect and work for the interests of nature). Together, both this generic and teleological ordering protect and safeguard nature from the reductionistic teleological construct which argues that nature is simply or primarily there to serve humanity's purposes or interests. Further, of course, nature is ordered by God to flourish as itself. Again this serves to protect nature from any arbitrary and destructive human activities that would threaten to undermine nature's own purposes of flourishing as itself.

Broadly, these various orderings allow space for my contention that nature, as ordered by God, is open to be worked by humanity. It is not solely there for the purposes of human work. Nonetheless, it is not simply a mature partner who tolerates human work simply because humanity is as yet, unfinished. Nature is rightly both subject and object.

Now with these critiques I do not mean to detract from the main point that Moltmann is making; namely that humanity should co-operate with nature as it works on nature so as to live in nature. I make these criticisms however, for they further help to critically identify the view of the human being and human purpose that Moltmann develops in this discussion. Here we have uncovered several indicators of what Moltmann considers human purpose to entail.

The vision of the person that emerges here is of the human being as a domiciliary worker. From this discussion it is clear that by constitution human beings are unfinished beings. They are beings which, as products of nature, are continually objects of it. Also at the same time, humans as unfinished beings are necessarily always subjects who need to work on and mold nature into a liveable environment. Human purpose then will necessarily include concepts involving work. This is so in as much as work (a particular kind of conciliatory work) is envisioned as a point of contact between the human and nature. I mean that the envisioned new conception of the inter-dependent relationship between the human and nature will be concretely realized primarily through harmonious working relationships between humans and nature. Herein the conflict between the two is supposed to dissipate, or at least become less problematic. In as much as the crisis of human purpose which Moltmann talks about will involve a theological re-orientation in human culture and activity toward a symbiotic and balanced relationship between humanity and nature, so too will work necessarily be included theologically as a part of this remedy for our ailing sense of human purpose. The naturalization of humanity will simply be the reflective part of humanity's purpose as we theologically seek to understand ourselves as a part of, rather than as over and against nature. Work will be the active side of human purpose, the application of this new understanding. On this view work becomes integral to a theological understanding of human purpose.

Functional Applications and Implications of the Imago Dei

The naturalization of the human being will involve developing a new theological conception that will relate human beings at the same time to both nature and God. Moltmann finds this new and needed conception in his version of the doctrine of the image of God which includes the concept of human beings as also *imago mundi*.

As already shown, Moltmann's view of this image is essentially relational. However function also plays a key role in his thought. For him, relationships and functions exist together so that it is often unnecessary, even impossible to differentiate between the two.

Following the implications of the dual subjectivity of human beings and nature, Moltmann develops a two fold interpretation of the human being. Not surprisingly, he talks about the human as created in the image of God. However, prior to this he posits that theology must begin, not with human beings in the image of God, but rather with the understanding that we are first created in the image of the world. Thus, the *imago mundi* is prior to the *imago Dei*. Here I shall briefly explore this concept.

Often theology has begun with the comparative question of the difference between the human being and the animals / the rest of creation. Moltmann argues that from the logic of creation itself it is better to begin with what links humans and non-humans together, that is, what they have in common. His suggestion is that the human is first a creature in the fellowship of creation. He or she is first the *imago mundi* and then, only subsequent to this, is he or she the *imago Dei*. (*GC*, p.186.)

Here is what Moltmann calls a 'strange double *function* on the part of human beings.' (*GC*, p.189. italics added) On the one hand, the human itself is an embodiment of all other creatures. This means that the human being contains all of the simpler systems found in creation. (*GC*, p.189.) 'These systems are present in him and he depends upon them. He is *imago mundi*.' (*GC*, p.190.) As *imago mundi* the human person becomes a 'microcosm in which all previous creatures are found again, a being that can only exist in community with all other created beings and which can only understand itself in that community.' (*GC*, p.186.) Further, as this microcosm, the human stands before God representing all other creatures. 'He lives, speaks and acts on their behalf. Understood as *imago mundi*, human beings are priestly creations and eucharistic beings.' (*GC*, p.190.)

On the other hand however, humans are also the *imago Dei*. He and she together are God's representative, or proxy in the community of creation. The human being represents God's glory and will on earth. Humans 'intercede before God for the community of creation.' (*GC*, p.190.) Herein, as God's counterpart and reflection, humans are distinguished from the rest of creation. Firstly, they have the divine charge to subdue the earth. This is understood by Moltmann simply as the commission to eat vegetable food. Secondly, they are supposed to name the animals so as to bring animals into the community of language with humans. Thirdly, unlike animals, humans are social beings and are dependent on the help of others. (*GC*, p.188.)

Humans are at once both the *imago mundi* and the *imago Dei*. With this concept firmly established, Moltmann then returns to his idea that the purpose of all of creation lies in the sabbath. Speaking of humanity's 'strange double function' he concludes that: 'In this double role they stand before the sabbath of creation in terms of time. They prepare the feast of creation.' (*GC*, p.190.) He later makes it clear that he understands the crown of creation to be God's sabbath and that: 'It is for this that human beings are created - for the feast of creation, which praises the eternal, inexhaustible God'. (*GC*, p.197.) Therefore, the 'enduring meaning of human existence lies in its participation in this joyful paean of God's creation.' (*GC*, p.197.)

What is most interesting for my purposes in this discussion is how function and roles are closely identified with the human being who is both the *imago mundi* and the *imago Dei*. Now Moltmann does not adopt a functional view of the image. His view is relational. Nonetheless, his whole discussion is permeated with descriptions of human 'being' and human purpose as centrally involving functions and the corresponding roles associated with them. We see for example, that the dual images (*mundi* and *Dei*) mean that humans have a 'strange double *function*'. Further, two of the three characteristics related to the *imago Dei* distinguish humans from animals by the functional activities of subduing and naming. Finally, through their 'double role' humans actually prepare the feast of creation. This implies that the preparation is a function upon which the very feast depends. (This then makes the fact, and type, of preparation very important for much depends upon this human activity.)

The point here is that while these characteristics could have each been described in terms of their relational dimensions, here Moltmann himself has chosen functional and active terminology. Indeed elsewhere, after arguing for the relational view of the image of God, Moltmann lists what he calls 'three fundamental relationships' involved with being in God's image. (*GC*, pp.220-221.) Yet upon examining the list we find again functional rather than purely relational descriptions: such as, ruling over earthly creatures as God's representative and in his name, being God's counterpart on earth and talking with and responding to him (both of which are activities rather than states of being), and being the appearance of God's splendor and his glory on earth. Ruling, representing, talking, responding, appearing, all of these concepts, which Moltmann rightly calls relationships, are also and at the same time functions derived from the role of being in God's image. Importantly however, in Moltmann's thinking the functions, specifically of ruling and subduing, are not understood to be identical to the image and likeness of God. (*GC*, p.224.) Nonetheless, we do find a very close connection between the image and likeness and these functions. I suggest that this connection can be described as the necessary application and implication of the image.

Now Moltmann's view of the *imago Dei*, as distinct from the *imago mundi*, is not yet complete but is also further defined and discussed. There is the image of God which is the trinitarian image. There is however, also the dimension to the image that can be called the *imago Christi,* or the image of Christ. And, in this image one finds the *gloria Dei est homo,* or, the eschatological glorification of human beings. (*GC,* p.215.) I will begin unpacking these ideas with Moltmann's description of the *imago Christi.*

As stated, for Moltmann the *imago Christi* is the *imago Dei* mediated through Christ. As such, they are not two distinct images. The former is theologically a more specific description of the latter. Further, with reference to how the image of Christ then relates to anthropology Moltmann says, 'christology is understood as the fulfillment of anthropology, and the anthropology becomes the preparation for christology.' (*GC,* p.218.) Therefore, Moltmann argues that: 'The true likeness to God is to be found, not at the beginning of God's history with mankind, but at its end; and as goal it is present in that beginning and during every moment of that history.' *GC,* p.225.)

Christ is the image of the invisible God and he fulfills this image as the mediator in creation, the reconciler of the world, and the Lord of the divine rule. (*GC,* p.226.) Further, 'the restoration or new creation of the likeness to God comes about in the fellowship of believers with Christ: since he is the messianic *imago Dei,* believers become *imago Christi,* and through this enter upon the path which will make them *gloria Dei* on earth.' (*GC,* p.226.) Two interpretive implications deserve mention here. First, believers correspond to Christ (and thus to God). In so doing, they will necessarily correspond to Christ's roles of mediation, reconciliation and lordship. Second, these roles are here summed up as leading to the eschatological glorification of human beings on earth.

These concepts of mediation, reconciliation and lordship come together in the imagery of God's appointment of humanity to rule over the animals. Moltmann is clear in arguing that the ruling talked about in initial creation is only properly understood eschatologically as ruling with Christ. Therefore, the rule of human beings will necessarily be in and with Christ, and as such it will be a liberating and healing rather than oppressive rule.

As a complement to this conception of ruling, Moltmann has already argued that nature's eschatological goal, its redemption, liberation, and glorification, will only be reached through humans. He argues that:

> Creation in the beginning started with nature and ended with the human being. The eschatological creation reverses this order: it starts with the liberation of the human being and ends with the redemption of nature. Its history is the mirror-image of the protological order of creation. Consequently, the enslaved creation does not wait for the appearance of Christ in glory in the direct sense; it waits for the revelation of the liberty of the children of God in Christ's appearance. Creation is to be redeemed through human liberty. (*GC,* pp.68-69, cf. p.189.)

Ruling with Christ then, a rule linked with humanity's and Christ's salvation of nature, becomes the eschatological glorification of human beings. Now Moltmann's logic develops as follows: Creation is creation for the sabbath.

Likewise human beings are created as the image of God for the divine glory. In glorifying God, creatures themselves 'arrive at the fulfillment of what they are intended to be.' (*GC*, p.228.) Combining these concepts, the human *telos* of glorifying God must include, but need not be limited to, our ruling with Christ. However, it is also important that this rule is likewise tied up with God's sabbath. Does this mean that the picture of God's sabbath is a parallel picture to Christ's, and thus our, healing and liberating rule? Although Moltmann himself does not directly make this connection, I suggest that it is so. I will examine shortly in more detail Moltmann's understanding of the sabbath. At this point however, the legitimate implication emerges that creation's goal of sabbath is not to be envisioned as an inactive state. Rather, it is a goal encompassing an active existence characterized by, and permeated with, the essence of God's sabbath rest.

So, again we have found that in Moltmann's depiction of the *imago Dei*, (this time as the *imago Christi*,) the concepts of function and role have moved to the forefront. Ruling, mediating, and redeeming, are all essentially functions of being in the divine image and each activity implies a corresponding role.

Is it fair however, to so emphasize the concepts of function and role in Moltmann's thought when, although he includes them as integral, he himself does not attribute to them the prominence that I am suggesting? Based on what has been already shown, I believe that such an emphasis is fair. However, there is more that may be said to strengthen my case.

In his discussion of the *imago Dei*, Moltmann himself has provided an additional collection of roles and functions to consider that are intended to illuminate further the implications of the image concept. One image, particularly associated with the concept of rule mentioned in Genesis 1:26, is that of 'justice of the peace'. (*GC*, pp.29-30. cf. p.224.) Further, two related images also appear. These are cultivator and steward of creation. The role of a cultivator is meant to conjure up the image of the protective work of a gardener. (*GC*, p.30.) The image of the steward is used to suggest that humans in God's image are meant to represent God and take care of God's earth for Him, they are tenants on His behalf. (*GC*, p.224.) Preservation and the continuation of the earthly side of creation are discussed here. (*GC*, p.224.) Interestingly, these two concepts are seen as firstly exemplified in the sabbath itself. (*GC*, p.224.) Yet, Moltmann is also clear that as the preservers and continuers of creation: 'Human beings become the authors of the further history of the earth.' (*GC*, p.224.) Again, sabbath is understood as a kind of rule rather than as an inactive existence.

These images (together with the ones already cited) give the warrant for concluding that in Moltmann's thought, function plays a key role in understanding the human person in the image of God. What however, does this further suggest concerning human purpose? The glory of God in God's sabbath is the goal of the whole creation, but it is tied closely with a kind of redemptive and healing rule. Human purpose then, even as derived from the concept of the image of God and as conceived of eschatologically rather than simply pro-tologically, includes the dimensions of human rule. Human rule as a concept necessarily implies some sort of active project; that is, it includes purposeful working.

On this view, to be in God's image through Christ includes, if not directly at least by implication and application, work. The ability, necessity, and orienta-tion for the human being to work then, (in initial creation) is viewed as funda-mentally a part of what it means to be a human being. Work is not simply an instrumental activity associated with survival or even spiritual progress. Rather, it is a fundamental condition of human created existence. It is ontological.

Human Purpose in the New Creation

Questions concerning the content of human purpose should in no way be lim-ited to the theology of the initial creation. Teleologically, human purpose nec-essarily includes conceptions of ends as well as origins. Theologically speak-ing, when contemplating human ends and the purposes contained therein, we are concerned with what it means to arrive at God's goal or destination for the human being. Yet, this goal should not primarily be understood as an end in the sense of a termination of that which has been. Neither, more importantly, should it be understood as if it meant the closing of a system (human life) that previously has been open. Rather, theologically the end for human beings should be envisioned as a consummation and a new beginning.

Christian hope for the human being, hope for the resurrection of the dead, is the hope of salvation and the new creation. This hope as an end is actually a beginning, and, a beginning which, although amply different from the previous existence, nonetheless also (in a transformed manner) incorporates that which has come before. This means that in addition to the obvious elements of discon-tinuity that the end introduces, it also embraces and perfects that which was originally there.

This vision of the eschatological new creation is important for explorations toward an ontology of work for it suggests that human purpose in the new crea-tion will be related to, although not in every way identical with, human purpose as found in the initial creation. As such there will remain important and genuine points of continuity as well as the obvious points of discontinuity.

The task now is to unpack and argue for this conception of the (human) new creation, and to explore further the implications of this vision. To this end, I suggest herein what are some of the essential points of continuity and disconti-nuity in human purpose between the initial and the new creation. Critical for the purposes of establishing an ontology of work will be to demonstrate that this scheme of continuity and discontinuity is also applicable with reference to human work and that work does continue in the new creation to be a fundamen-tal part of redeemed human existence and purpose. Further, I will suggest what this vision of work may look like given the transformation that is envisioned to take place on a cosmic level.

To accomplish these purposes I here continue a critical dialogue with Molt-mann's theology. I take up the exploration again with *God in Creation* but then continue the discussion from both *The Way of Jesus Christ* and *The Coming of God*. Particularly, I intend to establish further the ontology of work by examin-ing several doctrinal themes that cover both the transition from this creation to the new, and then the eschatological eternal state. I have organized these themes into two categories. These I am calling respectively: *Personhood and Gestalt: Resurrection and the Emerging Vision of Salvation*, and, *Salvation: The Sabbath and Shekinah.*

Personhood and Gestalt: Resurrection and the Emerging Vision of Salvation

So far Moltmann's discussion of what is personhood, or, what it is to be a hu-man person, is built upon a relational, trinitarian, and Christological conception of the image of God together with its various functional implications and appli-cations. As indicated, there is more that must be said in a Christian anthropol-ogy than these discussions alone can capture. Also important are questions con-cerning the nature and extent of the transition from this to the new creation for redeemed human beings. That is, questions concerning what is or is not saved, and how this is accomplished, must also be considered. Ultimately, my concern is for a vision of the eschatological eternal state of redeemed creation rather than for a view of the transition to it. The transition is simply the 'means through which' rather than the goal of the process. However, what one under-stands the eschatological eternal state to be concretely will to a large extent be directed and determined by what one envisions the transition from this creation to the new to entail; that is, what will it include and exclude from this life? Only that which is included in the transition, and not that which is excluded, can together with that which is completely and surprisingly new contribute to a vision of what the new creation will be ultimately. Therefore, before looking specifically at the eschatological eternal state of the redeemed human being, I will consider as an emerging vision of salvation what is involved in the transi-tion from the current to the new creation.

HUMAN CONSTITUTION AND GESTALT

I begin with Moltmann's understanding of the constitution of the human being in his discussion of anthropology in *God in Creation*. Moltmann argues for an essential unity of the body and the soul (with differentiation) rather than a strict dualism. The very fact that Moltmann takes up this discussion however, is not to be seen as a philosophical hijacking of his theology, or as an inconsistent regression into the realm and terminology of substantive metaphysics. Rather, the theme itself is essential for it is a practical and logical development from his assertion that 'embodiment is the end of all God's works'. (*GC*, pp.244ff.)

Moltmann argues that in Christian theology the 'soul' is in no way to be given primacy over the body. The spiritual is not more important than the material for both have an eschatological future. Ultimately, his vision is that of a 'perichoretic pattern of body and soul'. (*GC*, pp.258-262.) By this he means that the soul and body together exist in a mutual interpenetration and differentiated unity with no primacy of the one over the other (no hierarchy of spirit over matter). Rather, this perichoretic pattern of mutual interdependence should be understood as the Gestalt, or totality, of the human being. 'We are looking at the *Gestalt* – the configuration or total pattern – of the lived life.' (*GC*, p.259.) Here is introduced the Gestalt concept that will in Moltmann's writings from this point onward figure prominently in his view of the human being and human resurrection and salvation.

What however, does Moltmann more specifically mean by Gestalt? Building on terms developed by Gestalt psychology, he argues that a 'person's Gestalt emerges in the field formed by the human being and his environment.' (*GC*, p.259. note 40.) The dimensions involved here are many: 'nature' (genetic structure), the 'region of the world in which he is born', the 'society and culture in which the person grows up', the 'history which moulds his origins and conditions his future', the 'sphere of transcendence' (religion and value system). All of these, and similar factors, contribute to the formation of a person's Gestalt and thus, the person. (*GC*, p.259.)

Concerning what is commonly called personhood, Moltmann argues that 'in acquiring Gestalt, the person acquires both individuality and sociality.' (*GC*, p.259.) The understanding here is that the very identity of the person, both individually and socially, is constituted by the pattern of their total life, or Gestalt. To the degree that one changes any of these factors, one in effect and to that same degree changes the identity of the person. Now Moltmann comments that on some points Gestalt-formed identity is fixed. (Genetic structures would be one example of that which is essentially unalterable.) More importantly however, he further argues that identity and Gestalt are likewise 'historically open to considerable modification'. (*GC*, p.259.)

Another and equally important point to remember is that a human being's Gestalt is not merely a product of outward structures / environment. It is also constituted by the inward structures which are identified as the body and soul. Here Moltmann envisions as essential a person's conscious and unconscious (and dynamically open) relationship with himself or herself as a whole material and immaterial person. (*GC*, p.259.)

Not surprisingly, these outward and inward structures are argued to equally interpenetrate each other and thus together to form one's Gestalt. Body and soul, and our ever developing perceptions of them whether conscious or subconscious, together with our ever changing environment, contribute to the making of who we are as human persons.

Building on this discussion of Gestalt, Moltmann also makes some additional and related comments about the human that are important for my purposes. If a person (a Gestalt) is 'historically open to considerable modification', the question is how do we understand this openness? Moltmann argues that all living things can be described as 'open systems' and as such exist in the direction of their future. 'Their future is the scope of their open possibilities, limited by their past and their environment.' (*GC,* pp.264-265.) People, as people, live in the direction of their future. Because of this they are open to possibilities and to changing their historical futures. The important concept here for personhood is that the 'totality of the lived life', which will necessarily include change rather than a fixed 'static identity', will show itself in a person's alignment toward *the project* of his life. (*GC,* p.265.) This project is 'the project of his future' which in turn animates his life, and as a result, further forms his Gestalt. On this view a person is what he or she becomes, so that 'We can understand him if we understand the purpose of his life, his project.' (*GC,* p.265.) It is this project that gives meaning and orientation to his life. This project in turn involves his 'imaginative power'. Hence 'possibilities are explored and tried out in search of images and provisional projects, in anticipations and proleptic realizations of future conditions.' (*GC,* p.266.) Importantly, these projects are not just individual, but as they occur in the realm of social communication, they too become essentially social projects. (*GC,* p.266.)

This discussion of a person's life project as contributing to and growing out of his or her Gestalt has profound implications for an attempt to demonstrate that work is the ontological foundation of human purpose, not simply in the current creation but also in the new. It is a person's projects which are the applications and explorations of what and who that person is. As such these projects too, by way of expression and exploration, become part of the person's history, identity, and Gestalt. Now of course, these projects include more than simply the work involved in their undertaking. However, they also necessarily include the condition upon which they can be undertaken; that is, the active and applied processes which are foundational to their realization as projects. This means that the projects themselves include (although are not limited to) the work involved in achieving them. The ability and tendency to work then, while not in itself the project, is nonetheless a fundamental condition for the possibility of the project. Work therefore, is an ontological ground which is necessary for an open system if it is to remain open; meaning, open to its future and the projects that this future necessarily involves. An ontology of work is thus a basis upon which open systems can remain open. On this view, as long as persons are open systems, work ontologically remains a part of their fundamental existence and thus also a part of their essentially human purpose.

GESTALT, SALVATION AND 'TRANSITION' IN CHRIST

The necessary question to be addressed however, is whether a person in and through their ultimate salvation remains an open system? In human resurrection and salvation, is the totality of the person (as Gestalt) transformed into a new creation in such a way that essential humanness, and thus openness to the future, remains? Or, does the necessary discontinuity mean that somehow the fundamentally human category of openness is lost, and thus with it the concepts of future, project and work? These questions, concerning what is resurrected and saved, now need to be addressed.

When talking about human salvation, which is the resurrection of the dead to a new creation, the starting point for Christian theology must be the resurrection and new creation of Jesus Christ himself. I therefore, turn our attention away from Moltmann's *God in Creation* to his christology as found in *The Way of Jesus Christ*.

Appropriately, this discussion begins with Moltmann's section entitled 'Christ's Transition to the New Creation'. (*WJC*, pp.256.) Here, before speaking specifically of Christ, Moltmann summarizes his vision of the human in the initial creation.

> In the embodiment of a human being his nature and his history coincide, and the two together form the configuration or Gestalt of his life. Personhood is nature structured by the reflection of the mind and spirit, and by history... There are no human persons without nature, and there is no human nature without personhood. (*WJC*, p.256.)

The question however of what this human will become in and through his or her transition to the new creation depends upon what Christ became through his resurrection. Jesus Christ becomes the paradigm for humanity since in his embodiment he suffered both the historical and natural torments of death. Likewise, the nature of his embodiment in its risen form becomes the starting point for understanding what redeemed humanity can hope for. Christ was raised as a whole person, body and soul. We too expect to be raised in like manner, body and soul. What however, is involved in this? This question is really, 'how are we supposed to think of Christ's bodily resurrection?' (*WJC*, p.257.)

Moltmann summarizes the concepts encompassing the raising, resurrection, making alive, transfiguration, and transformation of Christ with the idea of 'transition'. (*WJC*, p.257.) The bodily risen Christ is the transition, the 'beginning of the new creation of mortal life in this world.' (*WJC*, p.257.)

> The raised body of Christ therefore acts as an embodied promise for the whole creation. It is the prototype of the glorified body. Consequently, a transfiguring efficacy emanates from it... (*WJC*, p.258.)

Interestingly for my purposes, Moltmann also here argues that Christ's body 'lives in the heaven of God's creative potencies and reigns with them and is no longer tied to the limited potentialities of earthly reality.' (*WJC*, p.258.) This implies ultimately that redeemed humans also will experience, in Christ and as we rule with him, God's 'creative potencies' and a new set of 'potentialities' which have hitherto not been available to us. Whatever this might entail, it at least suggests the vision that humanity will remain an open and active system since Christ's new life too has become eschatologically 'open' to these potentialities and creative potencies.

Here, have been outlined some initial points of continuity between this and the new creation. Before suggesting further points however, Moltmann also suggests where the main points of discontinuity lie. What will be done away with in the transition to the new creation? Because on the cross Christ conquered it, death itself (and all that is characterized by it) will be overcome. The 'death' and the 'mortality' of 'vulnerable human nature' will be done away with. (*WJC*, p.258.)

> With the raising of Christ, the vulnerable and mortal human nature we experience here is raised and transformed into the eternally living, immortal human nature of the new creation; and with the vulnerable human nature the non-human nature of the earth is transformed as well. This transformation is its eternal healing. But if this mortal human nature was accepted, raised, and transfigured like this, then Christ's resurrection also raised and gathered up the original good creation which is the ground of human nature, perfecting it in its own new creation. In Christ's resurrection human nature in its primordial form triumphs over its unnatural imprisonment in transience. (*WJC*, pp.258-259.)

Here we have gone from continuity to discontinuity and then back again to points of continuity. On this vision (and important to my own concerns) Christ's resurrection catches up and perfects our human nature and essence as we have experienced it in our lives. Likewise it does away with the transience and death which so far have been part of our existence. Does this also mean that the nature of human purpose (which we have argued includes work) will be completed and transformed rather than unrecognizably changed or irradiated? I believe that this follows.

'Eternal life can only be bodily life; if it is not it is not life at all.' (*WJC*, p.259.) The continuity here is essential in Moltmann's view and it lies in the fact that who we will be in eternity presupposes who and what we are and have been in this life. Moltmann captures this idea with the phrase 'enduring *somatic identity* in death.' God remembers the human being in his and her death, God knows their names, and death does not destroy their relationship (in his or her own particularity) with God. (*WJC*, p.261.) 'So what endures is the whole person, body and soul, in the Gestalt that has come into being through the history of his lived life, and in which God sees him.' (*WJC*, p.262.) However, is it simply that God 'remembers' a human in his Gestalt and that the particularities of the Gestalt themselves, once having been realized in this life, are then to be done away with in the new life? It seems not.

> What has changed? The vulnerability of this personal configuration, its mortality, its sins, its suffering and its grief will be overcome: '*This* perishable nature must put on the imperishable, and *this* mortal nature must put on immortality' (1 Cor. 15.53). Historical identity and eschatological transformation do not exclude one another, but are two sides of the one, single transition to eternal life.

When the sinfulness and the mortality are overcome, will other characteristics of the bodily existence in which men and women are created be set aside too? Will human needs and human dependence on food, air, climate and so forth be abolished? If we were to assume this, it would also mean an end to the earthly community of creation in which human beings live bodily and practically. Will human sexuality be abolished as well, so that there will no longer be 'male or female' (Gal. 3.28.), but all human beings will be 'like the angels' (Luke 20.35)? If we have to assume this, then it is not this creation which is going to be created anew, for in place of the human being who is created male and female there will be a different being altogether, and 'the second creation' will displace the first. But the eschatological new creation of this creation must surely presuppose *this whole* creation. For something new will not *take the place* of the old; it is *this same 'old'* [creation] *itself* which is going to be created anew (1 Cor. 15.39-42). The transformation into glory of this whole real creation takes place diachronically, from the last day to the first, on the day of the Lord. It is not something that happens *after* this world, but something that happens *with* this world. The life of created beings in the succession of the generations and times will *as such* be redeemed from guilt and grief and transformed into eternal joy. And from this neither human dependence on nature nor human sexuality can be excluded. (*WJC*, p.262. [ ] added.)

I have quoted Moltmann here at length for the concepts presented bring us to the heart of the discussion. The basic human characteristics of bodily existence, as well as a bodily existence itself, are seen as continuing into the new creation. The implications of this are immense. Moltmann even goes so far as to argue that the human need for food, and the like, will continue. Of course, in this vision we will not experience the transience and death which are currently associated with obtaining, preparing and eating this food. Nonetheless, the vision here, as with the garden of Eden, implies some sort of activity / cultivation and thus, work. I do not want to overstate myself at this point. I simply suggest that on the view presented above, human life in the new creation will still be fundamentally a recognizably human life. That which has gone before in human life, (here without the sin, mortality, suffering and grief) will also continue into the new, only it will be qualitatively new since it has been transformed. Human purpose therefore, will be transformed and freed from sin, mortality, suffering and grief, but it will still be the same human purpose that we currently experience. It will be the same 'open' human purpose which now includes among other things projects, and thus work. I suggest then, that the ontology of work is not a limited ontology in the sense that it is only an ontological reality in the present creation. Rather, the ontology of work is ontological because it is also a fundamental condition of being human in the new creation.

I, with Moltmann, have now made the transition however, from christology as such to eschatology, and particularly to personal eschatology. Admittedly these are fluid concepts and cannot be easily separated. However, I shall continue the discussion of personal eschatology from *The Coming of God*, Moltmann's volume specifically on eschatology.

The kinds of arguments about personal resurrection and salvation which Moltmann presents in *The Coming of God* are basically the same as those which have already been outlined. Therefore, I do not need to establish again the kind of eschatological vision that he proposes. In brief, the raising and transformation of this whole mortal life, its healing, reconciliation and completion, are the focus of his discussion. (*CoG*, p.70.) What this book adds to the earlier discussions however, is further detail to the vision and additional reflection which anticipates and answers some of the criticisms that could be made against his view. I will take up some of these points, not simply to develop Moltmann's view, but more importantly so that I can make further comment on my own construction concerning the continuation into the new creation of human purpose and thus, an ontology of work.

Early in his section on eternal life / personal eschatology Moltmann argues that our question concerning life 'is not whether our existence might possibly be immortal, and if so which part of it' (soul, mind or spirit). (*CoG*, p.53.) The question of life, and thus eternal life, is really 'will love endure, the love out of which we receive ourselves, and which makes us living when we ourselves offer it?' (*CoG*, p.53.) What does he mean by this however? He makes his argument as follows:

> But human life is livingness, and human livingness means to be interested, to be concerned. Concern in life is what we call love. True human life comes from love, is alive in love, and through loving makes something living of the other too. 'A person's real identity, we may say, is his love: his concern: his minding, not just his mind.' (*CoG*, p.53.)

Now this interest and love obviously include dimensions of interpersonal love and concern. The 'other' that is made living through love does include the personal other. This understanding is consistent with Moltmann's relational conception of being. However, here the other need not be limited to the personal other, nor could it be if life and personhood is understood as defined by our relationships with non-human reality as well as interpersonal relationships. The other here must also include all other entities. The surprise however, is that the impersonal too can become animated, and thus in a sense living, when our love embraces it. By our loving something, we give to it a new quality and significance, a new 'life'. It follows therefore, that as our life becomes an eternal life, so too, and tied up with this transition, does our concern and its object also become eternal. The vested significance which we offer to something in love thus becomes an eternal significance.

This proposal, that it is the impersonal as well as the personal which is the object of our concerns, love and interests is further suggested by the very way that Moltmann develops his discussion. In this context, because love will endure into eternal life, he is arguing for humans to fully engage in the totality of this life (including its materiality) and not to withdraw from it out of a fear of death. (*CoG*, pp.53-54.) The call is not simply to free oneself to love other persons. Rather, it is a call to embrace and love all of life and not to hold back out of a fear that it will all be lost in death.

Related to this call to life we find also the suggestion that a person's very identity is connected with his or her concerns or 'minding' about something, whatever this may be, whether human or non-human. As we have seen argued elsewhere, personal identity stems from our Gestalt, and this Gestalt includes our life's projects. In this present discussion Moltmann does not contradict his previous view. Here however, he does not refer specifically to life's projects. Rather, he addresses our concerns and 'minding' which are the motivational basis for this life of livingness / love. Here, the motivation for livingness rather than its application is in view. For consistency it must simply be assumed that this animated livingness will 'live' itself out in our life's projects as previously described.

The point is that on this view, as our love will continue into eternal life so too will our concern which is and has been embodied in our life's interests including both our relationships and projects. The implication is that not just we as persons will be saved in eternal life, but that so too will eternal life (in some way) be extended to the things that we love, the objects of our concern, including our projects. This must be the case for if it were not, we as persons would be so abstracted out of our life's contexts and thus so divorced from our Gestalts that in our disorientation and dislocation our very identities (stemming from our concerns our loves and interests) would be lost even as we were supposedly being saved.

This understanding of Moltmann's view and the implications that I (rather than he) have specifically drawn are further supported later in Moltmann's discussion of the 'immortality of the lived life'. (*CoG*, pp.71ff.) When again discussing the 'preservation of the person's identity' in the resurrection and transition to the new life, Moltmann introduces yet another line of reasoning which is meant to show that the continuity between this life and the life to come will necessarily involve our outward as well as inward realities.

> Everything that is bound up with a person's name – everything that the name means – is 'preserved' in the resurrection and transformed... What is meant here is not the soul, a 'kernel' of the person's existence, or some inward point of identity, but the whole configuration of the person's life, the whole life history, and all the conditions that are meant by his or her name. (*CoG*, p.75.)

Here the person's name is meant to represent all that a person is and has become in the context of that person's life. This use of 'name' is another reference to a person's total configuration or Gestalt, which we also call that person's 'spirit'. (*CoG*, p.75.) A person's body and soul, past and future, social and natural relationships, the 'fabric of the whole person's life' is to be preserved and transformed. (*CoG*, p.75.) 'In death, this Gestalt does not disintegrate into its several parts, but remains what it is "before God"; since the whole is more than the sum of its parts, it is also more than the disintegration of the parts.' (*CoG*, p.76.) Likewise, Moltmann later argues that 'everything that has put its mark on this life remains eternally.' (*CoG*, p.84.)

Now a few comments are in order. According to the picture here presented, and specifically according to the idea that everything that a person's 'name' means will be preserved and resurrected, it is important to recognize that this necessarily includes a person's roles, functions, purposes, webs of relationships, concerns and loves. All of these and the like having been transformed are envisioned as carrying over into the new creation. I as a totality, as the product of my life but also as an open being, will be preserved and transformed. Further, it is my natural as well as social relationships that are here specifically pointed to. It is not simply the 'inner' me, nor is it the me of my interpersonal relationships alone that will be preserved and transformed. It is the total me; the me who is a father, husband, churchman, scholar, friend, sportsman, builder, planner, dreamer, and so forth, in all of my particularity and concrete existence.

Is this however, good news? Does this understanding of the resurrection mean that I will be 'immortalized', not simply with all of my more positive qualities but also with all of my 'terrible experiences, faults, failings, and sicknesses?' Will the 'severely disabled human life' or the 'child who died young' simply as such be immortalized? (*CoG*, p.70.) Does this view – that all will be preserved and transformed that has made a mark on our lives – not lead to a vision of hell rather than heaven?

This would be so if immortalization rather than transformation were our hope. Thankfully however, 'raising' means a healing, reconciliation and completion, of all which is and has been, the good and bad. It does not mean its immortalization. (*CoG*, p.70.) Yes, resurrection means that nothing will be lost, neither our moments of happiness or pain. (*CoG*, pp.70-71.) Nor, on my view, will the concrete expressions of our beings be lost; that is, our projects and creations. These too become ontologically part of the actual created order once we have initiated them into existence out of the available possibilities, and once we have vested our love and concern upon them.

However, as I understand Moltmann's idea, this kind of preservation of all things has transformation, not immortalization, as its goal. This means the rectifying of our life histories and not their frozen preservation. (*CoG*, p.71.) If therefore, rectification forms part of the essence of salvation and transition, then it is essential that nothing (inwardly or outwardly, positively or negatively) be lost or ignored. All things stand in need of rectification: our 'best efforts', but also especially the negative and painful things that have become part of our lives. Salvation is the rectification of this life. It is not a substitution for it.

Another question however begins to emerge at this point. If the totality of this life is to be preserved and resurrected, and if the Gestalt of this life is understood to actually have a projective and formative effect upon the eventual particularity of our new and future life, does this not simply lead us to another version of justification by works? On this view of the preservation and resurrection / transformation of this lived life, are we not purely judged by our own lives? Do we not simply become slaves entrapped by what we have done or been involved with in this life? Do we not become products of our works (lived lives) in such a way that the principle of recompense rather than grace becomes the law?

Moltmann himself anticipates similar types of questions later in *The Coming of God* when dealing with the larger question of where the dead are, and specifically when he considers reincarnation. (*CoG*, pp.110-116.) Now my concern is not with Moltmann's discussion of reincarnation as such. Rather, I am interested in the general way that Moltmann answers the types of questions to which my questioning has led.

Moltmann is critical of what he calls the 'doctrine of karma'. Yet he recognizes that it is at once both close to the Abrahamic religions and remote from them. (*CoG*, p.114.) By the doctrine of karma he means the generally accepted 'law of act and destiny'. '"As one acts so one will be." "As a man sows, that he will also reap" (Gal. 6.7ff.).' (*CoG*, p.114.) Act and destiny here is not understood however, as a divine judgement. It is simply a law immanent in the world.

Moltmann's concern however, is not with this general principle as such. His concern comes when this idea is combined with Western anthropocentric ideas so that we conclude that we 'are responsible for our own fate in this world and beyond', and that we 'can save our own souls or destroy them.' (*CoG*, p.115.) He is concerned that the doctrine of karma leads in our Western context to self-justification through our works. Here Moltmann emphasizes that Christian theology sets grace over and against this view of karma. For him, and against this law of karma, grace means four things. Firstly, it is God who creates 'a new thing' and God who continually interrupts the chain of act and destiny and repeals the law of karma. Secondly, forgiveness of sins does not dispense with punishment, but is the repealing of the law of act and destiny. People are saved without the consequences of their works. Thirdly, grace means that judgment cannot consist of the consequences of evil action. God does not judge us according to what we have done. Fourthly, the

> principle of grace distinguishes very closely between person and act, and does so qualitatively. According to this principle, evil action is condemned, but the person is pardoned. People are no longer nailed down to what they have done and judged according to their works. They are freed from them in all their dignity. People are more than the sum of their works, and more than the sum of their sufferings. That is why being is more important than doing and having. (*CoG*, p.116.)

Notice here that Moltmann's view of the person, as one who has an existence in this concrete material world separate from actual applications of doing (function) and having, seems incongruous with his anthropology as sketched thus far in this chapter. (It is consistent however, with his anthropology in *On Human Dignity*.) Further, these concepts of a person's freedom from the concrete reality of his or her life seem to be at odds with his understanding of a person's preserved and resurrected Gestalt. For, up to this point Moltmann has been arguing precisely that it is the sum total of one's existence, inwardly and outwardly that must be preserved and transformed. People might be more than the sum of their works and sufferings, but as has been shown their identities include constitutionally their works and sufferings.

Here I shall not presume to reconcile the tensions for Moltmann. They may or may not be strictly resolvable within his arguments, (particularly by the qualification offered through the concept of transformation). Rather, what I shall do is to suggest both the reasons why it would be desirable to find a reconciliation of these ideas, and what the qualifications necessary for such a reconciliation might be.

It is essential for Christian theology and ethics to embrace both the ideas; the concept of grace and of a person's resurrected Gestalt. I have been arguing (throughout this section) reasons for the former. However, as the above discussion also suggests, in the process, it would be disastrous to fall into the trap of seeking self-justification through our own works. If the 'new life' is totally dependent on and deterministically established by what our Gestalts have become, rather than simply given shape by them, then this new life does become hell rather than salvation. The key question here is whether this, and ultimately Moltmann's, view of a person's Gestalt is understood as totally determining rather than simply providing the shape of the new life? For me, and I suspect for Moltmann, it would be the latter. The concept of the resurrected Gestalt is not understood as a totally determining factor of salvation. Such a concept does not rule out the fact that God, rather than humans, creates the new person. As influential as our own Gestalts are on the shape of the new life, they do not themselves due to some inherent transformative power produce the new life. Rather, God through his forgiving justifying grace creates new life from the old. The key concept in this discussion is transformation. Our new life does not depend strictly upon an act–destiny ordering. Rather, the picture is of an act - transformed (by God) destiny. The act is important not as a determinant, but because without the act there would be no concrete particularity for a transformed destiny. Now, if a particular act were different, that which would be transformed in the destiny would likewise be different. This does mean that the particularity of the person (an open system) too would be different if the act were different. At issue with grace however, is not the open particularity of the individual person as such. Rather, it is the qualitative effect that anything and everything in a person's life shall be transformed. Grace is total transformative and healing grace. No matter what the act, grace so permeates it that while incorporating the act into the new life it is transformed in such a way that it is released from the grip of death.

On this view and in this sense only, we have been and shall be formed / created by our past lives. However, we are not enslaved to or restricted by these lives. Here then, I can affirm the view of the relational / existential aspect of work as contributing to the becoming, identity, and self-realization of the person, while rejecting that this means a self-justification involving a closed 'act–destiny' ordering of human reality. Even the person who has become 'self-realized' through their work finds that this realized self is open to and indeed is still in need of transformation and rectification. The existential development of the person is not equal to his or her new life which only God's grace can bring.

Ultimately then, there is no difficulty in affirming both a person's preserved and resurrected Gestalt, and God's grace which saves us from hell, (even the hell of our current existence.) Christian theology and ethics needs both of these concepts.

With this I come to the conclusion of this section. Through these broader theological discussions I have been making the case that human purpose, as one important aspect of our Gestalt, will be preserved and transformed with the person in the transition to the new creation. Thus, work, understood as an ontological foundation of human purpose, will also be preserved and transformed with the person so that it will remain an ontological precondition of their humanness (the person is still an open system) even as they become a new creation.

The picture here has been primarily one of continuity. I have been emphasizing the similarities between humanness in this and the new creation. Yet, I have also made it clear that there are important discontinuities. Life and livingness point to the continuity, while sin, mortality and death point to the discontinuity. On this view therefore, the person will remain an open system, perfected and completed in the sense of being 'released from' sin, mortality and death and 'opened to' full flourishing as a real human person. Perfection and completion neither bring an end to human livingness, nor do they imply a radical change in the human from being an open to a closed system. Perfection and completion mean being released and given a new reality that (only as the new creation) enables the human to fully engage in penetrating the depths of humanness in a harmonious and active relationship with the rest of their environment. This environment will include relationships with both personal and non-human reality; personally humans will be in harmonious and active relationship with God and other persons, yet they will also be in harmonious, active, and mutual relationship with non-human creation. All of this 'living' will be done directly for the glory of God, but also the very process of living in this way will itself glorify God. In our glorification God is glorified. Here, then, the new creation is understood to be a new beginning rather than the end of living life for a truly human being.

This view has implications for work beyond what has already been said about its transformation and translation to the new life as an ontological precondition of eternal life. Our continued ability to take interest in, to love and thus live life will find its concrete expression in what in the new creation will be life's new projects. These projects, unlike their predecessors, will be released from transience; the conditions of sin, mortality and death. The curse on work that we find in the garden in Genesis 3 will be finally done away with in its totality so that we can both return to work as it should have been, and, go beyond what work in the initial creation could ever have been. Herein lies the newness. It is not simply a return to what should have been, but is a transition to that which can now be which simply could not have been in the original. This newness that will characterize work will involve our fully exploring life (ourselves, our environments, and God) through a new kind of active existence that could be called 'glorified work'. This exploration will involve our probing the newly recreated actualities but will also be open to new potentialities - and all will be done in the celebration of God and in celebration with God and the rest of creation.

The question now however, is whether this emerging vision of salvation that also saves human work remains consistent with the pictures of the new creation that scripture and broader theological reflection provide. I suggest that it is. Yet, it is not initially evident to many Christians that work (transformed and glorified work rather than either original or cursed work) will be part of the lived life in the new heaven and new earth. Therefore, my task is to demonstrate that this anthropology in the emerging vision of salvation is compatible with the anthropological vision of salvation as seen in the new heaven and new earth. To achieve this purpose I continue in dialogue with Moltmann. Specifically I am concerned with his vision of anthropology in the eternal state, and I will consider this through his paradigmatic categories of the sabbath and the Shekinah.

Salvation: The Sabbath and Shekinah

As I begin I need to emphasize, particularly on this topic, that in themselves Moltmann's discussions and imagery of the new creation do not directly take up or point to the question of whether work has a place within the new heaven and new earth. This is my question and not his. Therefore, the task is to generalize and extrapolate from his particulars, and to look for those characteristics in his imagery which relate either positively or negatively to my purposes. I shall demonstrate however, that there are basic elements in his imagery of the new creation that do suggest that this part of my hypothesis on the ontology of work (that there will be glorified work in the new creation) is appropriate.

Moltmann presents his vision of the new heaven and new earth in detail in *The Coming of God*. His entire discussion is structured around the differentiated yet related concepts of God's sabbath and Shekinah. He begins and ends his section on cosmic eschatology (new heaven – new earth) with these concepts and also refers to them throughout it. (*CoG*, pp.261, 317.) Therefore, I too will use and probe this structure in presenting his and my own view of creation, particularly the human, in the eternal state.

However, before looking at the meaning of these concepts in Moltmann's thought, it is important to mention initially that Moltmann's concern seems to be primarily what these sabbath and Shekinah mean for God. That is, these concepts are specifically presented and developed as God's sabbath and Shekinah. This suggests importantly that it is primarily the doctrine of God (his glory and his *telos*) and not anthropology, that Moltmann is exploring.

Nevertheless, this does not mean that it is inappropriate to ask anthropological questions in this theo-logical context. Since humans will be glorified in God, by examining God's glorified state we should also learn something about glorification for humans. Similarly, within Moltmann's view itself humans will be 'deified' in the sense that they will 'partake of the characteristics and rights of the divine nature through their community with Christ, the God-human being.' (*CoG*, p.272.) Therefore, even though Moltmann is reflecting within the doctrine of God, it becomes both possible and wholly appropriate to direct the reflections likewise to humans who will be in this sense God-like.

Having thus justified the task, I now turn to consider Moltmann's understanding of the doctrines of God's sabbath and Shekinah. In Moltmann's later thought the originally Jewish ideas of God's sabbath and God's Shekinah have become increasingly important. Yet, the complex and interdependent connections that Moltmann makes between these ideas renders understanding how he interprets and uses them somewhat of a challenge. Therefore, here I shall carefully trace Moltmann's presentation of the concepts, and where necessary I will add to it interpretive comments.

THE END IS MORE THAN THE BEGINNING

Moltmann begins his discussion of these two concepts by stating that creation should be understood in the light of redemption and not the other way around. (*CoG*, p.261.) It follows then, that the final consummation of creation is not to be primarily construed as the restoration of its initial conditions. Rather, initial creation should be understood to be completed in its consummation. The idea in Genesis of the 'completion' of the initial creation is not to be understood to mean that it was finished or perfect in the sense of being without any future. Rather, its initial completion means that it was fitting, appropriate, and corresponded to the Creator's will. On this view, its end completion will include more than was included in its beginning completion. 'The end is much more than the beginning.' (*CoG*, p.264.) This idea and the sense of movement captured in it is foundational for Moltmann's Christian interpretation of God's sabbath and Shekinah.

When Moltmann first introduces the idea of the sabbath, he presents it as the 'promise of future consummation built into the initial creation.' (*CoG*, p.264.) The sabbath itself is not creation's future glory. It is rather a built-in pointer to it. The future glory of the new creation is more than the original sabbath can capture. The future glory will involve the gathering up of the beginning (including the sabbath) into the end. Thus, there is a continuity established in that at the consummation God 'brings back everything that has ever been before.' (*CoG*, p.265.) Yet, there is also genuine newness (discontinuity) in the future glory that was not present in the old, at least not present in the same way. This newness is a going beyond that which was initially the case. The discontinuity then, is not simply the abolition of the negative. It is positively the introduction of a new good. How is this new good construed?

> What is the difference between the beginning and the consummation of creation, and what distinguishes the 'first heaven and the first earth' from the 'new heaven and the new earth'? It is the different presence of the Creator in the community of those he has created. (*CoG*, p.265.)

Here, rather than focusing upon the abolition of death as the difference between the old and the new creation, the different presence of God becomes the essential point of discontinuity. However, not only does this different presence distinguish the old from the new creation. It is also that which distinguishes the God's sabbath from his Shekinah.

THE SABBATH AND SHEKINAH INTERRELATED

According to Moltmann, the concept of God's sabbath is a way of referring to his presence. Yet it is described as a presence 'in the *time* of those he has created, or to put it more precisely, the dynamic presence of eternity in time, which links the beginning and end, thus awakening remembrance and hope.' (*CoG*, p.266.) This concept, 'in time', is the heuristic key for understanding what Moltmann believes the sabbath to be. It is a unique mode of being / temporality for God that allows God to be with us in created time in such a way that the beginning and end, the old and the new, are held together. It is this 'temporal' connectedness through God that is then supposed to awaken our remembrance and hope. This is the nature and purpose of the sabbath. The essence of the sabbath however, is that it is a particular kind of God's presence or dwelling.

The Shekinah, while similar to its sabbath counterpart, is nonetheless different. It still refers to a particular kind of God's presence / dwelling. However, as the 'eschatological indwelling of God in the "new heaven and the new earth"', it denotes God's presence in the '*space*' of his created beings. (*CoG*, p.266.) It is the idea that God is in our midst and therefore has brought eternal life. It is envisioned as the 'new Jerusalem' which becomes the 'home of God's Shekinah (Isa. 65; Ezek. 37; Rev. 21.).' (*CoG*, p.266.) The Shekinah then, is a spatial rather than a temporal concept. It deals with an understanding of God's presence in the space of creation rather than how God inter-connects and relates time in the flow of history to itself and to himself.

The sabbath then, is God's dwelling / presence in time, while the Shekinah is his dwelling / presence in space. In this respect the two concepts, sabbath and

Shekinah, are parallel. Both equally refer to God's presence. There is more to the parallel however than simply this. For Moltmann, these are also parallel concepts in that God has both a sabbath and corresponding Shekinah (a presence) in the initial creation, and a similar but different sabbath and corresponding Shekinah (a new presence) in the new creation or eternity.

In the initial creation there is the weekly sabbath and the sabbath year. However, this is also referred to by Moltmann as 'God's homeless Shekinah in the time of exile from Jerusalem, and in the far country of this world, estranged from God.' (*CoG*, p.266.) Here the sabbath and Shekinah are presented as parallel ways of viewing God's presence in the initial creation, the difference being in the perspective from which they are viewed, temporally or spatially.

As a parallel in the new creation, the new eschatological (rather than homeless) Shekinah is God's home with creation in the New Jerusalem. This is likewise represented as a new sabbath, 'the perfected sabbath in the spaces of the world.' (*CoG*, p.266.) Again eschatologically, the sabbath and Shekinah are construed as parallel ways (temporally and spatially) of referring to the same new reality of God's unified presence.

What emerges in these depictions therefore, are essentially three distinct yet interdependent parallelisms operating. The first is that the sabbath is God's presence expressed in temporal terms, while the Shekinah is God's presence expressed in spatial terms. The second is that God's presence, as both sabbath and Shekinah, is expressed and experienced in the new as well as the initial creation. The third parallel, building upon the first two, is that the sabbath is the Shekinah, and vice versa, expressed simply from a different perspective.

Now Moltmann also argues for an additional slightly different type of relationship between these concepts of God's presence, one embracing their symmetry yet doing so on a different plane. 'Sabbath and Shekinah are related to each other as promise and fulfillment, beginning and completion.' (*CoG*, p.266.) Moltmann is here referring to their complementing relationship with each other rather than their parallel nature. With reference to promise and fulfillment, the sabbath is reconstrued singularly and located solely in time in the initial creation. The Shekinah likewise has been made into a singular concept and is used solely to refer to the eschatological presence / indwelling of God in the new creation. The key point here is that the Shekinah is the 'end' that encompasses, but which is much greater than and thus transcends the beginning (the sabbath). Here surfaces the importance of the initial comments about the necessity of understanding creation in the light of redemption and not vice versa. The end, the redemption, the Shekinah, is the new and as such it is 'much greater' than the beginning, the initial creation, the sabbath. This does not mean that the Shekinah annihilates the sabbath. Rather, the former embraces the latter but then transforms it into something genuinely new so that the old, while still present, really has gone and the new has come. Its newness however is not to be understood as a realization of that which was inherent in the old. It is a genuinely new thing that is done by God with the old. Therefore the Shekinah, (still properly understood also as the eternal sabbath) is not simply a repetition of the initial sabbath in the new creation. It is something genuinely new and different but embracing the ethos of the old.

> In the sabbath, creation holds within itself from the beginning the true promise of its consummation. In the eschatological Shekinah, the new creation takes the whole of the first creation into itself, as its own harbinger and prelude, and completes it. Creation begins with time and is completed in space. The temporality of the first creation is itself its promise, and its openness for the new, eternal creation. (*CoG*, p.266.)

In this complementary rather than parallel scheme, the Shekinah rather than the sabbath becomes the predominant way of expressing the eschatological vision of the new heaven and new earth. This however, does not negate the vision of interchangeableness and balance that is generated by their parallel relationships. However, it does further define and in many ways limit what the nature of this parallel continuity can mean. The complementary relationship between these concepts as promise and fulfillment, is the relationship which moves the whole idea of God's presence forward to something genuinely new. Their parallel relationships, on the other hand, is that which preserves the continuity between the loci of movement. Herein lies the inner unity between the parallel and complementary aspects of these concepts. The continuity must be understood in the light of the direction of movement and not the other way around. For the end (the goal of the movement, the Shekinah) is much more than the similarity (the beginning, the sabbath). This way of interpretively combining both the parallel and complementary relationships between the sabbath and Shekinah will later be important, for it will guide my own conclusions concerning the vision of the new heaven and new earth.

Now Moltmann, similarly seeking to draw together the various relationships in his sabbath and Shekinah construct, suggests that there is 'inner unity' to the concepts themselves. (*CoG*, p.266.)

> It is to be found in the *menuhah,* the rest to which God came on the sabbath of creation and which he seeks when he desires to dwell in his creation. It does not only mean the end of God's creative and historical unrest; it is also in the positive sense the eternal bliss and eternal peace of God himself. That is why this repose of God's is often linked with 'God's desire'. That is the divine eschatology. Psalm 132.13f. shows the connection between sabbath and Shekinah: 'The Lord has chosen Zion; he has desired it for his habitation; "This is my resting place for ever; here will I dwell".' (*CoG*, p.266.)

The question of what exactly the idea of rest / God's rest means, both related to the initial and new creation, will be returned to shortly. Here I simply point out that the concept of rest, as the inner unity, is meant to accompany the idea of presence (expressed in terms of God's dwelling) as the key for understanding

Moltmann's Christian interpretation of the sabbath and Shekinah. The importance of this is its suggestion that God's dwelling, and thus ours in and with God, must be described and understood specifically in terms of rest.

Admittedly, by themselves these concepts of sabbath and Shekinah say little about what to envision concretely in the new heaven and new earth with respect to God, humanity, or non-human creation. Indeed, this does not even seem to be their purpose in Moltmann's discussion. Rather, for Moltmann they function as qualifiers rather than quantifiers. His usage of the concepts is as a kind of interpretative grid through which to filter the concepts and imagery associated with eternity. They are the guides which give the structure (or ethos) of the discussion rather than its building blocks. This is suggested by the very design of Moltmann's chapter on the new heaven and new earth as well as its content.

The actual building blocks for Moltmann's vision of the new heaven and new earth in this context include in order: the question of whether the world will be annihilated or consummated (*CoG*, pp.267-279.), a discussion of the end of time in the eternity of God (*CoG*, pp.279-295.), a parallel discussion of the end of space in the presence of God (*CoG*, pp.296-308.), and then finally an examination of the imagery of the cosmic temple, which is the heavenly Jerusalem (*CoG*, pp.308-319.).

I will here diverge from strictly tracing the development of Moltmann's discussion. Yet I will continue to examine portions of it as necessary for my own purposes. For the task of demonstrating that it is appropriate to posit a glorified form of work in the new heaven and new earth, I will need to build the following arguments around three fundamental questions; the question of time in God's eternity and ours, the question of rest in God's eternity and ours, and the question of the specific imagery associated with God's eternity and ours.

THE QUESTION OF TIME IN GOD'S AND OUR ETERNITY

The question of time in eternity asks, what will come with the end of our currently experienced time of this creation? What, if anything in the new creation will replace our currently experienced transient time? If we grant that the end is a new beginning, and that the end of time in the eternity of God is the beginning of something else, related to time but new and therefore different from it, then what will this 'transformed time' be and how will we, with God, experience it? Are eternity and eternal life to be depicted in terms of timelessness or in terms of a transformed and new time / temporality?

These questions are important for my purpose because the vision of eternity, which includes human participation in new projects in the new heaven and new earth (and thus a new and glorified form of work as their ontological basis) necessarily presupposes something like a corresponding new 'temporality' in and from which these projects can proceed. The idea of a project itself presupposes the necessity of some reality, which we usually depict in temporal terms. We must do something before, (decide, plan,) do something during (act, develop, construct) and do something at the end (conclude, reflect upon, enjoy and so forth) to have a project. If no such correspondingly new concept for temporality exists, then this part of the hypothesis, that the ontology of work exists in the new creation as well as the initial creation, is disproved. That is, if eternity is construed as timelessness, as having no alternative form of temporality at all, then it will be logically impossible to 'do' anything / to have an active livingness in eternal life. However, if there is a 'new temporality' which corresponds to eternal livingness, then it is logically possible to also posit a new and transformed ontology of work, call it what you will, that allows for human 'projects', in and with God, as a part of our new life's livingness.

What then, is the eschatological future of time? Moltmann's answer to this question is again a quite complex and nuanced argument. It is beyond my purpose here to offer a full and fully critical assessment of the totality of his view. Yet, his conclusions on this question of time have important implications for my hypothesis. What I propose to do therefore, is to sketch his reasoning so as to highlight and interact with his conclusions. Since my concerns are with his concluding picture as such, here I will simply assume rather than critique many of the details of his arguments.[7]

Essential for Moltmann's discussion of time is the apostle Paul's concept of the eschatological moment. (1 Cor. 15:52.) (*CoG*, p.279.) This moment is not to be understood abstractly, as it is in some theology, as that which can be existentialised to refer to an immediate religious experience. (*CoG*, pp.292ff.) Rather, it is that which comes with the end of time, the 'last day', the 'day of resurrection', the 'last trumpet'. It is the 'moment of eternity' when all of the dead will be raised diachronically. (*CoG*, pp.279-280.) 'In content it is defined as "the day of the Lord", to which all times are simultaneous.' (*CoG*, p.280.) This moment is 'the completion of history and creation, its perfecting into the kingdom of glory in which God himself "indwells" his creation.' (*CoG*, p.280.) It is when the temporal creation becomes the eternal creation. (*CoG*, p.294.)

What this eschatological moment means for time is that, strictly speaking, time shall be no more. However, it is not an annihilation of time or of all temporality as such that is in view. Rather, the picture here is that 'temporal creation will be transformed into eternal creation, and spatial creation into omnipresent creation.' (*CoG*, p.280.) Time in the eschatological moment will be 'gathered up, fulfilled and transformed through the eternity of the new creation.' (*CoG*, p.280.) It will not become, 'the absolute eternity of God himself; it is the relative eternity of the new creation, which participates in God's absolute eternity.' (*CoG*, p.280.) The word that Moltmann borrows from patristic and medieval theology to describe God's time rather than earthly time is *aeon* or *aevum*. (*CoG*, p.280.)

---

[7] Importantly, in his view of time and space here Moltmann is generally aware of and consistent with the tenor of the discussions of time and space currently being considered in physics. See for example: Davies, *About Time* (1995).

Clearly Moltmann envisions an appropriate counterpart to time in the new heaven and new earth. He argues for a transition from temporal to eternal creation, from our time to aeonic time. What then, is the nature of this aeonic time in relation to our current time?

In the classical and Platonic philosophical tradition, time is understood to have as its opposite timelessness. Here, temporality / time is opposed to eternity, as change is opposed to the unchanging. (*CoG*, p.281.) Theology too has often followed this path of definition. However, Moltmann argues that this is inappropriate. Christian theology should not continue to define time and eternity respectively as the opposites, as changeability and unchangeability. God's eternity is something other than 'the mere negation of temporality.' As Moltmann describes it, God's eternity is 'the fulness of creative life' and therefore, it is an 'opening for time in eternity.' (*CoG*, p.281.)

Moltmann presents two models for understanding this opening 'for' time 'in' eternity. The first, using personal metaphors, talks of God creatively resolving within himself, and in his 'eternal time', to create. The second, using spatial metaphors, talks of God's self-restricting to allow room for the other, for created time and space, within his eternity. (*CoG*, pp.281-282.) Both of these concepts, depicting a self-conscious and active God, are meant to suggest the same thing. God has made space for time and a time for time in his time which is eternity. Time and eternity are not opposites. Eternity is not to be understood as the mere negation of temporality or as timelessness. Rather, eternal time is a different mode of being than earthly time. Eternity (eternal time) as a mode of being (like temporal time with its transient past, present and future) is still a type of temporality in that it allows room for God to have an active, resolving existence within himself. Likewise, those who will eschatologically be included in eternal time will too still be able to have an acting and resolving existence.

In summarising the implications of Moltmann's pictures here, even God himself in his eternity experiences himself and creatively resolves to do certain things. For God to experience and resolve there is required some kind of condition within God, akin to temporality, (what Moltmann calls '*primordial aeon*') which provides the space metaphorically speaking for God to be the personal and active God expressed in the Bible. An eternal aeonic time construed as timelessness would simply preclude this idea of a personal and active God. Likewise, as we will be eschatologically included in God's eternity, timelessness would exclude a personal and active life on our part. Aeonic time then, cannot mean timelessness. It cannot be the negation of time.

Ultimately for Moltmann the difference between our time and aeonic time (including both God's absolute eternity – past and future, and our future relative eternity) lies in death, 'which is only earthly, not heavenly.' (*CoG*, p.282.) Death and the transience that death entails, rather than temporality itself, is the distinguishing factor between these two kinds of time. The fact that both are described as forms of time is important for it further demonstrates that the opposite of time is not timelessness but rather a different kind of temporality.

Aeonic time can be thought of as a time corresponding to the eternity of God: a time without beginning and end, without before and after. The figure, or configuration, of time that corresponds to the one, unending eternity is *cyclical* time, which has no end. (*CoG*, p.282.)

Care must be taken here not to attribute more to this metaphor of cyclical time than Moltmann himself does. He is simply trying to express the idea of a 'timeless form of time' to help us conceive of time without transience. (*CoG*, p.282.) Although I would argue that the image of cyclical time is ultimately inadequate, it at least allows us to preserve the sense of flow and movement of being which is necessary for existence while also avoiding the idea of loss (death) which is necessarily a part of transient time.

Moltmann's cosmology then presents us with a '*double form of time*' in creation. 'Earthly creation exists within the context of passing time, but this earthly time, for its part, belongs within the context of the aeonic time of 'the invisible world' continually touching it and being touched by it.' (*CoG*, p.283.) Again, eternity and time are not opposites. They are two corresponding forms of the same idea – time. They are inter-related through the latter's inclusion in the former, but they are still different in that time includes transience and death while eternity does not.

Interestingly, again in this context Moltmann employs his promise–fulfillment understanding of sabbath and Shekinah (with its internal logic) to illustrate the idea of created time's transience. Time in the initial creation is the 'time of promise' and the essence of this time is 'futurity'. That is, earthly time is an 'open, a-symmetrical, imbalanced system which is aligned towards its future.' (*CoG*, p.283.) As it is necessarily always aligned towards its future, it can never be fulfilled as such. If it were, it would cease to be time. Time, and thus creation, is directed toward its fulfilment, as the sabbath is directed toward the Shekinah. (*CoG*, p. 283.) Created time is a constant moving toward its fulfilment - eternal time.

However, the 'time pattern' in the initial creation does not only present time's forward moving and 'irreversible flow':

> it also confers time that is rhythmically interrupted and ordered through the sabbath days and the sabbath years. Rhythm is at once repetition and progress. In the rhythm of the sabbath interruptions of 'time's flow', earthly creation – human beings, animals and the earth – vibrate in the cosmic liturgy of eternity. The everflowing stream of time regenerates itself from the presence of eternity in the sabbath rhythm of the days, the years, and the seventh year, thus preparing for the messianic sabbath of the End-time creation and, through that, for the eschatological sabbath of the eternal creation. (*CoG*, pp.283-284.)

This observation is critical for my own purposes for in addition to further describing the nature of earthly time, it helps us to understand the ethos of the sabbath in the time of the initial creation; and it is this ethos that must be preserved in its eschatological transformation to Shekinah. The sabbath in the initial creation is not, as some understand it, simply a limitation on human work (although it does do this). More fundamental is the idea that the sabbath relativises work in the context of providing a rhythm to time which in turn is itself an eschatological anticipation of God's eternal presence. The issue of the sabbath then, and the sabbath rest, involves its being a temporal way of expressing God's presence in the rhythm of this created time's flow. Its rest is not first and foremost concerned with limiting human or Divine activity. It does this in the initial creation, but in the context of ordering time to reflect its ultimate eschatological transformation. When time and sabbath are eschatologically transformed, will the relativisation of and restriction on work too be transformed into something else? Theologically this is necessarily the case. I will return to this idea shortly when considering the question of the meaning of rest in the sabbath and Shekinah / initial and new creation.

What we have seen emerging in Moltmann's discussion of time's end, is a view that eternal life will include a corresponding eternal 'time' in which to live. Further, we also find that this new time is sufficient for living. Aeonic eternity is ultimately the eternity (time) 'of the new life of the future world.' (*CoG*, p.291. note 82.) 'Eternal life has nothing to do with timelessness and death, but is *full-filled life.*' (*CoG*, p.291.) Fulfilled life will take place in fulfilled time, and this fulfilled time is eternal aeonic time in the sense that it is time filled with eternity. (*CoG*, p.295.) Moltmann states:

> However we may imagine this, it is the very opposite of 'a deathlike silence'. If we have to think of it as the time of eternal life, then we have to imagine it as the time of eternal livingness... The purposeful time of history is fulfilled in the cyclical movement of life's eternal joy in the unceasing praise of the omnipresent God. The preferred images for eternal life are therefore dance and music, as ways of describing what is as yet hardly imaginable in this impaired life. (*CoG*, p.295.)

The one potential point of difficulty is Moltmann's image of eternal time as cyclical time. If this is simply understood to mean a rhythmic flow of time which excludes the loss that transient time necessarily entails, then there is little problem with the image. Indeed this appears to be his meaning with the expression a 'mutual perichoresis between eternity and time'. (*CoG*, p.295.) If however, the image is pushed so that this new time becomes a type of simultaneous circular existence, an eternal moment, which excludes also any re-conceived formulation of a transformed before, during, and after, then the image is inadequate. Then the notion of human 'project' disappears. For, as earlier suggested in the discussion of relational ontology, being necessarily includes the idea of relationship. Relationship necessarily includes the idea of reciprocity and the movement of mutuality (either moving something or being moved by something). Movement necessarily implies with it some kind of temporal space which allows something akin to progression; that is, some sort of before, during, and after. Indeed, even in Moltmann's account, there was a 'time', a *primordial moment*, in God's primordial aeonic time, when God decided to create. (*CoG*, p.282.) Likewise, eternal aeonic time, both absolute and relative, should also include this same possibility. What I envision here, is not a transient before, during, and after that is characterized by loss. Rather, it is an aeonic before, during and after, which preserves all of the movement so that nothing is lost. If Moltmann's image of cyclical time can embrace this concept, then I am happy to affirm it. If not, a new image is in order.

I now return to my initial questions concerning time and conclude with Moltmann that time too will be transformed in the new creation into something that allows for the active living of life. Transience and death rather than the 'temporal space' for living is what will be destroyed. Given this conclusion, I have no logical difficulty (with respect to the question of time) in affirming that since there will be a time in the new creation there can also be human projects, and thus work, as a part of life's new livingness. The view that human purpose, which includes work, will be transformed in the new creation need not then conflict with the view of time that we find in eternity. Rather they correspond to each other. With transformed human purpose comes the transformed condition / 'time' necessary for the realisation of this purpose. The risen life of Jesus, into which we enter, is not the end of activity, but the beginning of a new activity, the resurrection life.

Consequently, since work has already been demonstrated to be fundamental to humanness as ontologically part of human purpose, and since human purpose too will be preserved but transformed in the new creation, it is also appropriate to add glorified work (which becomes a type of eschatological play) to the list of eternal life's preferred images of dance and music. This is appropriate, even necessary, for glorified work has already been expressed in terms which make it too a type of aesthetic experience. It has been presented as a fundamental precondition for creative projects which themselves are the expressions and explorations of our total glorified humanness (and of glorified non-human nature) in harmonious communion with God in his glory, with other glorified humans, and with glorified nature. With this depiction, glorified work too became essentially both playful and artistic. It became an aesthetic category which, as such, should at least be located beside dance and music, if not made a more fundamental description of these celebrative activities.

THE QUESTION OF REST IN GOD'S AND OUR ETERNITY

Now the question becomes whether this vision of glorified work in aeonic time conflicts with another concept essential to the idea of the new creation; namely, that of God's eternal sabbath rest and ours? If glorified work cannot be understood as encompassed by the ethos of the eternal sabbath rest, (due primarily to the fact that it is further creative activity) then this part of my hypothesis either fails completely, or needs radical modification. Importantly, if the ethos of eternal sabbath rest precludes the vision of glorified work, then likewise will it preclude the images of dance and music since each of these three images involves intensely creative activity rather than simply reflection, contemplation or passivity. This means that if work fails the criterion of 'rest', then these other two preferred images likewise will fail and cease to be preferred images.

The primary concern however, is not with dance and music but with work. Yet the issues and questions involved are the same. Generally, they include what is particularly meant by God's eternal sabbath rest, and what are the applications of this for our eternal livingness as we participate with God in this sabbath rest? Specifically they ask whether God's eternal sabbath rest means the end of both human and divine activity and creativity?

Most of the theological resources needed to answer these questions have been developed already in the discussions with Moltmann about God's sabbath and Shekinah. What is needed by way of summary is to indicate what these resources are, and then apply them to the questions at hand.

As previously suggested, God's eternal sabbath, his eschatological dwelling in his new creation, must be described and understood specifically as his eternal rest. Therefore, so too must our eschatological existence in and with God be depicted as an eternal rest. As Moltmann has suggested, the inner unity of the dual modes of God's presence, sabbath and Shekinah, is found in God's *menuah*, his rest. (*CoG*, p.266.)

Rest then, is a common characteristic to both the initial sabbath and the eschatological sabbath. However, according to the logic of the new creation as Moltmann has presented it (the end is much more than the beginning) rest, even God's rest, like everything else will undergo an eschatological transformation and likewise become something new, something more than it was in the initial creation. For the initial sabbath rest is itself the promise of its future consummation. The consummated sabbath rest then, will be the beginning of a new and greater reality. It will be a completed rest and thus a new kind of rest both for God and for creation.

Moltmann himself appears to capture this idea of continuity yet newness when he comments that 'creation begins with time and is completed in space.'[8] (*CoG*, p.266.) Notice that the change from the beginning to the end involves here more than simply a movement occurring within a non-differentiated concept – time. The change from the beginning to the end, and thus from God's earthly sabbath presence (sabbath) to his eternal sabbath presence (Shekinah) will also involve a categorical transition – from time (history) to space (eternity). This is why the construct itself, sabbath-Shekinah is used, rather than simply the imagery of earthly sabbath - eternal sabbath. The idea is that the end needs to be understood as more than the beginning.

Another way to express this categorical change is to also notice the meta-

---

[8] This does not mean that Moltmann denies the reality of time and space in common-sense terms in the initial creation (where space-time is a unified concept).

phorical change that Moltmann employs. He initially represents the idea of God's earthly resting presence (sabbath) as God resting 'from' his work. The imagery here is of a rhythmic flow of God's presence metaphorically in time. First, God creates, next he withdraws from his creation, and in so doing he then again 'comes to himself'. (*GC*, pp.278-279.) The rhythm is represented by God first being free 'for' his works, and then becoming free 'from' them. This is the very work-rest rhythm which is to be repeated in time with the earthly sabbath. This metaphor then, is one expressing God's presence temporally. His final eschatological resting however, is metaphorically depicted differently. It is understood in terms of a resting place. Eschatologically, God rests 'in' his works, in the new Jerusalem. This is clearly a change from a temporal to a spatial metaphor. Again the idea is that there has been a transition for God's presence from time to space.

Now this categorical and metaphorical shift corresponds to the sabbath and Shekinah's complementary (promise–fulfillment) relationship. Of course, thinking in terms of their parallel relationships other things can be said. For example, even in the initial creation God rested both 'from' and 'in' his works. (*GC*, pp.279-280.) This corresponds to his having both a sabbath and Shekinah presence in the initial creation.

My interest however, is not with the implications of the parallel relationships between sabbath and Shekinah. Rather it is with the vision generated by the complementary relationship. Captured therein is the idea that the eschatological sabbath is something more than simply the original sabbath. As previously argued, the Shekinah is not simply a repetition of the initial sabbath, it is something much more, something genuinely new.

However, this new rest should not be seen as annihilating the former kind of rest. In as much as the initial sabbath rest will be taken up into the eschatological sabbath rest, its very ethos as rest (if not its specific application) will need to be preserved and encompassed within the new. How is this possible? How could such a transformation be described concretely which preserves the ethos of rest while also producing a new kind of rest? Here again the earlier conclusion must be kept in mind that the complementary relationship (promise-fulfillment) between the sabbath and Shekinah must be used to interpret its parallel relationships.

The earthly sabbath rest is the sabbath (God's presence) in the 'time' of the initial creation. As suggested, its construal as a temporal construct is the key for grasping its ethos in the initial creation. Since it is as such a temporal conception, the idea of the rhythms of time, that is, the rhythms of creative work and reflective rest, become a central application of its ethos. As long as there is a creation with and within transient time, this, or a similar rhythmic application of its ethos needs to be preserved. A sabbath rest from work is clearly part of its application for the initial creation.[9]

However, need the cessation of and from work also be an application of the sabbath ethos in the new creation which is no longer a creation in transient time? I suggest that it need not, and actually cannot be. In the new creation there will no longer be the rhythmic / temporal anticipation of perfect peace and harmony; that is, there will no longer be an earthly sabbath with its regulatory work–rest cycle. Nor will there be the need for such a sabbath. The eternal sabbath 'rest', which is more and greater than the initial, will have been fully realised and will have become the existent reality when God himself becomes wholly present 'in' and with his new creation. The limitation on work therefore, (as part of the earthly sabbath) will have served its purpose as a promise in time of both God's future Shekinah, and life's future and eschatological harmony and balance. Neither the limitation on work nor the earthly sabbath will any longer be needed. Nor will they any longer be appropriate to the new kind of space and time of eternal livingness. When God is all in all, all relationships will be characterised by full harmony and mutuality / rest. They will involve the active and creative give and take necessary for relationship. The inter-relationships between God, humanity, and the non-human creation will be so empowered with the divine life, so 'life generating', that both divine and human (and also even natural) creativity and activity can and necessarily will be released from all limitation for their full and harmonious expression, all to the greater glory of God.

What I am arguing then, is that with the transition from the earthly sabbath rest to the eschatological sabbath rest, we will find that the conditions of life have been so transformed that the very application of the earthly sabbath rest too will be changed. The restriction on work therefore, as part of the temporal rhythmic work-rest cycle of the sabbath, will pass away. The distinction between 'work', 'rest', and 'play' will disappear.

In what way however, will the 'rest' ethos be preserved if its concrete earthly application is bypassed? The key to answering this is found in the sabbath's transition from time to space and thus, in God's transition from dwelling with his creation in time to his indwelling creation in space. Rest, for God and us, will cease being a rhythmic resting 'from' in time, and become a resting

---

[9] This view is not only consistent with the conception of sabbath presented in *The Coming of God*. It is also consistent with the discussion of the sabbath presented by Moltmann in *God in Creation*. In this earlier book Moltmann argues that the whole work of creation was performed for the sake of the sabbath, as a feast without end. (*GC*, p.277.) Because of this, because in it the initial creation is blessed and sanctified and because it is the feast of redemption which Jesus too affirms, Christians should also retain a sabbath observance. (*GC*, pp.291-292.) This means among other things that 'in the sabbath stillness men and women should no longer intervene in the environment through their labour.' (*GC*, p.277.) The initial sabbath is a rest from creative and productive work in the initial creation.

place, a resting 'in'. Rest eschatologically first means that God comes to a set-tled habitation. He ceases his restless and creative wandering and his Shekinah finds its peaceful and harmonious home within his creation. We his creation find our rest correspondingly, in that as God is with us we receive our eternal life, our eternal happiness. (*CoG*, p.319.) Thus, eternal rest becomes redirected and applied as a kind of existence, as an eternal living of life characterised by perfect and harmonious relationships between God, humans, and nature.

With this redirection, the question of work becomes irrelevant to the ques-tion of rest. No longer at issue is whether eternal rest excludes the idea of glori-fied work. The question itself is mistaken for it commits the error of mixing categories. The point is that eternal 'rest' (peace or harmony) will completely permeate the entirety of the new life and new existence. Rather than being a restriction on creative activity and human projects, rest becomes the way to characterise them. Rest becomes their release to be. Glorified work then is glo-rified work precisely because it is characterised by the new eternal rest. An-other way to express this idea is that eschatologically work will become so permeated with the sabbath that it becomes freed and glorified work.[10]

This does not mean that glorified work is necessary, as such, to eternal rest. Just the opposite is true. Eternal rest is necessary for glorified work. That is, I am not suggesting that the condition of eternal rest establishes or even proves the idea of glorified work. This has not been the approach. Rather, the reason for positing glorified work lies in its being ontologically a part of our human-ness and livingness which will be preserved and transformed in eternal life. The point here is simply that my conception of glorified work in no way conflicts with the idea of eternal rest. Actually, more than simply the negation of the negative, I can state it affirmatively that glorified work positively corresponds to the theological vision of eternal rest in that it allows for the concrete particu-lar life for which rest becomes the characterization.

THE QUESTION OF THE SPECIFIC IMAGERY ASSOCIATED WITH GOD'S ETERNITY AND OURS

Having argued that neither the question of time nor the question of rest poses difficulties for the view that there will be glorified work (ontologically grounded in transformed humanness) in the new creation, what remains is the final question of whether the actual theological and biblical imagery associated with God's and our eternity precludes such an idea? I suggest that it does not, and to demonstrate this I will continue to dialogue with Moltmann specifically drawing upon his discussion in *The Coming of God* entitled 'The Cosmic Tem-ple: The Heavenly Jerusalem'. (*CoG*, pp.308-319.)

---

[10] I suggest that Barth in his discussion of the 'Hole Day' in his dogmatics, and with reference to the initial creation rather than the future new creation, was probing for an idea similar to this concept of work permeated with sabbath. See: Barth, *Church Dog-matics*, III 4 (1961), pp.50-63.

Now the specific imagery referring to the new heaven and new earth, particularly in Rev. 21-22, is not firstly meant to capture completely (in concrete material terms) all of the particulars of that coming reality. Its purpose is to serve primarily as a prophetic encouragement for those Christians in this world who are resisting its evils, the evils of Babylon / Rome. (*CoG*, p.308.)

To accomplish this purpose the biblical author employs the images (which Moltmann summarizes as) a heavenly Jerusalem, city of God, crystal temple and garden city. Each of these images is important for the project of resistance for each encourages believers with the promise of the coming reality of God's cosmic Shekinah, his 'immediate presence which interpenetrates everything', his 'unmediated and direct glory', and, their vindication. (*CoG*, p.317.)

This means that the imagery itself is not given specifically to answer my more speculative questions concerning what we might or might not do in eternity. However, modestly interpreted, the visions are nevertheless instructive for showing us something of the nature of eternity; for they show us something about both God and our eternal reality. Moltmann himself seems to concur when he writes: 'But the visions offer the cosmic image of a different world which accords wholly with God, because he himself dwells in it.' (*CoG*, p.308.) Therefore, to conceptualise more broadly this coming different world I shall explore briefly its general characteristics (rather than explore all of its particulars which have been given for a different purpose). Herein I shall find a vision of eternity that will be useful for many different purposes.

To begin to establish a wider vision of eternity I want to consider the foundational imagery of the heavenly Jerusalem. The heavenly Jerusalem to the theological eye is seen as a holy city; the city of God, cosmic temple, and garden city. (*CoG*, p.313.) Interestingly however, the prototype, the earthly Jerusalem, was viewed by the first Christians ambivalently as both a place of hope but likewise as a place of terror. It was a place of hope for it is where the risen Messiah appeared. (*CoG*, p.309.) (It is thus fitting that it would become a symbol of the new creation.) It was a place of terror however, in that it first was where the godless powers crucified God's Messiah. (*CoG*, p.308.) Eventually, after the destruction of the earthly Jerusalem in A.D. 70, the apocalyptic image of a heavenly Jerusalem became the preferred image of hope. It became the 'symbol of the hoped-for new creation of the world, God's dwelling'. (*CoG*, p.310.)

It is interesting to notice here how a normal and ambivalent product of human culture, a city, could come to symbolize God's new creation. Of course, the logic of redemption is again at work. The old is taken up into the new (there is continuity), but the new is genuinely something new (there is likewise discontinuity).

Now why was the image of a city chosen to represent God's eschatological indwelling? Moltmann, following Richard Bauckham, offers several important reasons specific to its role as a symbol of resistance. For my immediate purposes however, it is sufficient to note that at the very least it would have been an appropriate symbol because the ancient Christian world was a world of cities. (*CoG*, p.311. note 111.) The Christians were city dwellers and the heathen were called villagers. (*CoG*, p.311.) The political and social implications of this granted, the immediate thing to notice however, is that it is a city, a specifically human invention, which is chosen to represent and be the place of God's new indwelling. One might have expected to find a garden (Eden) as the preferred image for God's dwelling place since it would have been a divine rather than human creation. Would not God most appropriately dwell in his creation symbolically in something that he himself has created rather than in something created specifically by humans? This is not the case however. The biblical writers apparently did not have a problem using imagery that itself was an ambivalent product of human civilization and culture. I would not want to push this point too far, but this suggests again the idea that the eschatological transformation of human particularity, rather than its annihilation, is a goal of redemption. Human culture has produced something (a new ontological reality) - a city, which when transformed by God shall continue in the new creation. Further, it will be taken up by God and God himself will indwell his creation symbolically in it. Fundamentally this suggests according to the imagery that, as transformed, human projects are appropriate to the new creation and to God's presence.

This idea, of both continuity and discontinuity, of the human taken up into the divine, is further developed by an additional image for the eternal city that Moltmann highlights and explores.

> The city of God is the perfect '*garden* city'. In it the abundance of life and the beauty of the Garden of Eden return, but it is more than just paradise regained. As city, it fulfils the need and longing of men and women to build a living place of their own for human fellowship and culture. As the perfect city, it fulfills the history of human civilization, which according to the biblical saga began when Cain, the city-builder (Gen. 4.17), murdered his brother Abel, the nomadic shepherd. The new Jerusalem holds within itself the Garden of Eden ([Rev.] 22.1ff.) and is an image of perfect harmony between civilisation and nature. It thereby also consummates the history of earthly nature with human beings. The city of God lives in nature, and nature lives in the city of God. 'The garden city' was an ancient ideal of the *polis* for many peoples. (*CoG*, pp.314-315.)

This garden city (combining the realities created by both God and humans: garden and city) fulfils human civilization by being the perfect city, the perfect dwelling place for both God and humanity. As civilisation's fulfillment however it also suggests, not the annihilation or end of, but rather a new beginning to human civilization. It suggests a new communal livingness that shall again take form in what could be called transformed and freed, or, glorified human civilization. Thus, here is yet another way to express the idea that human projects (here cities) are appropriate to the nature of the new creation.

With this proposal I have returned again to the logic of redemption which takes up the old but produces with it something new. This logic is found in the vision of the new Jerusalem which is an envisioned garden city, but this city of God is likewise depicted, using this same logic, as God's crystal temple. How is this so?

Moltmann argues: 'As city of God, the new Jerusalem is paradise, at once the holy city and the cosmic temple.' (*CoG*, p.313.) It is a paradise in that it contains, like Eden, the water of life and the tree of life. (*CoG*, p.313.) Herein we find that the initial, the garden, is gathered up in the new. Further, the new Jerusalem is a holy city in that 'it fulfils the ideal of the ancient city, as a place where heaven and earth meet, at earth's central point, the point from which God rules his world and his humanity, not through power but through the force of attraction.' (*CoG*, p.313.) Here is found a combination of the old, an earthly city, taken up with the new, God's universal and yet attractive rule.

This city however, is further seen as a crystal temple. The temple signifies God's indwelling presence. It is crystal in that it is the city of light, transparent for the 'omnipresent light of God'. (*CoG*, p.314.) Herein is a specific allusion to the Shekinah, which was present in the temple in the initial creation, but which becomes much more in the temple in the new creation; a crystal temple.

With this I have returned to the idea that the primary importance of the imagery is to illustrate God's new Shekinah, his new indwelling presence with his creation. At issue is not simply a conception of the future earthly reality, but what kind of reality it will be with God indwelling it, when God is all in all. It must be admitted that initially the question of whether there will be glorified work in the new creation seems irrelevant to this specific imagery of the new creation. Yet this is not the case. Firstly, there is nothing in the imagery itself that would deny this hypothesis (and demonstrating this has been my first task). Actually, as we might expect, we have found in the imagery the same theological logic as we have found elsewhere (that the end gathers up but is more than the beginning). While this does not tell us specifically that the hypothesis is correct, it does at least suggest that since there is a strong case elsewhere for its plausibility, and since the logic there is the same as the logic here, then the burden of proof here is to show that the hypothesis cannot be reconciled with the imagery.

Secondly, the imagery generally suggests that human products and projects (here a city) are appropriate to the new creation (in as much as they are gathered up, and as long as they are transformed). Thirdly, the imagery of a fulfilled ancient city implies what I have also argued elsewhere, that there will be genuine community and continued but new human livingness in the new heaven and new earth. This livingness then, as also suggested, can only be concretely realised through the projects that are the concrete realisations of mutual relationships. Finally, the imagery of a garden city implies more than simply a new community between God, nature and humanity. It also is an allusion back to the Garden of Eden and suggests a gathering up and transformation of it. If this is so, would it not be legitimate to also posit that as in Eden there will be the transformed and corresponding task of the care and cultivation of the garden?

Does not the fact that Eden has an eschatological future also suggest that human work (which was initially mandated in Eden) likewise has an eschatological future? Without pushing this imagery too far this proposition, or something akin to it, seems to be in order.

Again therefore, we find that we have overcome a possible objection to the hypothesis that there will be glorified work (ontologically grounded in transformed humanness) in the new creation. Actually this imagery itself has shown itself to be useful for my purposes. The given images of the new creation do not argue against my hypothesis. They actually make room for it in that they suggest that human creations will be taken up and transformed in the new creation.

With this conclusion then, all three possible objections may be set aside, or, more specifically each together can be used positively to demonstrate the plausibility of the hypothesis. Having thus finally considered what are the most important potential objections to the second part of the book's overall hypothesis, I suggest that this part of the hypothesis has been adequately demonstrated.

Conclusions Concerning the Ontology of Work

I am now in a position to combine this portion of the hypothesis, that there shall be in the new creation glorified work ontologically grounded in transformed humanness, with the previous portion, that human work is ontologically part of humanness as it is theologically grounded in human purpose. When this is done what emerges is a quite strong case from within theological anthropology for a conception of work as ontological. This is what I have been most broadly seeking to demonstrate. I thus offer the theological conclusion that, ontologically work is so fundamental to created and human existence that it is necessarily a part of both this life and the life to come.

It is interesting to notice that while these arguments for an ontology of work have simply made the point that work is fundamental to a natural and human existence (both in this and the new creation), what the ontology of work itself does not tell us directly is the full nature or essence of that work. It does suggest what qualities should characterize work, primarily that work should be permeated with the sabbath, but beyond this and by itself it does not show a lot about what work should or should not include.

What this study of the ontology of work has done is to provide the theological (the created and eternal) basis and foundation for the totality of work; including here work's other aspects. For more detail concerning what the nature of work is, we must look additionally to work's instrumental and relational aspects. These provide most of the particulars about work.

Having said that however, what these particulars can legitimately suggest concerning truly Godly work will additionally be determined by what the ontology of work shows as needing to characterize work. Thus, what emerges is a somewhat dynamic vision of work where each of its three aspects informs and further shapes the others. This means that there is a mutual give and take necessitated with the relationships between the three aspects of work.

This picture of work then, (with reference to its three aspects) is decidedly not hierarchical in nature. Yes, the ontological aspect initially establishes the other two aspects. Nonetheless, the other two aspects in turn give the content to the ontological aspect (the form) thus bringing the ontological aspect itself into the broader and additionally defining relationships that exist between work's parts. What then is established with the ontology of work is a set of mutually defining (and restricting) relationships that together tell us what the normative nature and essence of work is to be.

Exploring what this might look like and suggesting what this means for both a broader theology of work and work ethics is now the task to be taken up in the concluding chapter.

CHAPTER 7

Conclusion: The Threefold Definition of Work and its Application

A Double Hypothesis Explored

Throughout this book I have explored and argued the case for a double hypothesis. In the first part of the book it was argued that theologically work should be depicted as a threefold non-hierarchical dynamic interrelationship of instrumental, relational, and ontological aspects. The appropriateness of this descriptive hypothesis for a more comprehensive theology of work was demonstrated by examining a few contemporary prominent theological understandings of work, both Protestant and Catholic. Through exploring the questions that theology had asked in relation to work, and through evaluating how theology has depicted human work, it became clear that a sufficiently broad yet unified framework for interpreting work was required: a framework that allows theologically for a multitude of sometimes diverse suggestions concerning work, and yet also holds these together in a meaningful way.

Likewise, in the process of investigating ideas related to each of the three outlined categories, each category emerged as necessary (practically and theoretically) for a fuller theological understanding of work. However, it was also discovered that, although the areas classified as work's instrumentality and relationality had been fairly well established theologically, its ontology had been largely underdeveloped. It was argued that many theological reflections on work have detected the need for and probed toward something like an ontology of work, (whether implying it from the doctrine of God or from anthropology) but that none had provided a satisfactorily comprehensive theological explanation and defense of it. This then led to the second part of the book and the second part of the hypothesis (that part upon which the first ultimately depends); that it is theologically appropriate and necessary to understand work ontologically, or, that there is an ontology of work. In the second half of the book it was demonstrated that human work is not only an instrumental activity undertaken to reach a secondary purpose whether that be survival, self-fulfillment, spiritual growth, the building of a society / civilization, or the like. Rather it was shown that work itself is a fundamental facet of our human and created existence and that this ontological status is derived teleologically (both protologically and eschatologically) from our essence (constitution and purpose) as humans. Because of this theology, work transcends its use value and becomes a valued entity in itself with its own particular 'isness' and *telos;* even if it necessarily always also has instrumental value and effects both in this world and the one to come.

Applying the Hypotheses to a Theology and Ethics of Work

The task of this book has been to demonstrate the validity of this double hypothesis. Now, in the final discussion it is important to show how this established hypothesis functions, and what its implications are for both a theology and an ethics of work.

The significance of this threefold understanding of the nature of work, for both a more comprehensive theology of work and then an ethics of work, lies in two areas. First, it provides a theological (and thereby an ethically normative) definition of work. Second, it offers a practical model, a theological ethics, for evaluating particular instances of work. I shall here consider both of these contributions in turn.

A Theological Definition of Work

In Chapter 1 of this book the concept of a theology of work was introduced and examined, as was the methodology I would use in working toward one. Likewise it was suggested that the contribution of this book toward that goal was to provide a theological definition of work; a theological explanation of work's essence and meaning. Rather than beginning with an existing definition of work derived primarily from some aspect of human experience (and then proceeding deductively toward a theology underpinning of it), I wanted to allow for a significantly higher level of induction and to let theology itself, in relationship to human experience, suggest a more comprehensive definition of work. The method of course was neither total deduction nor pure induction. Rather, within Chapter 1 I offered a broad hypothesis about work for exploration (one which of course was also itself initially developed through both induction and deduction). With its development however, what this hypothesis has become is a theological definition of work.

With each step in the exploration of the hypothesis there emerged a yet richer theological understanding of what work is currently, will be eschatologically, and thus should be ethically. Although no one sentence can ultimately capture the richness of what has been seen, I here offer as a definition a summarised statement of what has been concluded.

Human work is a transformative activity essentially consisting of dynamically interrelated instrumental, relational, and ontological dimensions: whereby, along with work being an end in itself, the worker's and others' needs are providen-

tially met; believers' sanctification is occasioned; and workers express, explore and develop their humanness while building up their natural, social and cultural environments thereby contributing protectively and productively to the order of this world and the one to come.

One value of this definition is that it pushes the field of a theology of work forward by incorporating a complex of issues, not hitherto always recognized, that a more comprehensive theology of work must address. As such, it redraws the boundaries for a theology of work.

Also, this definition makes a contribution to work ethics. It does this by making theologically and ethically normative statements about what human work is, and thus, should be. That is, it is a teleological definition with work's *is* also becoming its *ought*.

This Definition as a Model for Ethically Evaluating Work

This definition then is not only descriptive, it is also prescriptive. It becomes therefore, a practical model or framework for evaluating human work. Here I will pull together several observations made throughout the book to outline the substance of the model produced, and, I will look at what this model offers practically for a theological ethics of work.

THE COMPLEX TOTALITY OF WORK

According to the definition, human work is in essence (not incidentally) a threefold activity. The three dimensions of work (instrumentality, relationality, and ontology) are each distinct yet interrelated aspects within one complex to-tality called work. As suggested throughout the book, one way to express this idea is that the essence of work encompasses the mutual, non-hierarchical, in-terdependent relationships that exist between these three aspects. Applied ethi-cally, each aspect within work makes its own distinctive contribution to work's essential nature, yet in so doing it likewise qualifies and further defines (and therefore limits) the other aspects. Thus for example, it can be ethically de-duced from the relational aspect of work that work should be structured and carried out in such a way that workers may experience personal growth and development in and through their work. By making such a prescription how-ever, I have thus set some parameters around what we may legitimately posit ethically concerning both work's instrumentality and ontology. Instrumentality, for example, cannot therefore require that work be primarily about making the maximum amount of profit, if, by attempting to secure an excess amount of profit it would preclude or significantly hinder a worker's opportunity for per-sonal expression and development in and through work. Further, work's ontol-ogy cannot simply dictate that work is solely about 'the praise and Glory of God' (narrowly defined). Given work's relational aspect, the ontology of work must allow work essentially to be also about human development. In the same way then, each of work's aspects in its own turn will, by making its own claims, further qualify and somewhat dictate what we can ethically prescribe from its corresponding aspects. This dynamic and reciprocal process precludes the possibility that work, according to its aspects, can be construed hierarchically. In the model each aspect of work equally has a defining and qualifying contribution to make to work's essence, and thus to ethics.

Understood as functioning in this way, what this conception of work's essential nature primarily guarantees is resistance to any reductionistic ethical prescriptions related to work. It provides a set of checks and balances that will simply not allow one particular concern, as legitimate as it may be in its own right, to run roughshod over other important concerns. For example, some, following Adam Smith's defense of free markets and the division of labor, may argue that work is primarily or essentially concerned with human sustenance and that therefore questions of economics and economic efficiency must become the only (or primary) ethical criteria by which to judge particular forms of work – even though this tends to disadvantage the physical health and even the moral vision of the workforce. Others, following the lines of Marx's thought, may argue that work is primarily concerned with constructing a just social order or community and that therefore the only (or primary) criteria by which to judge forms of work will be the principles of social ownership and distribution. Both positions are correct to a point. However, according to this new model, individually both of these positions would be ethically unacceptable for each is equally reductionistic. Intrinsic to this new framework are ever present ethical challenges to such narrowly and singularly conceived concerns. In applying this normative definition of work, it becomes impossible to focus upon economic considerations alone for if we were to try we would immediately recognize that economic dictates will have other related social consequences that too need to be ethically evaluated. Here principles of social justice, without undermining the integrity of what some may call economic laws or realities, will nevertheless ethically limit (without prescribing) economics' dictates toward work. Conversely, it will be impossible to ethically focus solely upon supposed autonomous moral imperatives of social justice, for according to this model, we will also necessarily recognize the ethical implications which for example, the relative autonomy of economics as a normative discipline suggests for work. Here economics will not dictate, but will set some parameters for what we may meaningfully say about our understandings of social justice. Our normative definition or model of work then, approaching a form of ethics sometimes termed Christian realism, will simply not allow us to narrow the nature and meaning of work to one concern only (be that economics, social justice or the like). This is so even if one particular concern proves to be especially important at a particular time in a given context.

Of course in practice in the broken situations encountered in the real world, any one of work's three aspects might become the most ethically important. Flexibly, depending upon the concrete need at the time, a contextually determined hierarchy of aspects might be needed. For example, in a location where there is little food production and significant levels of starvation it will likely be necessary for work ethics to emphasize the instrumental (sustenance) aspect of work, and, thus possibly the economist side of work. Practically, a work ethics may initially need to legitimatise a host of economic activities and structures necessary for the provision of resources for basic life support for the greatest number of people. In so doing it may even legitimatise certain kinds of work which under less extreme circumstances would be deemed unethical. (For example, repetitive mechanized work in a factory.) The importance of my three-fold model however, is that even if exceptions are justified and overemphasised for a time (even ultimately destructive ones), there are nonetheless built into the model ethical correctives that will constantly and necessarily be pushing from within the context for more overall ethical structures and forms of work. The model will constantly be pushing toward an ethical equilibrium even though a perfectly harmonious balance may never be reached in the imperfections of this life.

So far however, I have simply been demonstrating the model's restricting and balancing (essentially) non-hierarchical function. Although this role is vital to the framework, I now will summarise what additionally the model offers to work ethics. Here I shall specifically look to each aspect of work; to what each suggests in itself and how it makes room for voices from other disciplines.

THE INSTRUMENTAL ASPECT OF WORK

Throughout this book I have referred to the instrumental aspect of work as incorporating two important dimensions. The first is the concern for sustenance. The second is the concern for a person's spiritual growth through work.

Sustenance concerns focus upon work as a means through which to provide the necessary resources for human survival and flourishing. It is clear that no theory or theology of work could be complete or meaningful without paying particular attention to issues relating to sustenance. Sustenance must be an elemental concern within any understanding of work. What however, does this mean practically? Here is where this theological work ethics model begins to open up to the wider world. Although being a normative view of work, it is not a closed view. It is at this point that voices from other disciplines are welcomed to make their contributions (though not to hijack the discussion). For example, when acknowledging that questions of sustenance are integral to any concept of work, we necessarily allow that the field of economics will have some normative prescriptions to offer. This does not mean that this theological work ethics will uncritically bow to whatever 'economics' at any given time is saying. Economic 'laws' are not autonomous, nor are they the only issues at stake. However, it does mean that questions concerning real conditions (the scarcity of resources, the need for the creation of wealth, markets, personal freedom and choice, efficiency and the like) will be recognised and tools appropriate to these questions will be used. Conclusions concerning issues like these will need to be made, and the discipline of economics will be invaluable in this process. In this sense it is fair to say that economics sets the agenda. Economics thus, though in a relativised way, will be allowed to establish some ethical parameters.

Practically stemming from its openness in this area the most appropriate context, or economic system, for the complex reality of work described in this book is, it seems to me, the market system (a version of market capitalism). I emphasis however, that it will need to be a version of market capitalism rather different to the one operating globally at the turn of the new millennium. This is so since it is the relational and ontological aspects of work, and not simply the instrumental, that set ethical parameters. These other two aspects require that the market system itself is subject to moral critiques and demands. The markets may need to be 'free' but these other aspects mean that they are neither autonomous nor unaccountable. Ultimately, the sustenance aspect of work's instrumentality functions best in an open market setting, yet in significant ways because of the other aspects we will want to moralize the markets; that is, make sure other values are brought into the economic sphere of existence. This challenge to market economics does not, as some may suggest, point to centralized planning, for in practical economic terms this most often leads to scarcity, diminished choice and the elimination of freedom, creativity, and self-exploration and presentation through work. Nor should we primarily or exclusively seek to moralize the markets through legislation that often times inadvertently stifles human risk and thus creativity and exploration. Rather, we will want to work toward moralizing the markets by working toward the spiritual and moral transformation of those who enter into the market structures. Here both spiritual conversion and some version of virtue ethics becomes indispensable. Nor is this an individualistic understanding of markets. People develop market structures. History shows that as people and their ideas and values change so do the nature of markets.

This then leads naturally to the next point dealing with work's instrumental aspect (one that if incorporated into a work ethics would contribute much to moralizing the markets). The second instrumental concern involves one's personal spiritual growth through their work. This may be referred to as work's contribution to sanctification. Starting with the Bible, throughout much of the history of theological reflections on work this has been a, if not the, primary concern. The idea is that work is an occasion for grace. In and through working a person grows spiritually through humble obedience to and dependence upon God, demonstrating to himself or herself and others the nature of their relationship to God, being kept from idleness and sin, having resources to share with others and so forth. Here yet broader concerns from spirituality and moral theology begin to contribute to work ethics. For example, ethical dictates that work must be able to incorporate should be derived from reflection on the nature of virtue and spirituality, the nature and demands of spiritual community life, and even sabbath principles.

THE RELATIONAL ASPECT OF WORK

In this book the relational aspect of work primarily refers to two other important dimensions of work. One is the concern for the existential development or self-fulfillment of the person through work. The other is the concern for the impact on, and value of, work for human social, structural and broader societal development.

Concerning a person's existential development or self-fulfilment through work I have argued that a theory or theology of work must allow room for human self-expression, self-exploration and personal development in and through human working activity. If humans are open beings, by their nature not yet finished beings, then all that they do and participate in will have an important effect upon their becoming and will ultimately contribute to who / what they become. Work, one of the primary ways (yet not the only way) that humans apply themselves to the task of living life, will thus be a central contributor to the evolution of the self both individually and socially.

If this is true then again we find this model for theological work ethics opening up to contributions from other disciplines. For example, when our concerns focus upon human development and flourishing, we will necessarily look to fields relating to human psychology and human development. What kinds of human effects will certain types of work have on the person? What kinds of conditions and opportunities will the person need to become fully humanised? Theological ethics, although not totally dependant upon psychology for its answers, will nonetheless enter with it into a dialogue to explore these types of issues. Further, especially related to questions of self-presentation and self-exploration, this work ethics will also look into questions of goodness and beauty, that is, to the arts and to the philosophical discipline of aesthetics to gain critical insights that can contribute additional ethical principles for evaluating work.

Concerning the impact on and value of work for human social, structural and broader societal development (civilization), I suggest that human societies are largely what they are as a result of human values which, in our vast array of personal and non-personal relationships, we make concrete through our work. Work ethics then will necessarily concern itself with the broader questions that address the kind of society or civilization that we want to live in. Ethically, what structures and organizational patterns do we want to produce and sustain so that we may flourish? What kinds of services and or goods should we recommend that humans value, and, how do we influence people to want these things as opposed to others that we have recognised to be more harmful? How do we combat racism or sexism that is embedded in the workplace?

Again as a theological work ethics begins to consider these types of questions it will open itself to dialogue, albeit critical dialogue, with a host of social sciences. Sociology, management theory, social anthropology and the like will all add their voices and suggest further ethical principles that will need to be considered within habits and patterns of working.

Finally, a large portion of this book has been concerned with what I have called the ontological aspect of work. While developing this idea, I pointed out several contributions that this aspect makes to a theological understanding of work. Here I want to highlight specifically what this means for an ethics of work.

The ontology of work suggests that work in its essence is more than the sum total of its instrumental and relational parts. 'Ontology' indicates that there is a greater reality and *telos* to work than its instrumentality and relationality, either individually or combined, can capture.

Although the ontology of work emerges from and is best developed from within human createdness and destiny (theological anthropology), the ontology of work means that work transcends and is more than a functional essence. Work cannot simply be made subordinate to the human as if it were only ordered to humanity. Work cannot be reductionistically construed as simply a means to an end; be these human or other natural ends. There is more to the essence of work than its useful results for humanity, other beings, and nature. Theologically the sabbath is the crown of God's creation. All work, therefore, is to be permeated with the ethos of the sabbath. This principle means that work is not simply an activity undertaken to achieve a derivative, albeit useful, human or natural end. Although emerging from human essence, work is a thing in itself, ordered to itself and standing in itself before God.

In this respect work does have its own normative character, transcending both its results and its use to workers. Yet, this is not a static essence, divorced from the process and results of work. The ontology of work cannot mean that work ceases to be a transformative activity. It is a transformation of the earth but in order that the Sabbath may be realised.

> A voice of one calling: 'In the desert prepare the way for the Lord; make straight in the wilderness a highway for our God. Every valley shall be raised up, every mountain and hill made low; the rough ground shall become level, the rugged places a plain. And the glory of the Lord will be revealed, and all mankind together will see it. For the mouth of the Lord has spoken.' (Isaiah 40:3-5.)

This spin on ontology means that all *positive* transformative action (for construction rather than destruction) may be considered to participate in the nature of the Sabbath or the fulfillment in the present of God's will on earth, which is the due preparation for the coming of the Messiah. In this sense work does transcend its 'normal' use value and is an end in itself. Work as a participation in the Sabbath has its own intrinsic value.

The ontology of work then, suggests that our work or works intrinsically become acts of worship, and that our works become entities which themselves, by flourishing as themselves, can praise God. Work is not simply a means to instrumental or relational ends. It is certainly not less than this, but in being these things, together with its ontological aspect, work also becomes more than these things. The whole does become more than the sum of its parts.

Having said these things, both that work has a kind of intrinsic value and that it also has extrinsic value, I want to further clarify what are the value and ethical prescriptions that follow from the ontology of work. Firstly, since work is in one respect an end in itself, any particular work (or product of work) must be treated and evaluated appropriately according to the dictates of its own being; so as to preserve its unique integrity as a particular work. For example, the product of one's work may be an evaluative report. The question here however, is whether it is a good report. Ethically we cannot only or simply evaluate work on the basis of its resultant functionality. The fact that it is a work itself with its own kind of being makes it ethically imperative that we treat each transformative act with a respect, reserve, or excitement which is appropriate to its own integrity and character as a work. I mean by this that work, as an end in itself, thrusts upon us certain ethical demands intrinsic to its being work; namely, that we are obliged to treat a work according to its ordering to flourish as itself.

Secondly however, since work ontologically also always has eternal value, (that is, since it necessarily contributes to the current world order, and as a part of that order when transformed will too affect the resultant nature and order of the new creation,) work must be ethically evaluated in terms of its success or failure to conform to the values of the new creation to which it is thus, necessarily linked. The ontology of work guarantees that work is not to be judged solely according to its current practical benefits. If it is to be fully ethical work it will also need to come into line with and promote the values theologically associated with the new creation. Of course no human endeavour can completely accomplish this goal. The question becomes however, to what degree a work or kind of work points in this direction.

THE LOGICAL RATHER THAN METAPHYSICAL PRIORITY OF THE ONTOLOGY OF WORK

Having thus looked separately at each aspect of work's essential nature I am finally in a position to step back and see one more important dynamic relationship within work itself that forms one more fundamental contribution of the ontological aspect of work. The concern here is again with how work's dimensions relate to each other (more positively rather than restrictively) in providing the framework for an ethics of work. Once again attention is turned to work's essentially dynamic, non-hierarchical, interrelated and interdependent nature.

In addition to the argument that each of the three aspects or work are equal: that each aspect of work is necessarily equal to the other and thus that each partially defines as well as holds the other mutually in check (both constitutionally and ethically), conceptually it is also important to see that the ontological aspect is logically prior (although not metaphysically prior) to the other aspects. How can this be so without the model ultimately turning into a hierarchical construct; something that has been vigorously argued against in this book?

Logically the ontological aspect functions as the foundational basis for the other two aspects. The instrumental and relational aspects find their ultimate legitimisation from their relationship to the ontological. What does this mean? The instrumental and relational aspects of work have obvious practical values in this life, especially with respect to continued human existence and human flourishing. However, a question may be asked as to whether, and if so how, can we suppose that these two results of work (continued human existence and human flourishing) are ultimately ethically good? What guarantees the goodness of human life itself? Radically, one might want to question whether human existence and flourishing are really goods at all given the apparent cost of these to the environment as a whole. Or less radically one could suggest that although these conditions are generically (and intuitively from our perspective) perceived to be ethical goods, they may indeed not ultimately or fundamentally be so. We might reason that they look like fundamental goods, but that in the light of the evolution of the whole cosmos they must be understood as simply emotivist wishes that we ourselves have understandably invented. In a universe of chance, how could they be absolute or necessary goods?

Alternatively, it may be theologically argued that although work (instrumentally and relationally conceived) has some current value, in the light of eternity it is not really in itself significant. Work might be important now and even important eternally in as much as it relates to or affects one's individual spiritual development. However, beyond this, work in itself simply has an earthly and limited, and not eternal value.

To each of these lines of reasoning the ontology of work responds negatively. The ontological aspect of work locates both work's instrumental and relational aspects totally and resolutely into an eternal, and thus an absolute framework. The ontology of work means that work as a whole, including its constituent parts, is embedded into the fabric of both this world and the one to come. This legitimates both the instrumental and relational aspects of work in such a way that their results (continued human existence and human flourishing) can be claimed to be absolute and fundamental ethical goods. Continued human existence and flourishing are goods not simply from an emotivist perspective. When work's instrumental and relational dimensions are placed in an eternal framework, both human flourishing and existence become bound up with and a part of God's eternal *telos* for his creation. That is, they make a contribution to and become part of God's new creation. Therefore, they have an ultimate heavenly and not simply earthly existence and resultant value. The ontology of work means that work's parts (as well as the whole) have eternal significance in themselves. With the ontological aspect then, the other two aspects of work (instrumental and relational) and their results (continued human existence and human flourishing) are guaranteed an ethical grounding and ultimate value from an eternal perspective.

Importantly, there is no reason why this role ascribed to the ontology of work, its logically prior legitimisation of work's instrumental and relational aspects, would necessitate a resultant metaphysical hierarchy between work's constituent aspects. Indeed in this book I have already argued why such a hierarchy (whether only affirming the metaphysical priority of the ontological aspect, or whether also derivatively affirming the metaphysical priority of the relational over the instrumental aspect) would be dangerous, and why it cannot be the case. Here I simply conclude that being the logically foundational aspect of work's essential nature does not require any further metaphysical moves or commitments. Rather, such a role simply suggests one more unique and necessary contribution of the ontology of work to the complex totality of work.

Final Comments

I have now come to the end of my explorations into a theology of work. To what end have I written this book on work? I am convinced that the Church of Jesus needs to provide Christ's followers with yet more encouragement to explore and to imaginatively experiment with how our daily 'normal' working activity (which occupies most of our waking lives) relates to the whole of our lives (in our various relationships), to our spirituality, to God, to the rest of creation, and to eternity. I believe that the Church's effectiveness in witness, and her continued relevance to the lives of her children depends to a large extent upon how well she moves toward this goal. I am convinced that her task must increasingly be to guide all of her children into a deeper integrative understanding of the nature and meaning of human work.

Bibliography

Adams, Robert M. 'Vocation.' *Faith and Philosophy* 4 (1 Oct. 1987): pp.448-62.

Adeney, Bernard. 'Work: Necessity, Vocation and Strategy.' *Radix* 15 (Jan./Feb. 1984): pp.13-15.

Agrell, Göran. *Work, Toil and Sustenance: An Examination of the View of Work in the New Testament, Taking into Consideration Views Found in Old Testament, Intertestamental, and Early Rabbinic Writings.* Translated by Stephen Westerholm. Lund: Hakan Ohlsons, 1976.

Ahlers, Rolf. 'Theory of God and Theological Method.' *Dialog* 22 (Sum. 1983): pp.235-240.

Alexander, John F, and others, eds. 'What Are We Doing with Our Lives.' *Other Side* No 95 (Aug. 1979): pp.6-63.

Alkire, Sabina. 'This Unemployment: Disaster or Opportunity?' *Theology* 97 (Nov. / Dec. 1994): pp.402-413.

von Allmen, J.J., ed. *Vocabulary of the Bible.* English ed., London: Lutterworth Press, 1958.

Almen, Louis T. 'Vocation in a Post-Vocational Age.' *Word & World* 4 (Spr. 1984): pp.131-140.

Althaus, Paul. *The Ethics of Martin Luther.* Translated by Robert Schultz. Philadelphia: Fortress Press, 1972.

Anderson, Bernhard W. *From Creation to New Creation: Old Testament Perspectives.* Overtures to Biblical Theology, eds. Walter Brueggemann, John R. Donahue, Sharyn Dowd, and Christopher R. Seitz. Minneapolis: Fortress Press, 1994.

Anderson, Ray S. *On Being Human: Essays in Theological Anthropology.* Grand Rapids: Eerdmans, 1982.

Arendt, Hannah. *Between Past and Future.* New York: Viking Press, 1961.

Aristotle. *Nicomachean Ethics.* Indianapolis: Hackett, 1985.

Arneson, Richard J. 'Meaningful Work and Market Socialism.' *Ethics* 97 (Apr. 1987): pp.517-545.

Atkinson, David. 'A Christian Theology of Work.' In *Pastoral Ethics: A Guide to the Key Issues of Daily Living*, pp.104-111. Oxford: Lynx Communications, 1994.

Attwood, David. *The Spade and the Thistle: The Place of Work Today.* Grove Booklet on Ethics, Bramcote: Grove Books, 1980.

Badcock, Gary D. *The Way of Life: A Theology of Christian Vocation.* Grand Rapids: Eerdmans, 1998.

Ballard, Paul H. *Towards a Contemporary Theology of Work.* Collegiate Center of Theology. Faculty of Theology, University College: Cardiff, 1982.

Banks, Robert. 'The Place of Work in the Divine Economy: God as Vocational Director and Model.' In *Faith Goes to Work: Reflections from the Marketplace*, ed. R Banks. pp.18-29. New York: Alban Inst., 1993.

— *Redeeming the Routines: Bringing Theology to Life.* Wheaton: Bridgepoint (Victor), 1993.

Barnette, Henlee H. *Christian Calling and Vocation.* Grand Rapids: Baker, 1965.

Barr, William R. 'Life: Created in the Image of God.' *Mid-Stream* 21 (Oct. 1982): pp.473-484.

Barth, Karl. *Church Dogmatics,* III 4. Edinburgh: T&T Clark, 1961.

— *The Humanity of God.* Translated by J.N. Thomas and T. Weiser. London: Collins, 1961.

— *Ethics.* Translated by Geoffrey Bromiley. ed. Dietrich Braun. Edinburgh: T&T Clark, 1981.

Bauckham, Richard. *Moltmann: Messianic Theology in the Making.* Basingstoke: Marshall Pickering, 1987.

— *The Theology of Jürgen Moltmann.* Edinburgh: T&T Clark, 1995.

Bauer, J.B., ed. *Encyclopedia of Biblical Theology.* Vol. 3. London: Sheed and Ward, 1970.

Baum, Gregory, ed. *Work and Religion. Concilium* 131 (1/1980). Edinburgh: T&T Clark, 1980.

Bellah, R.N., ed. *Habits of The Heart: Individualism and Commitment in American Life.* New York: Harper & Row, 1985.

Berkhof, Hendrikus. *Christ: The Meaning of History.* Translated by Buurman, L. Richmond: John Knox Press, 1966.

— *Well Founded Hope.* Richmond: John Knox Press, 1969.

Berkouwer, G.C. *Man: The Image of God.* Grand Rapids: Eerdmans, 1962.

— *Studies in Dogmatics: The Return of Christ.* Translated by Van Oosterom, James. ed. Marlin J. Van Elderen. Grand Rapids: Eerdmans, 1972.

Bernbaum, J.A. and S.M. Steer. *Why Work: Careers and Employment in Biblical Perspective.* Grand Rapids: Baker, 1986.

Bienert, Walter. *Die Arbeit nach der Lehre der Bibel. Eine Grundlegung evangelischer Sozialethik.* Stuttgart: 1954.

Biggar, Nigel, ed. *Reckoning With Barth: Essays in Commemoration of the Centenary of Karl Barth's Birth.* London: Mowbray, 1988.

— *The Hastening That Waits: Karl Barth's Ethics.* Oxford Studies in Theological Ethics, ed. Oliver O'Donovan. Oxford: Claredon Press, 1993.

— 'Work ...on Not Making a Tyranny Out of a Necessity.' In *Good Life: Reflections on What We Value Today,* pp.46-56. London: SPCK, 1997.

Bonhoeffer, Dietrich. *Ethics.* Based on German sixth edition, 1963 ed., Translated by Smith, Neville Horton. London: SCM Press, 1955.

— *Letters and Papers from Prison,* ed. Eberhard Bethge. London: SCM Press, 1971.

Bottomore, Tom, ed. *A Dictionary of Marxist Thought.* Oxford: Basil Blackwell, 1983.

Breclaw, Keith. '*Homo Faber* Reconsidered: Two Thomist Reflections on Work.' *Thomist* 57 (4 1993): pp.579-607.

Bromiley, G.W., ed. *The International Standard Bible Encyclopedia.* Fully revised ed., Vol. 4. Grand Rapids: Eerdmans, 1978-88.

Brown, Colin, ed. *The New International Dictionary of New Testament Theology.* English ed., Vol. 3. Grand Rapids: Zondervan, 1978.

Brunner, Emil. *The Divine Imperative: A Study in Christian Ethics.* English ed., Translated by Olive Wyon. Lutterworth Library, London: Lutterworth Press, 1937.

Bube, Richard H. 'Tension in Theology: Creation Vs. Redemption.' *JASA* 32 (Mar. 1980): pp.1-4.

Cain, Clifford C. 'Omega: Some Reflections on the Meaning of the Afterlife.' *Faith and Philosophy: Journal of the Society of Christian Philosophers* 1 (3 1984, Jl.): pp.327-

335.

Cairns, David. *The Image of God in Man.* Revised ed., London: SCM Press, 1973.

Calvin, John. *Institutes of the Christian Religion.* Translated by Ford Lewis Battles. The Library of Christian Classics, ed. John McNeill. London: SCM Press, 1960.

— *Sermons on the Epistle to the Ephesians.* Edinburgh: Banner of Truth Trust, 1973.

Carnley, Peter. 'A Theology of Vocation to Work.' *St Mark's Review* No 97 (Mar. 1979): pp.11-15.

Carter, Kenneth H, Jr. 'Of Human Toil, Daily Bread, and Common Life: Review of 5 Books.' *Books and Religion* 14 No 8 (Oct. 1986): p.7.

Chapman, G Clark. 'Jürgen Moltmann and the Christian Dialogue with Marxism.' *Journal of Ecumenical Studies* 18 (Sum. 1981): pp.435-450.

Chenu, Marie-Dominique. *The Theology of Work: An Exploration.* Translated by Lilian Soiron. Dublin: Gill and Son, 1963.

Chewning, Richard C., ed. *Biblical Principles & Business.* Vol. 1. Christians in the Marketplace Series. Colorado Springs: Navpress, 1989.

—, ed. *Biblical Principles & Economics.* Vol. 2. Christians in the Marketplace Series. Colorado Springs: Navpress, 1989.

Childs, James M. Jr. *Christian Anthropology and Ethics.* Philadelphia: Fortress Press, 1978.

Chilton, David. *Paradise Restored.* Tyler Texas: American Bureau for Economic Research, 1984.

Chirico, Peter. 'Revelation and Natural Law.' *Theological Studies* 52 (S. 1991): pp.539-540.

Chmielewsky, Philip J. 'Review: Work in the Spirit. by Miroslav Volf.' *Thomist* 57 (14, Oct. 1993): pp.708-714.

Clark, Dennis. *Work and the Human Spirit.* New York: Sheed & Ward, 1967.

Clines, D.J.A. 'The Image of God in Man.' *Tyndale Bulletin* 19 (1968): pp.53-54.

Cochrane, James R. and Gerald West, eds. *The Three-fold Cord: Theology, Work and Labour.* Hilton, South Africa: Cluster Pubns, 1991.

Cole, Graham. 'Ethics and Eschatology: Paley's System Reconsidered.' *Reformed Theological Review* 47 (My.-Aug. 1988): pp.33-43.

Coles, Robert. 'On the Meaning of Work.' *The Atlantic* (Oct. 1971): pp.103-4.

Conway, Jeremiah P. 'Murphy's Law and the Humanization of Work.' *Religious Humanism* 16 (Aug. 1982): pp.187-192.

Cottingham, David C. 'Rosen, Moltmann, and the Anticipatory Paradigm: Biological Modelling Processes Compared to Psychological Archetypes and Biblical Typology.' *Perspectives on Science and Christian Faith* 42 (Dec. 1990): pp.239-245.

Cruz, Virgil P. 'The Beatitudes of the Apocalypse: Eschatology and Ethics.' In *Perspectives on Christology: Essays in Honor of Paul K. Jewett*, ed. M Shuster and R Muller. pp.269-283. Grand Rapids: Zondervan, 1991.

Cullmann, Oscar. *Christ and Time: The Primitive Christian Conception of Time and History.* Revised ed., Translated by Floyd V. Filson. Philadelphia: Westminster Press, 1964.

Curran, Charles. *Directions in Fundamental Moral Theology.* Notre Dame: University of Notre Dame Press, 1985.

—, and Richard McCormick, eds. *Official Catholic Social Teaching. Readings in Moral Theology No. 5.* New York: Paulist Press, 1986.

Dale, E.S. *Bringing Heaven Down to Earth: A Practical Spirituality of Work.* New

York: Peter Lang, 1991.

Das, Somen. 'A Theology of the Future and Christian Ethics.' *Bangalore Theological Forum* 15 (My.-Aug. 1983): pp.63-86.

David, J.J. *Christ's Victorious Kingdom: Postmillennialism Reconsidered.* Grand Rapids: Baker, 1986.

Davidson, James C. and David P. Caddell. 'Religion and the Meaning of Work.' *Journal for the Scientific Study of Religion* 33 (Jn. 1994): pp.135-147.

Davies, J. G. 'Work and the Making of a Christian World.' *Irish Theological Quarterly* 35 (1968): pp.93-116.

Davies, Paul. *About Time: Einstein's Unfinished Revolution.* London: Viking, 1995.

Davies, W. D. and D. Daube, eds. *The Background of the New Testament and Its Eschatology.* Cambridge: Cambridge University Press, 1956.

Davis, H. and D. Gosling, eds. *Will the Future Work? Values for Emerging Patterns of Work and Employment.* Geneva: WCC, 1985.

DeKoster, Lester. *Work, the Meaning of Your Life.* Grand Rapids: Christian's Library Press, 1982.

Donagan, Alan. 'Teleology and Consistency in Theories of Morality as Natural Law.' In *The Georgetown Symposium on Ethics: Essays in honor of Henry Babcock Veatch - April 1983,* ed. R Porreco. pp.91-107. Lanham, Md: University Press of America, 1984.

Dooyeweerd, Herman. *The Christian Idea of the State.* Translated by J. Kraay Nutley, NJ: Craig Press, 1968.

Duffy, Stephen J. *The Dynamics of Grace: Perspectives in Theological Anthropology.* Vol. 3. New Theology Studies, ed. Peter C. Phan. Minnesota: The Liturgical Press, 1993.

Eller, Vernard. 'A Voice on Vocation.' *Reformed Journal* 29 (My. 1979): pp.16-20.

Ellul, Jacques. 'Work and Calling.' *Katallagete* 4 (Fall/Winter 1972): pp.8-16.

Erickson, Millard J. *Christian Theology.* Single volume ed., Grand Rapids: Baker, 1983-5.

Evans, C. Stephen. 'Healing Old Wounds and Recovering Old Insights: Toward a Christian View of the Person Today.' In *Christian Faith and Practice*, ed by M. Noll and D. Wells, pp.68-86. Grand Rapids: Eerdmans, 1988.

Ezell, Douglas. 'Eschatology and Ethics in the New Testament.' *Southwestern Journal of Theology* 22 (2 Spr. 1980): pp.72-95.

Fairweather, Ian C.M. and James I.H. McDonald. *The Quest for Christian Ethics: An Enquiry into Ethics and Christian Ethics.* Edinburgh: The Handsel Press, 1984.

Finnis, John. *Natural Law and Natural Rights.* Oxford: Oxford University Press, 1980.

Flannery, Austin, ed. *Vatican Council II: The Conciliar and Post Conciliar Documents.* Dublin: Dominican Publications, Saint Savior's, 1975.

The Forgotten Trinity: 1 The Report of the BCC Study Commission on Trinitarian Doctrine Today. British Council of Churches, 1989.

Forrester, W.R. *Christian Vocation: Studies in Faith and Work.* London: Lutterworth, 1951.

Fromm, Erich. *Marx's Concept of Man.* New York: Fredrick Ungar, 1961.

Gavin, F. 'The Catholic Doctrine of Work and Play.' *Theology* 21 (1930): pp.14-40.

Genovesi, Vincent J. *Expectant Creativity: The Action of Hope in Christian Ethics.* Washington: University Press of America, 1982.

Geoghegan, A.T. *The Attitude Toward Labor in Early Christianity and Ancient Culture.*

Vol. 6. Studies in Christian Antiquity, ed. J. Quasten. Washington: Catholic University of America, 1945.

Gibbs, J.R. 'The Challenge of Transformation-Toward a Theology of Work in Light of the Thought of H. Richard Niebuhr.' Ph.D., Cambridge, 1990.

Gibbs, Mark. 'Vocation, Work, and Work for Pay.' *Word & World* 4 (Spr. 1984): pp.126-130.

Gillet, Richard W. *The Human Enterprise: A Christian Perspective on Work.* Kansas City: Leaven, 1985.

Gorringe, Timothy. 'Work Leisure and Human Fulfillment.' In *Capital and the Kingdom: Theological Ethics and Economic Order*, pp.59-78. London: SPCK, 1994.

Gregorios, Paulos. *The Human Presence: An Orthodox View of Nature.* Geneva: World Council of Churches, 1978.

Gremillion, Joseph. *The Gospel of Peace and Justice: Catholic Social Teaching Since Pope John.* New York: Maryknoll, Orbis Books, 1976.

Grenz, Stanley J. *Theology for the Community of God.* Carlisle: Paternoster Press, 1994.

— and Roger E Olsen. *20th Century Theology: God & the World in a Transitional Age.* Carlisle: Paternoster Press, 1992.

Griffiths, Brian. *The Creation of Wealth.* Downers Grove: Inter-Varsity Press, 1984.

Gunton, Colin E. *The Promise of Trinitarian Theology.* Edinburgh: T& T Clark, 1991.

— 'Trinity, Ontology and Anthropology: Towards a Renewal of the Doctrine of the Imago Dei.' In *Persons, Divine and Human: King's College Essays in Theological Anthropology*, eds. Christoph Schwöbel and Colin E. Gunton. pp.47-61. Edinburgh: T& T Clark, 1991.

— *The One, The Three and the Many: God, Creation and the Culture of Modernity.* 1992 Bampton Lectures, University of Oxford, Cambridge: Cambridge University Press, 1993.

Gustafson, James M. *Christian Ethics and the Community.* Introduction by Charles Sweezey ed., New York: Pilgrim Press, 1979.

— *Theology and Ethics.* Oxford: Basil Blackwell, 1981.

— *Ethics From a Theocentric Perspective.* Chicago: University of Chicago Press, 1981-84.

Hall, Douglas John. *Imaging God. Dominion as Stewardship.* Grand Rapids: Eerdmans, 1986.

Halton, Mark R. 'Theology of Work: Survey of Recent Literature.' *Christian Ministry* 20 (2 1989): pp.16-17.

Harcourt-Norton, Clive. 'Work and Unemployment: A Biblical Perspective.' *St Mark's Review* No 97 (Mar. 1979): pp.17-23.

Hardy, Lee. *The Fabric of This World: Inquiries into Calling, Career Choice, and the Design of Human Work.* Grand Rapids: Eerdmans, 1990.

— 'Book Review: Work in the Spirit. by Miroslav Volf.' *Calvin Theological Journal* 28 (#1 Apr. 1993): pp.191-196.

Harrelson, Walter. 'Eschatology and Ethics in the Hebrew Bible.' *Union Seminary Quarterly Review* 42 (1-2 1988): pp.43-48.

Hart, Ian. 'The Teaching of Luther and Calvin about Ordinary Work: 1. Martin Luther (1483-1546).' *Evangelical Quarterly* 67 (1 1995): pp.35-52.

— 'The Teaching of Luther and Calvin about Ordinary Work: 2. John Calvin (1509-64).' *Evangelical Quarterly* 67 (2 1995): pp.121-135.

— 'The Teaching of the Puritans about Ordinary Work.' *Evangelical Quarterly* 67 (3

1995): pp.195-209.

Hauck, F. 'Die Stellung des Urchristentumas zur Arbeit und Geld.' In *BFChTh* 2:3, Gutersloh, 1921.

Hauerwas, Stanley. *The Peaceable Kingdom: A Primer in Christian Ethics.* Notre Dame: University of Notre Dame Press, 1983.

— 'Work as Co-Creation: A Critique of a Remarkably Bad Idea.' In *Co-Creation and Capitalism: John Paul II's 'Laborum Exercens'*, eds. Houck and Williams. Washington: University Press of America, 1983.

— and Alasdair MacIntyre, eds. *Revisions: Changing Perspectives in Moral Philosophy.* Vol. 3. A Series of Books on Ethics. Notre Dame: University of Notre Dame Press, 1983.

Haywood, Carol Lois. 'Does Our Theology of Work Need Reworking?' *Currents in Theology and Missions* 8 (Oct. 1981): pp.298-301.

Heinecken, Martin J. 'When Working is Over: Or, When Working Takes on a Unique Transformation.' *Word & World* 4 (Spr. 1984): pp.165-172.

Hendry, George S. *Theology of Nature.* Philadelphia: Westminster Press, 1980.

Herzog, Frederick, ed. *The Future of Hope: Theology as Eschatology.* New York: Herder & Herder, 1970.

Hiltner, S. 'Needed: A New Theology of Work.' *Theology Today* 31 (1974): pp.243-247.

Hinze, Bradford E. 'A Prophetic Vision: Eschatology and Ethics.' In *Praxis of Christian Experience: An Introduction to the Theology of Edward Schillebeeckx,* eds. E. Schillebeeckx and R. Schreiter. pp.131-146. San Francisco: Harper & Row, 1989.

Hoekema, Anthony. *The Bible and the Future.* Grand Rapids: Eerdmans, 1979.

Holden, Mark. *Called by the Gospel.* Minneapolis: Augsburg, 1983.

Holmes, Arthur. 'Wanted: A Christian Work Ethic for Today.' *The Reformed Journal* 28 (Oct. 1978): pp.17-20.

Horosz, William and Tad S Clements, eds. *Religion and Human Purpose: A Cross Disciplinary Approach.* Dordrecht, Netherlands: Martinus Nijhoff, 1987.

Horton, John and Susan Mendus, eds. *After MacIntyre: Critical Perspectives on the Work of Alasdair MacIntyre.* Notre Dame: University of Notre Dame Press, 1994.

Hultgren, Arland J, ed. 'Working.' *Word & World* 4 (Spr. 1984): pp.115-172.

Hummel, Gert. 'Morality and Beyond: Anthropology and New Ethics in Tomorrow's Information Society.' In *Being and Doing: Paul Tillich as Ethicist,* ed. J Carey. pp.125-154. Macon: Mercer University Press, 1987.

Hunsinger, George. *How To Read Karl Barth: The Shape of His Theology.* New York: Oxford University Press, 1991.

Hurst, Anthony. *Rendering Unto Caesar: An Exploration of the Place of Paid Employment within the Framework of Christian Belief.* Worthing: Churchman Publishing, 1986.

Illanes, Jose Luis. *On the Theology of Work.* Translated by M. Adams. Dublin: Scepter Books, 1967.

Janzen, Waldemar. 'The Theology of Work from an Old Testament Perspective.' *Conrad Grebel Review* 10 (Spr. 1992): pp.121-138.

Johnstone, Brian. 'Eschatology and Social Ethics: A Critical Survey of the Development of Social Ethics in the Ecumenical Discussion 1925-1968.' In *Sylloge Excerptorum Dissertationibus Vol 49: ad Gradum Doctoris in Sacra Theologia vel in Lure Canonico,* ed. et al B Johnstone. pp.47-85. Leuven: Katholieke Universiteitte, 1979.

Jungel, Eberhard. *Death: The Riddle and the Mystery.* Translated by Iain and Ute Nicol. Philadelphia: Westminster Press, 1974.

Juros, Helmut. 'The Object of the Theology of Work.' *Communio* (US) 11 (Sum. 1984): pp.136-144.

Kaiser, E.G. *Theology of Work.* Westminster, MD: Newman Press, 1966.

Kamenka, Eugene, ed. *The Portable Karl Marx.* New York: Penguin Books, 1983.

Kerr, Fergus. 'Moral Theology After MacIntyre.' *Studies in Christian Ethics* 8 (1 1995): pp.33-44.

Klein, Lisl. *The Meaning of Work.* Fabian Society, 1963.

Kolden, Marc. 'Work and Meaning: Some Theological Reflections.' *Interpretation* 48 (Jl. 1994): pp.262-271.

Kuhn, Harold B. 'The Christian Mind and the Work Ethic.' *The Asbury Seminarian* 25 (Apr. 1971): pp.3-5.

Kung, Hans and Jürgen Moltmann, eds. *Why Did God Make Me?* Vol. 108. *Concilium: Religion in the Seventies.* New York: The Seabury Press, 1978.

Kuzmic, P. 'History and Eschatology: Evangelical Views.' In *In Word and Deed: Evangelism and Social Responsibility*, ed. B.J. Nicholls. pp.135-164. Exeter: Paternoster Press, 1985.

Leith, John H. *John Calvin's Doctrine of the Christian Life.* Louisville: Westminster/John Knox Press, 1989.

Limouris, Gennadios. 'Orthodoxy Facing Contemporary Social Ethical Concerns.' *Ecumenical Review* 43 (4 1991): pp.420-429.

Lindbeck, George A. *The Nature of Doctrine.* Philadelphia: Westminster Press, 1984.

Lossky, Vladimir. *In the Image and Likeness of God.* London: Mowbrays, 1974.

Lovatt, John. 'Jesus in the Workplace: Towards a Better Theology of Work.' *Modern Churchman* 34 (2 1992): pp.10-16.

MacIntyre, Alasdair. *After Virtue: A Study in Moral Theory.* Second ed., London: Duckworth, 1985.

— *Whose Justice? Which Rationality?* London: Duckworth, 1988.

Macmurray, John. *Persons in Relation.* Gifford Lectures Glasgow, 1954, London: Faber and Faber, 1961.

— *The Self as Agent.* Gifford Lectures Glasgow, 1953, London: Faber and Faber, 1961.

Macquarrie, John. 'A Theology of Personal Being.' In *Persons and Personality: A Contemporary Enquiry*, eds. Author Peacocke and Grant Gillett. pp.172-179. New York: Basil Blackwell, 1987.

Mare, W Harold. 'The Work Ethic of the Gospels and Acts.' In *Interpretation and History: Essays in Honor of Allan A. MacRae*, eds. R Harris, S-H Quek, and R Vannoy. pp.155-168. Singapore: Christian Life Publishers, 1986.

Maritain, Jacques. *True Humanism.* Translated by M.R. Adamson. London: Geoffrey Bles: The Centenary Press, 1938.

— *The Rights of Man and Natural Law.* London: Geoffrey Bles: The Centenary Press, 1944.

— *The Person and the Common Good.* Translated by John J. Fitzgerald. London: Geoffrey Bles: The Centenary Press, 1948.

Marshall, I. H. 'Slippery Words (I) Eschatology.' *Expository Times* 89 (8 1978): pp.264-269.

Marshall, Paul, ed. *Labour of Love: Essays on Work.* Toronto: Wedge Publishing Foundation, 1980.

— 'Work and Vocation.' *The Reformed Journal* 30 (Sept. 1980): pp.16-20.

— *Thine is the Kingdom: A Biblical Perspective on the Nature of Government and Politics Today.* Grand Rapids: Eerdmans, 1984.

— 'Calling, Work, and Rest.' In *Christian Faith and Practice*, ed by M. Noll and D. Wells, pp.199-217. Grand Rapids: Eerdmans, 1988.

Marx, Karl. *Grundrisse: Foundations of the Critique of Political Economy* (Rough Draft). Translated by Martin Nicolaus. London: Allen Lane, 1973.

— *Karl Marx, Frederick Engels: Collected Works.* Vol. 31, Capital vol. 1. London: Lawrence & Wishart, 1975.

— *Karl Marx, Frederick Engels: Collected Works.* Vol. 3: 1843-1844. London: Lawrence & Wishart, 1975.

Mayr, Ernst. 'The Idea of Teleology.' *Journal of the History of Ideas* 53 (Jan.-Mar. 1992): pp.117-135.

McClendon, James Wm., Jr. *Systematic Theology: Ethics.* Nashville: Abingdon Press, 1986.

— *Systematic Theology, Doctrine* Vol. II. Nashville: Abingdon Press, 1994.

McFadyen, Alistair I. *The Call to Personhood: A Christian Theory of the Individual in Social Relationships.* Cambridge: Cambridge University Press, 1990.

McGovern, Arthur F. 'Pope John Paul II on "Human Work".' *Telos* 58 (1983-4): pp.215-218.

McLellan, David. *Marx's Grundrisse.* London: MacMillan, 1971.

Meeks, M. Douglas. *Origins of the Theology of Hope.* Philadelphia: Fortress Press, 1974.

— 'God and Work.' In *God the Economist: The Doctrine of God and Political Economy,* pp.127-155. Minneapolis: Fortress Press, 1989.

Metteer, Charles A. 'A Survey of the Theology of Work.' *Evangelical Review of Theology* 25:2 (2001) pp.154-169.

Meyer, John R. 'Striving for Personal Sanctity Through Work.' *Thomist* 61 (No 1 1997): pp.85-106.

Middelmann, Udo. *Pro-existence.* Downers Grove: Inter-Varsity, 1974.

Middleton, Robert G. 'Revising the Concept of Vocation for the Industrial Age.' *Christian Century* 103 No 32 (Oct. 29 1986): pp.943-945.

Migliore, Daniel L. 'Hope for the Kingdom and Responsibility for the World.' *Princeton Seminary Bulletin suppl no. 3* (1994): pp.1-152.

Moberg, David O. 'Christian Perspectives on Work and Leisure.' In *Quest for Reality: Christianity and the Counter Culture,* ed. et al C.F.H. Henry. pp.107-113. Downers Grove: Inter-Varsity Press, 1973.

Moltmann, Jürgen. *Theology of Hope: On the Ground and Implication of a Christian Eschatology.* Translated by James W. Leitch. New York: Harper & Row, 1967.

— *Religion, Revolution, and the Future.* Translated by M. Douglas Meeks. New York: Charles Scribner's Sons, 1969.

— *Hope and Planning.* Translated by Margaret Clarkson. London: SCM Press, 1971.

— *Theology of Play.* Translated by Reinhard Ulrich. New York: Harper & Row, 1972.

— *Theology and Joy.* Translated by Reinhard Ulrich. London: SCM Press, 1973.

— *The Crucified God: The Cross of Christ as the Foundation and Criticism of Christian Theology.* Translated by R.A. Wilson and John Bowden. New York: Harper & Row, 1974.

— *Man: Christian Anthropology in the Conflicts of the Present.* Translated by John

Sturdy. Philadelphia: Fortress Press, 1974.

— *The Experiment of Hope.* Translated by John Sturdy. Philadelphia: Fortress Press, 1975.

— 'Creation and Redemption.' In *Creation Christ and Culture: Studies in Honor of T. F. Torrance*, ed. Richard McKinney. Edinburgh: T&T Clark, 1976.

— *The Church in the Power of the Spirit: A Contribution to Messianic Ecclesiology.* Translated by Margaret Kohl. New York: Harper & Row, 1977.

— *The Future of Creation: Translated Essays.* Translated by Margaret Kohl. Philadelphia: Fortress Press, 1979.

— *The Trinity and the Kingdom: The Doctrine of God.* Translated by Margaret Kohl. San Francisco: Harper & Row, 1981.

— 'An Interview: By Miroslav Volf.' *Christian Century* 100 (Mar. 16 1983): pp.246-249.

— *On Human Dignity.* Translated by with Introduction M. Douglas Meeks. Philadelphia: Fortress Press, 1984.

— *God in Creation: An Ecological Doctrine of Creation.* Translated by Margaret Kohl. The Gifford Lectures 1984-1985, London: SCM Press, 1985.

— 'The Ecological Crisis: Peace with Nature?' *The Scottish Journal of Religious Studies* 9 (No 1 1988): pp.5-18.

— *The Way of Jesus Christ: Christology in Messianic Dimensions.* Translated by Margaret Kohl. London: SCM Press, 1990.

— *The Spirit of Life: A Universal Affirmation.* Translated by Margaret Kohl. London: SCM Press, 1992.

— 'Christ in Cosmic Context.' In *Christ and Context: The Confrontation Between Gospel and Culture,* eds. H. D. Regan and A. J. Torrance. pp.180-191, 205-209. Edinburgh: T&T Clark, 1993.

— *The Coming of God: Christian Eschatology.* Translated by Margaret Kohl. London: SCM Press, 1996.

Moore, Jeffrey Scott. 'A Theology of Work for Contemporary Christians.' *Sewanee Theological Review* 36 (Michaelmas 1993): pp.520-526.

Mouw, Richard J. *Politics and the Biblical Drama.* Grand Rapids: Baker, 1983.

— *The God Who Commands.* Notre Dame: University of Notre Dame Press, 1990.

Murphy, James Bernard. *The Moral Economy of Labor: Aristotelian Themes in Economic Theory.* London: Yale University Press, 1993.

Nash, Elizabeth J. 'A New Model for a Theology of Work.' *Modern Churchman* 29 (1 1986): pp.23-27.

Nelson, O. *Work and Vocation: A Christian Discussion.* New York: Harper & Row, 1954.

Neuhaus, Richard John. 'Wealth and Whimsy: On Economic Creativity.' *First Things* 5 (Aug.-Sept. 1990): pp.23-30.

Nicol, Iain G. 'Vocation and the People of God.' *Scottish Journal of Theology* 33 (No 4 1980): pp.361-373.

Niebuhr, Reinhold. *Moral Man and Immoral Society.* New York: Scribner, 1932.

— *An Interpretation of Christian Ethics.* New York: Meridian Books, 1956.

— *The Nature and Destiny of Man.* New York: Charles Scribner's Sons, 1960.

Noll, Mark A. & Wells, David F., eds. *Christian Faith & Practice in the Modern World: Theology from an Evangelical Point of View.* Grand Rapids: Eerdmans, 1988.

Northcott, Michael S. *The Environment & Christian Ethics.* New Studies in Christian

Ethics, ed. Robin Gill. Cambridge: Cambridge University Press, 1996.

Novak, Michael. *The Spirit of Democratic Capitalism.* New York: American Enterprise Institute / Simon and Schuster, 1982.

— 'Creation Theology.' In *Co-Creation and Capitalism: John Paul II's 'Laborum Exercens'*, eds. Houck and Williams. pp.17-41. Washington: University Press of America, 1983.

O'Donovan, Oliver. 'The Natural Ethic.' In *Essays in Evangelical Social Ethics,* ed. D. Wright. pp.19-35. Exeter: Paternoster Press, 1978.

— *Resurrection and Moral Order: An Outline for Evangelical Ethics.* Leicester: Inter-Varsity Press, 1986.

Oldham, J. H., ed. *Foundations of Ecumenical Social Thought: The Oxford Conference Report. 1937* with Introduction by Harold L. Lunger ed., Philadelphia: Fortress, 1966.

— *Work in Modern Society.* London: SCM Press, 1950.

Ollman, Bertell. *Alienation: Marx's Conception of Man in Capitalist Society.* Cambridge: Cambridge University Press, 1971.

'The Oxford Declaration on Christian Faith and Economics.' *Transformation* 4 (No 2 1990): pp.1-9.

Page, Ruth. *God and the Web of Creation.* London: SCM Press, 1996.

Pannenberg, Wolfhart. *Anthropology in Theological Perspective.* First U.K. ed., Translated by Matthew J. O'Conell, Edinburgh: T& T Clark, 1985.

— *Systematic Theology.* Vol. 1&2. Edinburgh: T&T Clark, 1991.

Parker, S. *Leisure and Work.* London: Allen and Unwin, 1983.

Pelikan, Jaroslav, ed. *Luther's Works.* Vol. 1-54. Saint Louis: Concordia Publishing House, 1958-67.

Pennington, M. Basil. *Called: New Thinking on Christian Vocation.* New York: Seabury, 1983.

Peters, Ted F. 'Creation, Consummation, and the Ethical Imagination.' In *Cry of the Environment: Rebuilding the Christian Creation Tradition,* ed. P. Joranson and K. Butigan. pp.401-429. Sante Fe: Bear & Co, 1984.

Piper, O.A. 'The Meaning of Work.' *Theology Today* 14 (1957): pp.174-194.

Plamenatz, John. *Karl Marx's Philosophy of Man.* Oxford: Clarendon Press, 1975.

Plantinga, Cornelius, Jr. 'Images of God.' In *Christian Faith and Practice*, ed by M. Noll and D. Wells, pp.51-67. Grand Rapids: Eerdmans, 1988.

Pope, John Paul II. *Redemptor Hominis: Encyclical Letter.* London: Catholic Truth Society, 1979.

— 'Laborem Exercens: Encyclical Letter (1981).' In *Gregory Baum, The Priority of Labor*, pp.95-152. New York: Paulist Press, 1982.

Pope, John XXIII. *Mater et Magistra: Encyclical Letter.* London: Catholic Truth Society, 1961.

Pope, Leo XIII. *Rerum Novarum: Encyclical Letter.* London: Catholic Truth Society, 1891.

Pope, Paul VI. *Populorum Progressio: Encyclical Letter.* London: Catholic Truth Society, 1967.

Pope, Pius XI. *Quadragesimo Anno: Encyclical Letter.* London: Catholic Truth Society, 1931.

Porter, Jean. *The Recovery of Virtue: The Relevance of Aquinas for Christian Ethics.* London: SPCK, 1994.

— 'Christianity, Divine Law and Consequentialism.' *Scottish Journal of Theology* 48 (4 1995): pp.415-442.

Preisker, H. *Das Ethos der Arbeit im Neuen Testament.* Gnadenfrei in Schlesien, 1936.

— *Das Ethos des Urchristentums.* 2nd ed., Gutersloh, 1949.

Preston, Ronald H. 'Pope John Paul II on Work.' *Theology* 82 (1983): pp.19-24.

von Rad, Gerhard. *Genesis: A Commentary.* Rev. ed., Translated by John H. Marks, OTL, London: SCM Press, 1972.

Rahner, Hugo. *Man at Play: Or Did You Ever Practice Eutrapelia?* Translated by Brian Battershaw and Edward Quinn. London: A Compass Book: Burns and Oats, 1965.

Rahner, Karl. 'The Hermeneutics of Eschatological Assertions.' In *Theological Investigations: More Recent Writings*, pp.323-346. 4. London: Darton, Longman & Todd, 1966.

Raines, John C. 'Capital, Community and the Meaning of Work.' In *The Public Vocation of Christian Ethics*, eds. B. Harrison, Stivers R., and Stone R. pp.211-222. The Pilgrim Press, 1986.

— 'Tools and Common Grace.' *Cross Currents* 40 (Fall 1990): pp.314-327.

— 'Book Review: Work in the Spirit. by Miroslav Volf.' *Journal of Church and State* 35 (Sum. 1993): pp.624-625.

— and D.C. Day-Lower. *Modern Work and Human Meaning.* Philadelphia: Westminster Press, 1986.

Reck, Donald W. 'The Theoretical Bases of a Theology of Work.' *Irish Theological Quarterly* 31 (1964): pp.228-239.

Richardson, A. *The Biblical Doctrine of Work.* London: SCM Press, 1952.

Rolnick, Philip A. 'Polanyi's Progress: Transcendence, Universality, and Teleology.' *Tradition & Discovery* 19 (2 1993): pp.13-31.

Roos, L. 'On a Theology and Ethics of Work.' *Communio* 11 (1984): pp.100-119.

Roschin, Mikhail. 'Old Belief and Work.' *The Keston Journal: Religion State and Society* 23 (3 1995): pp.263-267.

Ruether, Rosemary. *Liberation Theology: Human Hope Confronts Christian History and American Power.* New York: Paulist Press, 1972.

— *To Change the World: Christology and Cultural Criticism.* London: SCM Press, 1981.

— *Sexism and God Talk: Toward a Feminist Theology.* London: SCM Press, 1983.

Ryken, Leland. *Work and Leisure in Christian Perspective.* First British Edition (1989) ed., Leicester: Inter-Varsity Press, 1987.

Sayers, Dorothy. *Creed or Chaos?* New York: Harcourt, Brace, 1947.

Scanzoni, John. 'The Christian View of Work.' *Applied Christianity* (Sept. 1974): pp.16-23.

Schilling, S Paul. 'Ernst Bloch: Philosopher of the Not-Yet.' *The Christian Century* 84 (Nov. 15 1967): pp.1455-1458.

Schulze, Ludi. *Calvin and 'Social Ethics': His Views on Property, Interest and Usury.* Pretoria: Kital, 1985.

Schumacher, Christian. *To Live and to Work: A Theological Interpretation.* London: MARC Europe, 1986.

Schuurman, Douglas J. 'Creation, Eschaton, and Ethics: An Analysis of Theology and Ethics in Jürgen Moltmann.' *Calvin Theological Journal* 22 (1 1987): pp.42-67.

— *Creation, Eschaton, and Ethics: The Ethical Significance of the Creation-Eschaton Relation in the Thought of Emil Brunner and Jürgen Moltmann.* American University

Studies, Series VII - Theology and Religion- Vol. 86, New York: Peter Lang, 1991.

— 'Creation, Eschaton, and Social Ethics: A Response to Volf.' *Calvin Theological Journal* 30 (No 1 April 1995): pp.144-158.

Schwartz, Adina. 'Meaningful Work.' *Ethics* 92 (No 4 Jl. 1982): pp.634-646.

Schwöbel, Christoph. 'Human Being as Relational Being: Twelve Theses for a Christian Anthropology.' In *Persons, Divine and Human: King's College Essays in Theological Anthropology,* eds. Christoph Schwöbel and Colin E. Gunton. pp.141-165. Edinburgh: T& T Clark, 1991.

— 'Introduction.' In *Persons, Divine and Human: King's College Essays in Theological Anthropology*, eds. Christoph Schwöbel and Colin E. Gunton. pp.1-29. Edinburgh: T& T Clark, 1991.

Scotchmer, Paul. 'The Christian Meaning of Work.' *New Oxford Review* 47 (My. 1980): pp.12-18.

Shepherd, P. 'Karl Barth and the Contemporary Crisis of Work.' M.A., Leeds, 1988.

Sherman, Doug and William Hendricks. *Your Work Matters to God.* Colorado Springs: Navpress, 1987.

Sherman, Douglas Richard. 'Towards a Christian Theology of Work.' Th.M, Dallas Theological Seminary, 1984.

Shillington, V George. 'A New Testament Perspective on Work.' *Conrad Grebel Review* 10 (Spr. 1992): pp.139-155.

Shriver, Donald W., Jr. 'Vocation and Work in an Era of Downsizing.' *The Christian Century* 12 No 17 (My. 17 1995): pp.538-545.

Soelle, Dorothee and S. Cloyes. *To Work and To Love.* Philadelphia: Fortress, 1984.

Soper, David W. 'The Theology of Work of Robert Calhoun.' In *Major Voices in American Theology*, pp.193-217. Philadelphia: Westminster, 1953.

Stott, J. 'Work and Unemployment.' In *Decisive Issues Facing Christians Today*, pp.164-185. 2nd ed., London: Marshall Pickering, 1990.

— 'Reclaiming the Biblical Doctrine of Work.' *Christianity Today* (My. 4 1979): pp.36-39.

Strum, Douglas. 'Praxis and Promise: On the Ethics of Political Theology.' *Ethics* 92 (No 4 Jl. 1982): pp.733-750.

Swinburne, Richard. *The Evolution of the Soul.* Oxford: Claredon Press, 1986.

— 'The Structure of the Soul.' In *Persons and Personality: A Contemporary Enquiry,* eds. Author Peacocke and Grant Gillett. pp.33-55. New York: Basil Blackwell, 1987.

Sykes, S. W. 'Life After Death: The Christian Doctrine of Heaven.' In *Creation Christ and Culture: Studies in Honor of T. F. Torrance,* ed. Richard McKinney. pp.250-271. Edinburgh: T&T Clark, 1976.

de Tavernier, Johan. 'Eschatology and Social Ethics.' In *Personalist Morals: Essays in Honor of L Janssens,* ed. J. Selling. pp.279-300. Louvain: Leuven University Press, 1988.

Tawney, R.H. *Religion and the Rise of Capitalism.* 1937 ed., New York: Penguin Books, 1922.

Taylor, Charles. *Sources of the Self: The Making of the Modern Identity.* Cambridge: Cambridge University Press, 1989.

Terkel, Studs. *Working: People Talk About What They Do All Day and How They Feel About What They Do.* New York: Pantheon Books, 1972.

Thatcher, Adrian. 'Christian Theism and the Concept of a Person.' In *Persons and Personality: A Contemporary Enquiry*, eds. Author Peacocke and Grant Gillett. pp.180-

196. New York: Basil Blackwell, 1987.

Thielicke, Helmut. *Theological Ethics.* English ed., Translated by Lazareth, William H. Grand Rapids: Eerdmans, 1979.

Thompson, Thomas R. 'Trinitarianism Today: Doctrinal Renaissance, Ethical Relevance, Social Redolence.' *Calvin Theological Journal* 32 (#1 1997): pp.9-42.

Thrall, Margaret. 'Christian Vocation Today.' *Theology* 59 (Mar. 1976): pp.84-89.

Tilgher, Adriano. *Work: What It Has Meant to Men Through the Ages.* New York: Arno Press, 1977.

Todd, John M., ed. *Work: Christian Thought and Practice.* London: Darton Longman and Todd, 1960.

Torrance, Alan J. *Persons in Communion: An Essay on Trinitarian Description and Human Participation.* Edinburgh: T& T Clark, 1996.

Torrance, T.F. *Calvin's Doctrine of Man.* London: Lutterworth Press, 1949.

Traffas, John, R. 'The Spirit of Community and the Spirituality of Work: A Note on Laborem Exercens.' *Communio* 10 (1983): pp.407-411.

Trathen, D A, ed. 'The Work Ethic.' *St Mark's Review* No 97: (Mar. 1979): pp.1-34.

Truesdale, A. 'Last Things First: The Impact of Eschatology on Ecology.' *Journal of the American Scientific Affiliation* 46 (2 1994): pp.116-120.

Unemployment and the Future of Work: an Inquiry for the Churches. London: Council of Churches for Britain and Ireland: CCBI Inter-Church House, 1997.

Umholtz, Thomas F. 'Vocation and Work.' *The Christian Century* 102 (Aug. 28-Sept. 4 1985): pp.767-768.

Vatican, II. *Gaudium et Spes: Pastoral Constitution on the Church in the World Today.* London: Catholic Truth Society, 1966.

Vidler, A. R. *A Century of Social Catholicism.* London: SPCK, 1964.

Volf, Miroslav. 'Doing and Interpreting: An Examination of the Relationship Between Theory and Practice in Latin American Liberation Theology.' *Themelios* 8 (No 3 1983): pp.11-19.

— 'On Human Work: An Evaluation of the Key Ideas of the Encyclical Laborem exercens.' *SJTh* 37 (1984): pp.67-79.

— 'Arbeit und Charisma. Zu einer Theologie der Arbeit.' *Zeitschrift fur Evangelische Ethik* 31 (1987): pp.411-433.

— 'Human Work, Divine Spirit, and New Creation: Toward a Pneumatological Understanding of Work.' *Pneuma* 9 (1987): pp.173-193.

— 'Materiality of Salvation: An Investigation in the Soteriologies of Liberation and Pentecostal Theologies.' *Journal of Ecumenical Studies* 26 (Sum. 1989): pp.447-467.

— 'God, Freedom, and Grace: Reflections on the Essentiality of Atheism for Marx and Marxism.' *Occasional Papers on Religion in Eastern Europe* 10 (Jl. 1990): pp.15-31.

— 'On Loving With Hope: Eschatology and Social Responsibility.' *Transformation* 7 (3 1990): pp.28-31.

— *Work in the Spirit: Toward a Theology of Work.* Oxford: Oxford University Press, 1991.

— 'Eschaton, Creation, and Social Ethics.' *Calvin Theological Journal* 30 (No 1 Apr. 1995): pp.130-143.

Wall, James M, ed. 'The Church in the Workplace.' *Christian Ministry* 20 (Nov.-Dec. 1989): pp.9-15.

Wallace, Ronald S. *Calvin's Doctrine of the Christian Life.* London: Oliver and Boyd, 1959.

Wallis, Wilber B. 'Eschatology and Social Concern.' *Journal of the Evangelical Theological Society* 24 (Mar. 1981): pp.3-9.

Ware, Kallistos. 'The Unity of the Human Person According to the Greek Fathers.' In *Persons and Personality: A Contemporary Enquiry*, eds. Author Peacocke and Grant Gillett. pp.197-206. New York: Basil Blackwell, 1987.

Weber, Max. *The Protestant Ethic and the Spirit of Capitalism*. Translated by Talcott Parsons. London: Unwin University Press, 1930.

Weigel, George and Robert Royal, eds. *A Century of Catholic Social Thought*. Washington: Ethics and Public Policy Center, 1991.

Wendell, Francois. *Calvin: The Origins and Development of His Religious Thought*. Translated by Philip Mairet. London: Collins, 1963.

West, Philip. 'Cruciform Labour: The Cross in Two Recent Theologies of Work.' *Modern Churchman* 28 (4 1986): pp.9-15.

— 'Karl Barth's Theology of Work: A Resource for the Late 1980s.' *Modern Churchman* 30 (3 1988): pp.13-19.

— 'Toward A Christian Theology of Work: A Critical Appropriation of the Theology of Jürgen Habermas.' Ph.D, Cambridge, 1986.

Westermann, Claus. *Creation*. Translated by John J. Scullian. Philadelphia: Fortress Press, 1974.

— *Genesis*. Translated by D. E. Green. Edinburgh: T& T Clark, 1974.

— *Genesis 1-11: A Commentary*. Translated by John J. Scullian. London: SPCK, 1984.

Williams, S. 'The Partition of Love and Hope: Eschatology and Social Responsibility.' *Transformation* 7 (3 1990): pp.24-27.

Williamson, Clark M. 'Notes on a Theology of Work.' *Encounter* 37 (Sum. 1976): pp.294-307.

Wingren, Gustaf. *The Christian's Calling: Luther on Vocation*. Translated by Carl Rasmussen. London: Oliver and Boyd, 1957.

Wojtyla, Karol (Pope John Paul II). *The Acting Person*. Translated by A. Potocki. London: Reidel, 1979.

Wolff, Hans Walter. *Anthropology of the Old Testament*. English ed., Translated by Margaret Kohl. London: SCM Press, 1974.

Wolters, Al. *The Foundational Command: Subdue the Earth*. Toronto: Institute for Christian studies, 1973.

Wolters, Albert W. *Creation Regained*. Grand Rapids: Eerdmans, 1985.

Wolterstorff, Nicholas. 'More on Vocation.' *Reformed Journal* 29 (My. 1979): pp.20-23.

— *Art in Action: Toward a Christian Aesthetic*. Grand Rapids: Eerdmans, 1980.

— *Until Justice and Peace Embrace*. Grand Rapids: Eerdmans, 1983.

— 'Christianity and Social Justice.' *Christian Scholars Review* 16 (1987): pp.211-228.

— 'Evangelicalism and the Arts.' *Christian Scholars Review* 17 (1988): pp.449-473.

Zizioulas, John D. 'On Being a Person. Towards an Ontology of Personhood.' In *Persons, Divine and Human: King's College Essays in Theological Anthropology*, eds. Christoph Schwöbel and Colin E. Gunton. pp.33-46. Edinburgh: T& T Clark, 1991.

— *Being as Communion: Studies Personhood and the Church*. New York: St Vladimir's Seminary Press, 1993.

Author Index

Subject Index

Paternoster Biblical Monographs

(All titles uniform with this volume)

Joseph Abraham
Eve: Accused or Acquitted?
A Reconsideration of Feminist Readings of the Creation Narrative Texts in Genesis 1–3

Two contrary views dominate contemporary feminist biblical scholarship. One finds in the Bible an unequivocal equality between the sexes from the very creation of humanity, whilst the other sees the biblical text as irredeemably patriarchal and androcentric. Dr. Abraham enters into dialogue with both camps as well as introducing his own method of approach. An invaluable tool for anyone who is interested in this contemporary debate.

2002 / ISBN 0-85364-971-5 / xxiv + 272pp

Paul Barker
The Triumph of Grace in Deuteronomy
This book is a textual and theological analysis of the interaction between the sin and faithlessness of Israel and the grace of Yahweh in response, looking especially at Deuteronomy chapters 1–3, 8–10 and 29–30. The author argues that the grace of Yahweh is determinative for the ongoing relationship between Yahweh and Israel and that Deuteronomy anticipates and fully expects Israel to be faithless.

2004 / ISBN 1-84227-226-8 / xxii + 270pp

Jonathan F. Bayes
The Weakness of the Law
God's Law and the Christian in New Testament Perspective
A study of the four New Testament books which refer to the law as weak (Acts, Romans, Galatians, Hebrews) leads to a defence of the third use in the Reformed debate about the law in the life of the believer.

2000 / ISBN 0-85364-957-X / xii + 244pp

Mark Bonnington
The Antioch Episode of Galatians 2:11-14 in Historical and Cultural Context
The Galatians 2 'incident' in Antioch over table-fellowship suggests significant disagreement between the leading apostles. This book analyses the background to the disagreement by locating the incident within the dynamics of social interaction between Jews and Gentiles. It proposes a new way of understanding the relationship between the individuals and issues involved.

2004 / ISBN 1-84227-050-8 / approx. 350pp

May 2004

Mark Bredin
Jesus, Revolutionary of Peace
A Nonviolent Christology in the Book of Revelation
This book aims to demonstrate that the figure of Jesus in the Book of Revelation can best be understood as an active nonviolent revolutionary.
2003 / ISBN 1-84227-153-9 / xviii + 262pp

Daniel J-S Chae
Paul as Apostle to the Gentiles
His Apostolic Self-awareness and its Influence on the Soteriological Argument in Romans
Opposing 'the post-Holocaust interpretation of Romans', Daniel Chae competently demonstrates that Paul argues for the equality of Jew and Gentile in Romans. Chae's fresh exegetical interpretation is academically outstanding and spiritually encouraging.
1997 / ISBN 0-85364-829-8 / xiv + 378pp

Luke L. Cheung
The Genre, Composition and Hermeneutics of the Epistle of James
The present work examines the employment of the wisdom genre with a certain compositional structure and the interpretation of the law through the Jesus' tradition of the double love command by the author of the Epistle of James to serve his purpose in promoting perfection and warning against doubleness among the eschatologically renewed people of God in the Diaspora.
2003 / ISBN 1-84227-062-1 / xvi + 372pp

Andrew C. Clark
Parallel Lives
The Relation of Paul to the Apostles in the Lucan Perspective
This study of the Peter-Paul parallels in Acts argues that their purpose was to emphasize the themes of continuity in salvation history and the unity of the Jewish and Gentile missions. New light is shed on Luke's literary techniques, partly through a comparison with Plutarch.
2001 / 1-84227-035-4 / xviii + 386pp

Andrew D. Clarke
Secular and Christian Leadership in Corinth
A Socio-Historical and Exegetical Study of 1 Corinthians 1–6
This volume is an investigation into the leadership structures and dynamics of first-century Roman Corinth. These are compared with the practice of leadership in the Corinthian Christian community which are reflected in 1 Corinthians 1–6, and contrasted with Paul's own principles of Christian leadership.

2004 / ISBN 1-84227-229-2 / xii + 188pp

Stephen Finamore
God, Order and Chaos
René Girard and the Apocalypse
Readers are often disturbed by the images of destruction in the book of Revelation and unsure why they are unleashed after the exaltation of Jesus. This book examines past approaches to these texts and uses René Girard's theories to revive some old ideas and propose some new ones.

2004 / ISBN 1-84227-197-0 / approx. 344pp

Scott J. Hafemann
Suffering and Ministry in the Spirit
Paul's Defence of His Ministry in II Corinthians 2:14–3:3
Shedding new light on the way Paul defended his apostleship, the author offers a careful, detailed study of 2 Corinthians 2:14–3:3 linked with other key passages throughout 1 and 2 Corinthians. Demonstrating the unity and coherence of Paul's argument in this passage, the author shows that Paul's suffering served as the vehicle for revealing God's power and glory through the Spirit.

2000 / ISBN 0-85364-967-7 / xiv + 262pp

Douglas S. McComiskey
Lukan Theology in the Light of the Gospel's Literary Structure
Luke's Gospel was purposefully written with theology embedded in its patterned literary structure. A critical analysis of this cyclical structure provides new windows into Luke's interpretation of the individual pericopes comprising the Gospel and illuminates several of his theological interests.

2004 / ISBN 1-84227-148-2 / approx. 400pp

Stephen Motyer
Your Father the Devil?
A New Approach to John and 'The Jews'
Who are 'the Jews' in John's Gospel? Defending John against the charge
of anti-semitism, Motyer argues that, far from demonizing the Jews, the
Gospel seeks to present Jesus as 'Good News for Jews' in a late first
century setting.
1997 / ISBN 0-85364-832-8 / xiv + 260pp

Esther Ng
Reconstructing Christian Origins?
The Feminist Theology of Elizabeth Schüssler Fiorenza: An Evaluation
In a detailed evaluation, the author challenges Elizabeth Schüssler
Fiorenza's reconstruction of early Christian origins and her underlying
presuppositions. The author also presents her own views on women's roles
both then and now.
2002 / ISBN 1-84227-055-9 / xxiv + 468pp

Robin Parry
Old Testament Story and Christian Ethics
The Rape of Dinah as a Case Study
What is the role of story in ethics and, more particularly, what is the role of
Old Testament story in Christian ethics? This book, drawing on the work
of contemporary philosophers, argues that narrative is crucial in the ethical
shaping of people and, drawing on the work of contemporary Old
Testament scholars, that story plays a key role in Old Testament ethics.
Parry then argues that when situated in canonical context Old Testament
stories can be reappropriated by Christian readers in their own ethical
formation. The shocking story of the rape of Dinah and the massacre of the
Shechemites provides a fascinating case study for exploring the parameters
within which Christian ethical appropriations of Old Testament stories can
live.
2004 / ISBN 1-84227-210-1 / approx. 350pp

David Powys
'Hell': A Hard Look at a Hard Question
The Fate of the Unrighteous in New Testament Thought
This comprehensive treatment seeks to unlock the original meaning of
terms and phrases long thought to support the traditional doctrine of hell. It
concludes that there is an alternative – one which is more biblical, and
which can positively revive the rationale for Christian mission.
1997 / ISBN 0-85364-831-X / xxii + 478pp

Rosalind Selby
The Comical Doctrine
Can a Gospel Convey Truth?
This book argues that the Gospel breaks through postmodernity's critique
of truth and the referential possibilities of textuality and its gift of grace.
With a rigorous, philosophical challenge to modernist and postmodernist
assumptions, it offers an alternative epistemology to all who would still
read with faith *and* with academic credibility.
2004 / ISBN 1-84227-212-8 approx. 350pp

Kevin Walton
Thou Traveller Unknown
The Presence and Absence of God in the Jacob Narrative
The author offers a fresh reading of the story of Jacob in the book of Genesis through the paradox of divine presence and absence. The work also
seeks to make a contribution to Pentateuchal studies by bringing together a
close reading of the final text with historical critical insights, doing justice
to the text's historical depth, final form and canonical status.
2003 / ISBN 1-84227-059-1 / xvi + 238pp

Alistair Wilson
When Will These Things Happen?
A Study of Jesus as Judge in Matthew 21–25
This study seeks to allow Matthew's carefully constructed presentation of
Jesus to be given full weight in the modern evaluation of Jesus'
eschatology. Careful analysis of the text of Matthew 21–25 reveals Jesus to
be standing firmly in the Jewish prophetic and wisdom traditions as he
proclaims and enacts imminent judgement on the Jewish authorities then
boldly claims the central role in the final and universal judgement.
2004 / ISBN 1-84227-146-6 / xvi + 292pp

Lindsay Wilson
Joseph Wise and Otherwise
The Intersection of Covenant and Wisdom in Genesis 37–50
This book offers a careful literary reading of Genesis 37–50 that argues
that the Joseph story contains both strong covenant themes and many
wisdom-like elements. The connections between the two helps to explore
how covenant and wisdom might intersect in an integrated biblical
theology.
2004 / ISBN 1-84227-140-7 approx. 350pp

Stephen I. Wright
The Voice of Jesus
Studies in the Interpretation of Six Gospel Parables
This literary study considers how the 'voice' of Jesus has been heard in different periods of parable interpretation, and how the categories of figure and trope may help us towards a sensitive reading of the parables today.
2000 / ISBN 0-85364-975-8 / xiv + 280pp

Paternoster Theological Monographs

(All titles uniform with this volume)

Emil Bartos
Deification in Eastern Orthodox Theology
An Evaluation and Critique of the Theology of Dumitru Staniloae
Bartos studies a fundamental yet neglected aspect of Orthodox theology: deification. By examining the doctrines of anthropology, christology, soteriology and ecclesiology as they relate to deification, he provides an important contribution to contemporary dialogue between Eastern and Western theologians.
1999 / ISBN 0-85364-956-1 / xii + 370pp

James Bruce
Prophecy, Miracles, Angels *and* Heavenly Light?
The Eschatology, Pneumatology and Missiology of Adomnán's Life of Columba
This book surveys approaches to the marvellous in hagiography, providing the first critique of Plummer's hypothesis of Irish saga origin. It then analyses the uniquely systematized phenomena in the *Life of Columba* from Adomnán's seventh-century theological perspective, identifying the coming of the eschatological Kingdom as the key to understanding.
2004 / ISBN 1-84227-227-6 / approx. 400pp

Colin J. Bulley
The Priesthood of Some Believers
Developments from the General to the Special Priesthood in the Christian Literature of the First Three Centuries
The first in-depth treatment of early Christian texts on the priesthood of all believers shows that the developing priesthood of the ordained related closely to the division between laity and clergy and had deleterious effects on the practice of the general priesthood.
2000 / ISBN 1-84227-034-6 / xii + 336pp

May 2004

Iain D. Campbell
Fixing the Indemnity
The Life and Work of George Adam Smith
When Old Testament scholar George Adam Smith (1856–1942) delivered the Lyman Beecher lectures at Yale University in 1899 he confidently declared that 'modern criticism has won its war against traditional theories. It only remains to fix the amount of the indemnity.' In this biography, Iain D. Campbell assesses Smith's critical approach to the Old Testament and evaluates its consequences, showing that Smith's life and work still raises questions about the relationship between biblical scholarship and evangelical faith.
2004 / ISBN 1-84227-228-4 / approx. 276pp

Sylvia W. Collinson
Making Disciples
The Significance of Jesus' Educational Strategy for Today's Church
This study examines the biblical practice of discipling, formulates a definition, and makes comparisons with modern models of education. A recommendation is made for greater attention to its practice today.
2004 / ISBN 1-84227-116-4 / approx. 320pp

Stephen M. Dunning
The Crisis and the Quest
A Kierkegaardian Reading of Charles Williams
Employing Kierkegaardian categories and analysis, this study investigates both the central crisis in Charles Williams's authorship between hermetism and Christianity (Kierkegaard's Religions A and B), and the quest to resolve this crisis, a quest that ultimately presses the bounds of orthodoxy.
2000 / ISBN 0-85364-985-5 / xxiv + 254pp

Keith Ferdinando
The Triumph of Christ in African Perspective
A Study of Demonology and Redemption in the African Context
The book explores the implications of the gospel for traditional African fears of occult aggression. It analyses such traditional approaches to suffering and biblical responses to fears of demonic evil, concluding with an evaluation of African beliefs from the perspective of the gospel.
1999 / ISBN 0-85364-830-1 / xviii + 450pp

Andrew Goddard
Living the Word, Resisting the World
The Life and Thought of Jacques Ellul
This work offers a definitive study of both the life and thought of the French Reformed thinker Jacques Ellul (1912-1994). It will prove an indispensable resource for those interested in this influential theologian and sociologist and for Christian ethics and political thought generally.
2002 / ISBN 1-84227-053-2 / xxiv + 378pp

Ruth Gouldbourne
The Flesh and the Feminine
Gender and Theology in the Writings of Caspar Schwenckfeld
Caspar Schwenckfeld and his movement exemplify one of the radical communities of the sixteenth century. Challenging theological and liturgical norms, they also found themselves challenging social and particularly gender assumptions. In this book, the issues of the relationship between radical theology and the understanding of gender are considered.
2004 / ISBN 1-84227-048-6 / approx. 304pp

Roger Hitching
The Church and Deaf People
A Study of Identity, Communication and Relationships with Special Reference to the Ecclesiology of Jürgen Moltmann
In *The Church and Deaf People* Roger Hitching sensitively examines the history and present experience of deaf people and finds similarities between aspects of sign language and Moltmann's theological method that 'open up' new ways of understanding theological concepts.
2003 / ISBN 1-84227-222-5 / xxii + 236pp

John G. Kelly
One God, One People
The Differentiated Unity of the People of God in the Theology of Jürgen Moltmann
The author expounds and critiques Moltmann's doctrine of God and high-lights the systematic connections between it and Moltmann's influential discussion of Israel. He then proposes a fresh approach to Jewish-Christian relations building on Moltmann's work using insights from Habermas and Rawls.
2004 / ISBN 0-85346-969-3 / approx. 350pp

Mark F.W. Lovatt
Confronting the Will-to-Power
A Reconsideration of the Theology of Reinhold Niebuhr
Confronting the Will-to-Power is an analysis of the theology of Reinhold Niebuhr, arguing that his work is an attempt to identify, and provide a practical theological answer to, the existence and nature of human evil.
2001 / ISBN 1-84227-054-0 / xviii + 216pp

Neil B. MacDonald
Karl Barth and the Strange New World within the Bible
Barth, Wittgenstein, and the Metadilemmas of the Enlightenment
Barth's discovery of the strange new world within the Bible is examined in the context of Kant, Hume, Overbeck, and, most importantly, Wittgenstein. MacDonald covers some fundamental issues in theology today: epistemology, the final form of the text and biblical truth-claims.
2000 / ISBN 0-85364-970-7 / xxvi + 374pp

Gillian McCulloch
The Deconstruction of Dualism in Theology
With Reference to Ecofeminist Theology and New Age Spirituality
This book challenges eco-theological anti-dualism in Christian theology, arguing that dualism has a twofold function in Christian religious discourse. Firstly, it enables us to express the discontinuities and divisions that are part of the process of reality. Secondly, dualistic language allows us to express the mysteries of divine transcendence/immanence and the survival of the soul without collapsing into monism and materialism, both of which are problematic for Christian epistemology.
2002 / ISBN 1-84227-044-3 / xii + 282pp

Leslie McCurdy
Attributes and Atonement
The Holy Love of God in the Theology of P.T. Forsyth
Attributes and Atonement is an intriguing full-length study of P.T. Forsyth's doctrine of the cross as it relates particularly to God's holy love. It includes an unparalleled bibliography of both primary and secondary material relating to Forsyth.
1999 / ISBN 0-85364-833-6 / xiv + 328pp

Nozomu Miyahira
Towards a Theology of the Concord of God
A Japanese Perspective on the Trinity
This book introduces a new Japanese theology and a unique Trinitarian formula based on the Japanese intellectual climate: three betweennesses and one concord. It also presents a new interpretation of the Trinity, a co-subordinationism, which is in line with orthodox Trinitarianism; each single person of the Trinity is eternally and equally subordinate (or serviceable) to the other persons, so that they retain the mutual dynamic equality.
2000 / ISBN 0-85364-863-8 / xiv + 256pp

Eddy José Muskus
The Origins and Early Development of Liberation Theology in Latin America
With Particular Reference to Gustavo Gutiérrez
This work challenges the fundamental premise of Liberation Theology, 'opting for the poor', and its claim that Christ is found in them. It also argues that Liberation Theology emerged as a direct result of the failure of the Roman Catholic Church in Latin America.
2002 / ISBN 0-85364-974-X / xiv + 296pp

Anna Robbins
Methods in the Madness
Diversity in Twentieth-Century Christian Social Ethics
The author compares the ethical methods of Walter Rauschenbusch, Reinhold Niebuhr and others. She argues that unless Christians are clear about the ways that theology and philosophy are expressed practically they may lose the ability to discuss social ethics across contexts, let alone reach effective agreements.
2004 / ISBN 1-84227-211-X / xvi + 320pp

Ed Rybarczyk
Beyond Salvation
Eastern Orthodoxy and Classical Pentecostalism on becoming like Christ
At first glance eastern Orthodoxy and Classical Pentecostalism seem quite distinct. This groundbreaking study shows that they share much in common, especially as it concerns the experiential elements of following Christ. Both traditions assert that authentic Christianity transcends the wooden categories of modernism.
2003 / ISBN 1-84227-144-X / xii + 356pp

Signe Sandsmark
Is World View Neutral Education Possible and Desirable?
A Christian Response to Liberal Arguments
(Published jointly with The Stapleford Centre)
This book discusses reasons for belief in world view neutrality, and argues that 'neutral' education will have a hidden, but strong world view influence. It discusses the place for Christian education in the common school.

2000 / ISBN 0-85364-973-1 / xiv + 182pp

Hazel Sherman
Reading Zechariah
The Allegorical Tradition of Biblical Interpretation through the Commentaries of Didymus the Blind and Theodore of Mopsuestia
A close reading of the commentary on Zechariah by Didymus the Blind alongside that of Theodore of Mopsuestia suggests that popular categorising of Antiochene and Alexandrian biblical exegesis as 'historical' or 'allegorical' is inadequate and misleading.

2004 / ISBN 1-84227-213-6 / approx. 280pp

Andrew Sloane
On Being a Christian in the Academy
Nicholas Wolterstorff and the Practice of Christian Scholarship
An exposition and critical appraisal of Nicholas Wolterstorff's epistemology in the light of the philosophy of science, and an application of his thought to the practice of Christian scholarship.

2003 / ISBN 1-84227-058-3 / xvi + 274pp

Daniel Strange
The Possibility of Salvation Among the Unevangelised
An Analysis of Inclusivism in Recent Evangelical Theology
For evangelical theologians the 'fate of the unevangelised' impinges upon fundamental tenets of evangelical identity. The position known as 'inclusivism', defined by the belief that the unevangelised can be ontologically saved by Christ whilst being epistemologically unaware of him, has been defended most vigorously by the Canadian evangelical Clark H. Pinnock. Through a detailed analysis and critique of Pinnock's work, this book examines a cluster of issues surrounding the unevangelised and its implications for christology, soteriology and the doctrine of revelation.

2002 / ISBN 1-84227-047-8 / xviii + 362pp

G. Michael Thomas
The Extent of the Atonement
A Dilemma for Reformed Theology from Calvin to the Consensus
This is a study of the way Reformed theology addressed the question, 'Did Christ die for all, or for the elect only?', commencing with John Calvin, and including debates with Lutheranism, the Synod of Dort and the teaching of Moïse Amyraut.

1997 / ISBN 0-85364-828-X / x + 278pp

Mark D. Thompson
A Sure Ground on which to Stand
The Relation of Authority and Interpretive Method in Luther's Approach to Scripture
The best interpreter of Luther is Luther himself. Unfortunately many modern studies have superimposed contemporary agendas upon this sixteenth-century Reformer's writings. This fresh study examines Luther's own words to find an explanation for his robust confidence in the Scriptures, a confidence that generated the famous 'stand' at Worms in 1521.

2004 / ISBN 1-84227-145-8 / xvi + 322pp

Graham Tomlin
The Power of the Cross
Theology and the Death of Christ in Paul, Luther and Pascal
This book explores the theology of the cross in St Paul, Luther and Pascal. It offers new perspectives on the theology of each, and some implications for the nature of power, apologetics, theology and church life in a postmodern context.

1999 / ISBN 0-85364-984-7 / xiv + 344pp

Graham J. Watts
Revelation and the Spirit
A Comparative Study of the Relationship between the Doctrine of Revelation and Pneumatology in the Theology of Eberhard Jüngel and of Wolfhart Pannenberg
The relationship between revelation and pneumatology is relatively unexplored. This approach offers a fresh angle on two important twentieth century theologians and raises pneumatological questions which are theologically crucial and relevant to mission in a post modern culture.

2004 / ISBN 1-84227-104-0 / xxii + 232pp

Nigel G. Wright
Disavowing Constantine
Mission, Church and the Social Order in the Theologies of
John Howard Yoder and Jürgen Moltmann
This book is a timely restatement of a radical theology of church and state
in the Anabaptist and Baptist tradition. Dr Wright constructs his argument
in dialogue and debate with Yoder and Moltmann, major contributors to a
free church perspective.
2000 / ISBN 0-85364-978-2 / xvi + 252pp

The Paternoster Press
PO Box 300,
Carlisle,
Cumbria CA3 0QS,
United Kingdom
Web: www.paternoster-publishing.com

May 2004